D1534909

WITHDRAWN

CONCEPTS IN JUDGEMENT AND DECISION RESEARCH

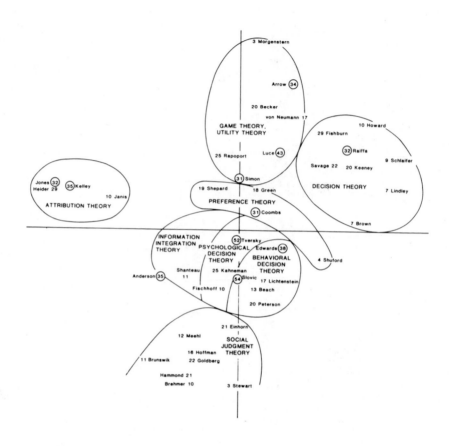

3 Morgenstern

Arrow (34)

20 Becker
von Neumann 17

GAME THEORY,
UTILITY THEORY

10 Howard
29 Fishburn

25 Rapoport   Luce (43)

(32) Raiffa
9 Schlaifer
Savage 22   20 Keeney

(31) Simon

DECISION THEORY
7 Lindley

Jones (32) (35)Kelley
Heider 29   19 Shepard   18 Green
                10 Janis
ATTRIBUTION THEORY   PREFERENCE THEORY

(31) Coombs

7 Brown

INFORMATION
INTEGRATION   (52)Tversky
THEORY   PSYCHOLOGICAL   Edwards(38)
                DECISION
                THEORY   BEHAVIORAL   4 Shuford
                            DECISION
        Shanteau   THEORY
           11   25 Kahneman
Anderson(35)   (54)Slovic 17 Lichtenstein
        Fischhoff 10   13 Beach

                              20 Peterson

                    21 Einhorn

    12 Meehl   SOCIAL
                      JUDGMENT
        16 Hoffman   THEORY
11 Brunswik   22 Goldberg

    Hammond 21
    Brehmer 10   3 Stewart

CONCEPTS IN JUDGEMENT AND DECISION RESEARCH

Definitions, Sources, Interrelations, Comments

Barry F. Anderson
Donald H. Deane
Kenneth R. Hammond
Gary H. McClelland
James C. Shanteau

PRAEGER

PRAEGER SPECIAL STUDIES • PRAEGER SCIENTIFIC

Library of Congress Cataloging in Publication Data
Main entry under title:

Concepts in judgement and decision research.

  1. Decision-making--Addresses, essays, lectures.
I. Anderson, Barry F.
HD30.23.C66   658.4'03   81-7345
ISBN 0-03-059337-9   AACR2

Published in 1981 by Praeger Publishers
CBS Educational and Professional Publishing
A Division of CBS, Inc.
521 Fifth Avenue, New York, New York 10175 U.S.A.

123456789   145   987654321

Printed in the United States of America

PREFACE

Judgment and decision making is an intellectual crossroads. Researchers and practitioners from economics, mathematics, experimental psychology, social psychology, management science, and policy science all come to exchange ideas. Yet the exchange is only partial, for the conversants speak, if not in different tongues, certainly in a variety of dialects. They use the same word--"risk", "tradeoff", "utility", "independence", "weight", "attribute"--for different concepts. They use different words--"composition rule", "integration rule", and "organizing principle"; "configural", "synergistic", and "nondecomposable"; "classical", "analytical", and "canonical probability"--for the same concepts. And they make use of words--"judgment", "choice", "decision making", "rationality"--that, while widely shared, are seldom given any precise definition. Partly as a consequence of this diversity in language, those interested in judgment and decision making tend to converse in small groups, finding it difficult to gain from or contribute to groups other than their own. For the newcomer, of course, the problem can be especially great.

This book is the second part of a three-part effort intended to unify the field of judgment and decision making. The first was K. R. Hammond, G. H. McClelland, and J. Mumpower's *Human Judgment and Decision Making*, which provides a theoretically neutral framework that facilitates description and comparison of six major approaches. The third will be a book by K. R. Hammond that will present a theory of cognition within which each of the approaches are seen as having a complementary function.

This book presents the major concepts in this field and provides definitions, information about sources and interrelationships, and comments on current status. Each entry typically consists of several parts: a definition or definitions, in the form of quotations or close paraphrases from authoritative sources; a denotative example; a list of synonyms; a comment on the origins and current usage of the concept; and, finally, a list of related concepts that should help the user to explore the conceptual structure of the field.

Terms treated in this book are typed in all capitals the first time they appear in any entry, the use of boldface caps indicating that the term is treated in that entry and the use of lightface caps indicating that it is treated elsewhere in the book. (The term that is capitalized will in some cases be a slight grammatical variant of the exact title of the entry, for example, "conservative" instead of "conservatism", "independent" instead of "independence".)

An additional feature of the book is a graphic representation in the Frontispiece of the similarity relations (in terms of frequency of bibliographic co-citation) of the major researchers in judgment and decision making. This graph was prepared by Howard White and Belver Griffith of Drexel University. It should enable the user more quickly to comprehend the conceptual structure of the field and, thus, to search this structure more effectively and to grasp better the reasons for differences in use and definitions of terms. A discussion by White and Griffith of the method of co-citation analysis is included at the end of the book.

We would like to thank Martin Tolcott for suggesting the need for this book and for providing encouragement during its development. We would also like to thank Norman H. Anderson, Ward Edwards, Robyn M. Dawes, Edward E. Jones, Lola L. Lopes, Kenneth R. MacCrimmon, Robert J. Quinn, Martin K. Starr, Donald A. Wehrung, and Detlof von Winterfeldt for reviewing portions of the manuscript. Since none read the entire manuscript, however, and since we did not heed all their advice, we must bear the full responsibility for whatever errors remain. Finally, we would like to thank Doreen Victor for obtaining permissions for an unusually large number of quotations and proofreading and correcting an unusually large bibliography; Janet Grassia for editing the text; Mary Luhring for supervising the preparation of the illustrations and coordinating the details of production; and Michael O'Reilly for writing the many computer programs used to check the text for consistency and produce the final copy.

This work is based upon research supported by the Engineering Psychology Programs, Office of Naval Research, Contract N00014-77-C-0336, Work Unit Number NR 197-038. This project was also supported in part by BRSG Grant No. RR07013-14 awarded by the Biomedical Research Support Program, Division of Research Resources, National Institute of Health.

ACKNOWLEDGEMENTS TO PUBLISHERS

Acknowledgements are made to the following publishers for use of quotations in this volume.

Page 5.   Plott, Axiomatic social choice theory, *American Journal of Political Science*. Copyright © 1976 by the University of Texas Press.

Page 16.   Kahneman & Tversky, Subjective probability, *Cognitive Psychology*. Copyright © 1972 by Academic Press.

Page 30.   Simon, *Models of thought*. Copyright © 1979 by Yale University Press.

Page 52.   Krantz, Luce, Suppes & Tversky, *Foundations of measurement* (Vol. 1). Copyright © 1971 by Academic Press.

Page 53.   Luce, Conjoint Measurement: A brief survey, *Conflicting objectives in decisions,* edited by Bell, Keeney & Raiffa. Copyright © 1977 by John Wiley & Sons, Ltd. Reprinted by permission.

Page 80.   Reproduced from *The Delphi Method: Techniques and Applications,* 1975, edited by Harold A. Linstone and Murray Turoff with permission of publishers, Addison-Wesley, Advanced Book Program, Reading, Massachusetts, U.S.A.

Page 87.   Reprinted by permission of the publisher from Kim & Roush, *Mathematics for social scientists*. Copyright © 1980 by Elsevier North Holland, Inc.

Page 104-   Weber, *The methodology of the social sciences*, translated
105.   by Shils and Finch. Copyright © 1949 by The Free Press, renewed 1977, Edward A. Shils.

Page 105.   Simon, *Administrative behavior*. Copyright © 1976 by Herbert A. Simon. Reprinted by permission of Macmillan Publishing Company, Inc.

Page 130.   von Neumann & Morgenstern, *Theory of games and economic behavior*. Copyright © 1944, 1972 by Princeton University Press. Reprinted by permission.

Page 131.   Polya, *Mathematics and plausible reasoning* (Vol. 1). Copyright © 1954 by Princeton University Press. Reprinted by permission of Princeton University Press.

A POSTERIORI DECOMPOSITION.

See DECOMPOSITION.

A POSTERIORI PROBABILITY.

See POSTERIOR PROBABILITY.

A PRIORI DECOMPOSITION.

See DECOMPOSITION.

A PRIORI PROBABILITY.

See PRIOR PROBABILITY.

ABSOLUTE.

See SCALES of MEASUREMENT.

ABSOLUTE WEIGHT.

See WEIGHT.

ACCOUNTING PRICE.

See COST-BENEFIT ANALYSIS.

ACHIEVEMENT.

See LENS MODEL, LENS MODEL EQUATION.

ACT FORK.

See DECISION TREE.

ACT NODE.

See DECISION TREE.

ACTUARIAL PREDICTION

definition: Prediction based on statistical data (as opposed to judgments) which are aggregated mathematically (as opposed to intuitively). In actuarial prediction, the individual, object, or event is assigned to a class on the basis of objective criteria. Predictions of behaviors, characteristics, or events are made on the basis of the frequencies with which they have been observed to occur in that class. "The mechanical combining of information for classification purposes, and the resultant PROBABILITY figure which is an empirically determined relative frequency, are the characteristics that define the actuarial or statistical type of prediction" (Meehl, 1954, p. 3.)

comment: Actuarial prediction is frequently contrasted with CLINICAL PREDICTION. Actuarial predictions are generally more accurate than clinical predictions (Sarbin, Taft, & Bailey, 1960; Meehl, 1954; Dawes, 1979; Sawyer, 1966.)

synonym: STATISTICAL PREDICTION

related terms: CLINICAL PREDICTION, BOOTSTRAPPING, OBJECTIVE PROBABILITY.

ADAPTIVE.
———————

See FEEDBACK, RATIONALITY.

ADDING MODEL
—————— —————

definition: A LINEAR MODEL that AGGREGATES information from different
VARIABLES by (a) multiplying each input variable by a CONSTANT (which
may vary from input variable to input variable and which may be 1),
(b) summing the products, and then (c) adding a constant (which may be
0) to the sum. Thus,

$$Y = a + b_1X_1 + b_2X_2 + \ldots + b_kX_k.$$

It is important to note that the transformation of variables (for
example, by VALUE or UTILITY FUNCTIONS) is a separate matter from
their aggregation. Linear aggregation rules, such as adding, can take
as inputs the outputs of either linear or nonlinear transformations.

examples: An example of an adding model would be subtracting (which
is the same kind of aggregation rule as adding) the VALUE of one
alternative from that of another to obtain the difference in
PREFERENCE between them (Shanteau & Anderson, 1969). Another would be
the addition of height and width, by children, in estimating area
(Anderson & Cuneo, 1978).

comment: In an analysis of variance, the way in which the independent
variables combine is said to be **ADDITIVE** when there are main effects
but no INTERACTION (Hoffman, Slovic, & Rorer, 1968, pp. 340f).   An
adding model is indicated graphically by PARALLELISM (see figure on
next page) (Anderson, 1981) among the functions relating X_1 to Y at
different levels of X_2. Despite their simplicity, adding models (more
generally, linear models) are very robust prediction models (Yntema &
Torgerson, 1961; Dawes & Corrigan, 1974), at least when the predictors
are not negatively correlated (McClelland, 1978).

synonym: **ADDITIVE MODEL**.

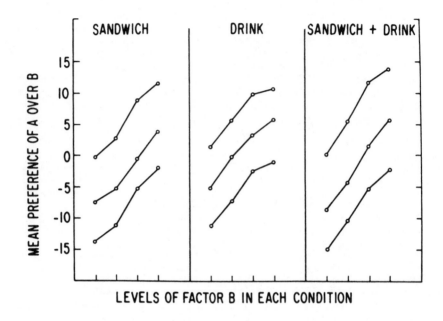

Parallelism

From Shanteau & Anderson, 1969. Copyright 1969 by Academic Press. Reprinted by permission.

related terms: PARALLELISM, AVERAGING MODEL, LINEAR MODEL, INDEPENDENCE, FUNCTION FORM, WEIGHT.

ADDITIVE.

   See ADDING MODEL.

ADDITIVE MODEL.

See ADDING MODEL.

ADMISSABLE SET.

See PARETO FRONTIER.

AGENDA PROBLEM

definition: The fact that the alternative chosen can depend on the order in which the alternatives are considered, especially when the CHOICE is defined by majority vote (Plott, 1976).

example: Consider a public of three persons, P1, P2, and P3, and a set of three POLICY alternatives, X, Y, and Z, which are ranked by these three persons as follows (example from Plott, 1976):

	X	Y	Z
P1	3	2	1
P2	1	3	2
P3	2	1	3

A 1 represents the lowest order of PREFERENCE, and a 3 the highest. If the agenda calls for voting on policies X and Y first and then choosing between the winner of that vote and Z, X will win the first round, and Z will win the second and be declared overall winner. If, however, the agenda calls for voting on X and Z first and then on the winner of that vote and Y, Z will win the first round, and Y will win the second and be declared overall winner! As a final possibility, if the agenda calls for voting on Y and Z first and then on the winner of that vote and X, Y will win the first round, and X will win the second and be declared overall winner.

comment: "'...How often will such a crazy case occur?' If everything is random, the answer is not what the asker expected to hear. In this case the answer is simply 'almost always.' The PROBABILITY of this event approaches *one* as the number of alternatives approaches infinity and it approaches it *very* rapidly. In this sense the cycle is *the* case and *not* the exception" (Plott, 1976, p. 514). Though this is clearly an unsatisfactory state of affairs, it is one that politicians are keenly aware of: In practical politics, who controls the agenda often controls the election.

synonyms: MAJORITY RULE CYCLE, MAJORITY PREFERENCE CYCLE.

related terms: ARROW's PARADOX, SOCIAL WELFARE FUNCTION.

AGGREGATION

definition: Combining information. For example, combining VALUE JUDGMENTS on different DIMENSIONS to yield an overall MEASURE of value, or combining PROBABILITY estimates based on different sets of data to arrive at an overall estimate of probability. Such combination may be either within or across persons.

comment: Information can be combined according to a variety of rules or principles. CONJOINT MEASUREMENT calls these rules COMPOSITION RULES and distinguishes among ADDITIVE, distributive, and dual-distributive rules. IIT calls them INTEGRATION RULES, and distinguishes among ADDING, AVERAGING, and MULTIPLYING rules. SJT calls them ORGANIZING PRINCIPLES and distinguishes between ADDITIVE and CONFIGURAL principles. BDT uses two kinds of combining rules: the multiplicative rule of BAYES' THEOREM and an AVERAGING rule for combining value judgments.DT also uses Bayes' Theorem; however, it employs both additive and multiplicative MULTIATTRIBUTE VALUE or UTILITY FUNCTIONS.

Anderson (1974c, p. 237) observes that attempts at a "unified theoretical system" of aggregation, or integration processes have been relatively limited. "Systematic developments have been made by Garner (1962; see also Garner & Morton, 1969) using statistical information theory, by Edwards (e.g., 1968a) using BAYESIAN theory of mathematical statistics, and by Brunswik (1956; see also Hammond, 1966) using MULTIPLE REGRESSION analysis. ...All three share a predominant concern with normative analysis in which the mathematical model is used as a standard against which to measure the success or ACHEIVEMENT of the organism rather than as a description of the psychological processes themselves. The present approach [IIT], in contrast, is primarily descriptive in nature."

If information is to be aggregated across dimensions that are measured in different units, the problem of COMMENSURATION must be addressed. If information is to be aggregated across different individuals to arrive at, for example, a SOCIAL WELFARE FUNCTION, the problems of INTERPERSONAL COMPARABILITY and ARROW's PARADOX must be addressed.

Because the number of items of information that humans can process simultaneously is severely limited (Miller, 1956; Broadbent, 1975), it is difficult to aggregate information across dimensions (Goldberg, 1965; Shepard, 1964; Slovic & Lichtenstein, 1971).

Aggregation is necessary in the case of both A PRIORI and A POSTERIORI DECOMPOSITION.

synonyms: COMPOSITION, INFORMATION INTEGRATION, ORGANIZATION.

related terms: DECOMPOSITION, COMMENSURATION, INTERPERSONAL COMPARABILITY, LINEAR MODEL, MULTILINEAR MODEL, ADDING MODEL, AVERAGING MODEL, MULTIPLYING MODEL, CONFIGURAL MODEL.

AGREEMENT.

See LENS MODEL EQUATION.

ALGEBRAIC TRANSITIVITY.

See TRANSITIVITY.

ALGORITHM.

See HEURISTIC.

ALLAIS' PARADOX

definition: A choice problem, constructed by Allais (1953a), to which people typically respond in ways inconsistent with UTILITY theory. The problem involves two hypothetical decision situations, the first of which is as follows:

Situation A. Choose between

Gamble 1. $500,000 with probability 1.00.

Gamble 2. $2,500,000 with probability .10,
$500,000 with probability .89,
$0 with probability .01.

Most people prefer Gamble 1 to Gamble 2, thus implying that

u($500,000) > .10u($2,500,000) + .89u($500,000) + .01u($0)

and hence that

.11u($500,000) > .10u($2,500,000) + .01u($0).

The second situation is as follows:

Situation B. Choose between

Gamble 3. $500,000 with probability .11,
$0 with probability .89.

Gamble 4. $2,500,000 with probability .10,
$0 with probability .90.

Most prefer Gamble 4 to Gamble 3, thus implying that

.10u($2,500,000) + .90u($0) > .11u($500,000) + .89u($0)

and hence that

.10u($2,500,000) + .01u($0) > .11u($500,000).

This is clearly inconsistent with the implication of the choice in the first situation.

comment: Allais' paradox argues that utility theory is flawed as a DESCRIPTIVE MODEL of human DECISION MAKING. Whether it is flawed as a NORMATIVE MODEL for decision making is another question. Savage (1954; see Coombs, Dawes, & Tversky, 1970, p. 127) has shown another way of looking at Allais' paradox that makes the prescriptions of utility theory intuitively acceptable and thus seems to take the force out of Allais' paradox on this point.

related terms: UTILITY, REVEALED PREFERENCE, CERTAINTY EFFECT.

ANALYTIC PROCESSES.

  See QUASI-RATIONALITY.

ANALYTIC THOUGHT.

  See QUASI-RATIONALITY.

ANALYTICAL APPROACH to PROBABILITY.

  See OBJECTIVE PROBABILITY.

ANCHOR

definition: A stimulus or thought that provides a reference or
starting point for judgment.

comment: Kahneman & Tversky use the term to refer to a starting point
for the ANCHORING and ADJUSTMENT heuristic. Torgerson (1958, p. 80)
defines anchor as "those conditions that determine the origin and unit
of the subjective continuum which the subject will use in reporting
his judgments of magnitude." He lists three kinds of anchors: the
past experiences of the subject, the instructions, and the range and
distribution (see Parducci, 1963, 1965, 1968) of the stimuli being
judged.

     Unambiguous anchoring of stimulus (information, cue) and response
scales is necessary for interpretation and interpersonal comparison of
magnitude judgments (Nunnally, 1967, p.   526; Torgerson, 1958, p.
80).

related terms: ANCHORING and ADJUSTMENT.

ANCHORING and ADJUSTMENT

definition: A judgmental HEURISTIC, identified by Tversky and Kahneman (1974), in which people make estimates by starting from an initial VALUE (ANCHOR) and then adjusting it, usually to an insufficient degree, to yield the final answer. For example, subjects asked to estimate the percentage of African countries in the United Nations, starting with an arbitrary initial value of 10% produced an estimate of 25%, while those starting with an arbitrary initial value of 65% produced an estimate of 45%. (The initial value was established by spinning a wheel of fortune in the subject's presence and then first asking the subject whether the actual value was higher or lower than the value on which the wheel had stopped.)

comment: SUBJECTIVE PROBABILITY distributions for a given quantity, such as the Dow-Jones, can be obtained in two ways that, while formally equivalent, seem to lead to adjustment from different anchors. (Tversky & Kahneman, 1974)

      a. FRACTILE ESTIMATION. Asking the subject to select values for the Dow-Jones that correspond to specified percentiles of his PROBABILITY distribution.

      b. PROBABILITY ESTIMATION. Asking the subject to assess the probability that the true value of the Dow-Jones will exceed some specified values.

In fractile estimation, the JUDGE states his answer in units of the assessed quantity, and the natural starting point is his best estimate. This procedure yields probability distributions that are too tight. In probability estimation, the answers are stated in probabilities or ODDS, and the natural starting point is a probability of one-half or even odds. This procedure yields probability distributions that are too flat. The difference in the way the anchoring-and-adjustment heuristic seems to be applied to FRACTILE ESTIMATION and PROBABILITY ESTIMATION suggests the possibility that an appropriate combination of the two methods could yield properly CALIBRATED probability distributions.

Similarly, REVEALED PREFERENCE can be measured in two ways that, while formally equivalent, seem to lead to adjustment from different anchors (Slovic & Lichtenstein, 1968). If a person is asked *which bet he prefers*, strength of PREFERENCE correlates most highly with the probability of winning, suggesting anchoring and adjustment on a probability scale. However, if he is asked *how much he is willing to bid for a bet*, the amount of money bid correlates most highly with amount to win and amount to lose, suggesting anchoring and adjustment on a money scale, as illustrated by the following subjective report:

> If the odds were...heavier in favor of winning... rather than losing..., I would pay about 3/4 [adjustment] of the amount I would expect to win [anchor]. If the reverse were true, I would ask the experimenter to pay me about...1/2 [adjustment] of the amount I could lose [anchor] (Slovic & Lichtenstein, 1968.)

Both the probability estimation and the revealed preference examples point to the wisdom of TRIANGULATION.

related terms: HEURISTIC, SUBJECTIVE PROBABILITY, ANCHOR, CONSERVATISM, FUNDAMENTAL ATTRIBUTION ERROR, AVAILABILITY, REPRESENTATIVENESS.

ARCHIMEDEAN AXIOM.

See AXIOM.

ARROW's PARADOX

definition: The paradox, pointed out by Arrow (1951, 1963), that if the possibility of INTERPERSONAL COMPARABILITY (which see) of UTILITY is excluded, then the only methods of arriving at a SOCIAL WELFARE FUNCTION on the basis of individual PREFERENCES which (a) will be defined for a wide range of sets of individual orderings, (b) will not reflect individuals' preferences negatively, (c) will be TRANSITIVE, and (d) will be INDEPENDENT of irrelevant alternatives are either imposed or dictatorial (Arrow, 1963, p. 59). (A social welfare function is said to be "dictatorial" if there exists an individual whose preferences determine the social welfare function (Arrow, 1963, p. 30) and "imposed" if there is some pair of alternatives such that the community can never express a preference for one over the other (Arrow, 1963, p. 28)).

example: The following example deals with the problem of dependence **IRRELEVANT ALTERNATIVES** (alternatives that are logically irrelevant to the decision) on (see Arrow, 1963, p. 26; Plott, 1976, pp. 513ff.) See AGENDA PROBLEM for another example.

Consider a public of seven persons, P1 through P7, and a set of four POLICY alternatives, A, B, C, and D, which are ranked by these seven persons as follows:

	A	B	C	D
P1	4	3	2	1
P2	1	4	3	2
P3	2	1	4	3
P4	3	2	1	4
P5	4	3	2	1
P6	1	4	3	2
P7	2	1	4	3
Sum	17	18	19	16

Clearly, C is the most peferred and D the least preferred, with A and B falling in between.

Now, let us see what happens when we exclude one of these alternatives, say D, from the voting process. Whether or not D is taken into consideration should be quite irrelevant to judgments of the relative preferability of A, B, and C.

What the set of figures on the next page shows is that, even though this may be true for the individual rankings (each person's ranking of the remaining policies below is perfectly consistent with his ranking of these same policies in the full set of four above), it is not necessarily true for a social welfare function based on these rankings. Whereas before the ordering was A < B < C, it is now C < B < A, quite the reverse!

comment: Arrow's paradox poses a problem for social planners: How

	A	B	C
P1	3	2	1
P2	1	3	2
P3	2	1	3
P4	3	2	1
P5	3	2	1
P6	1	3	2
P7	2	1	3
Sum	15	14	13

are plans to be ordered in terms of contribution to social welfare if INTERPERSONAL COMPARISONS cannot be made and if not making interpersonal comparisons leads to Arrow's paradox? A number of suggestions have been made for avoiding Arrow's paradox (e.g., Black, 1948a, b; Coombs, 1964; Flood, 1978; Harsanyi, 1955; Luce & Raiffa, 1957; Pattanaik, 1971; Sen, 1973.) However, none of these has gained general acceptance.

synonyms: **V**OTING **P**ARADOX.

related terms: INTERPERSONAL COMPARABILITY, SOCIAL WELFARE FUNCTION, CARDINAL UTILITY, AGENDA PROBLEM.

ASPIRATION LEVEL.

See GOAL.

AT.

See ATTRIBUTION THEORY.

ATTITUDE TOWARD RISK.

See VON NEUMANN-MORGENSTERN UTILITY.

ATTRIBUTE.

See DIMENSION, MULTIATTRIBUTE DECISION MAKING.

ATTRIBUTE LEARNING.

See CONCEPT LEARNING.

ATTRIBUTION

definition: "The assignment of causes to behavior" (Jones, Kanouse, Kelley, Nisbett, Valins, & Weiner, 1971), for example, ascribing behavior to personal causes (dispositions) or to impersonal causes (roles). "The perception or INFERENCE of cause" (Kelley & Michela, 1980, p. 458). See ATTRIBUTION THEORY.

comment: This term was introduced by Heider (1958) and was later selected for emphasis by Kelley (1967a,b) and Jones & Davis (1965).

related terms: ATTRIBUTION THEORY, FUNDAMENTAL ATTRIBUTION ERROR, CORRESPONDENT INFERENCE, DISCOUNTING, INFERENCE, CLINICAL PREDICTION, SUBJECTIVE PROBABILITY.

ATTRIBUTION THEORY

definition: A DESCRIPTIVE approach to JUDGMENT deriving from the work of Fritz Heider (1958) and associated primarily with the names of Harold Kelley and Edward Jones (see Jones, Kanouse, Kelley, Nisbett, Valins, & Weiner, 1971; Kelley, 1967a,b; Jones & Davis, 1965; Harvey, Ickes, & Kidd, 1976, 1978). Attribution Theory (**AT**) seeks to describe the processes by which people arrive at causal explanations, or ATTRIBUTIONS, for behavior. A primary concern is with how people distinguish between personal and impersonal causes (see FUNDAMENTAL ATTRIBUTION ERROR).

comment: Attribution theory can be thought of as being concerned with the naive observer's descriptive model of CHOICE behavior (including his/her own; see Bem, 1972). As such, it speaks to the BELIEFS, or PROBABILITY judgments, on which the naive observer bases his/her DECISIONS. Many of the effects obtained by AT appear to be explainable in terms of the HEURISTICS described by PDT (Jones, 1979).

synonym: AT.

related terms: JUDGMENT vs. DECISION THEORIES, ATTRIBUTION,

CORRESPONDENT   INFERENCE,   DISCOUNTING,   COVARIATION   PRINCIPLE,
HEURISTICS.

AUTOCORRELATION

definition: Correlation   between   "values   of   the   same VARIABLE at
different time lags" (Makridakis & Wheelwright, 1977, p.   23).   For
example,   correlation   between   profits   in   January   and   profits   in
February, between February and March, between January and March,   etc.
Used   to   detect   temporal   patterns   in   the   data   (Makridakis   &
Wheelwright, 1977, p.   23).

comment: If the data are *stationary*, no pattern will   be   evident   in
the   autocorrelations.   If   there   is   a   LINEAR   trend,   the
autocorrelations will decrease regularly with increasing separation in
time,   and no pattern will be evident in the autocorrelations of first
differences (differences between the first VALUE of the series and the
second,   between the second and the third, and so forth.)   If there is
a NONLINEAR trend, there will be a pattern in the autocorrelations   of
first differences, but this can usually be eliminated by taking second
or third differences.   If   there   is   a   *cyclical*   pattern   (called   a
seasonal   pattern if the cycle length is not greater than a year), the
autocorrelations will peak at regular intervals (e.g.,   the   January-
January,   February-February,   etc.   correlations might be higher than
the others)(Makridakis & Wheelwright, 1977, pp.   15-31.)

related terms: FORECASTING, LINEAR, NONLINEAR.

AUTO CORRELATION ANALYSIS.

    See FORECASTING.

AVAILABILITY

definition: A   judgmental   HEURISTIC,   identified   by Kahneman   and
Tversky   (1973),   in which a person evaluates the frequency of classes
or the SUBJECTIVE   PROBABILITY   of   events   by   the   ease   with   which
relevant   instances   come   to   mind."   (p.   207) For example, one may
assess the RISK of heart attack among middle aged people by   recalling

such occurrences among one's acquaintances. (See SCRIPT.) In one experiment, subjects who heard a list of names of famous women and an equal number of names of men who were not famous judged there to have been more names of women in the list than names of men. Similarly, it is a common experience that the subjective probability of an accident rises temporarily when one sees a car overturned by the side of the road.

comment: The major difference between availability and REPRESENTATIVENESS is that the former evaluates subjective probability by "the difficulty of retrieval and construction of instances," thus focusing on "the particular instances, or the denotation of the event"; whereas the latter evaluates subjective probability by "the degree of correspondence between the sample and the population, or between an occurrence and a model," thus focusing on "the generic features, or the connotation, of the event." "Thus, the representativeness heuristic is more likely to be employed when events are characterized in terms of the their general properties; whereas the availability heuristic is more likely to be employed when events are more naturally thought of in terms of specific occurrences." (Kahneman & Tversky, 1972, pp. 451-452.)

related terms: HEURISTIC, SUBJECTIVE PROBABILITY, SCRIPT, REPRESENTATIVENESS, ANCHORING and ADJUSTMENT.

AVERAGING MODEL

definition: A MODEL that AGGREGATES information from different VARIABLES by (a) multiplying each input variable by a *relative* CONSTANT (i.e., a constant from a set that has been normalized to sum to 1), (b) summing the products, and then (c) adding a constant (which may be 0) to the sum. Thus,

$$Y = a + (b_1/B)X_1 + (b_2/B)X_2 + \ldots + (b_k/B)X_k.$$

(See Anderson, 1981, p. 71.) It is important to note that the transformation of variables (for example, by VALUE or UTILITY FUNCTIONS) is a separate matter from their aggregation. Linear aggregation rules, such as the equal-weights (see below) averaging model, can take as inputs the outputs of either linear or nonlinear transformations.

comment: The averaging model, like the ADDING MODEL, yields no INTERACTION in analysis of variance. Adding and averaging models are distinguished by changing the size of the stimulus set. The figure below illustrates the logic:

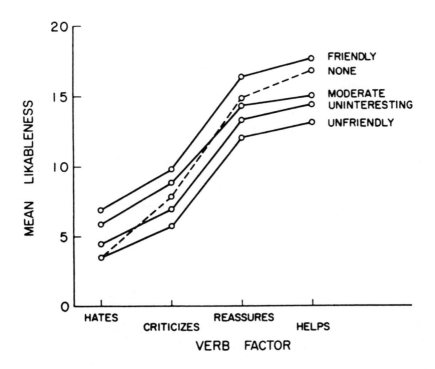

A Crossover

From Anderson, 1981. Copyright 1981 by Academic Press. Reprinted by permission.

(From Anderson, 1981, p. 68a.) "...The near-PARALLELISM of the four solid curves supports a linear-type model, either adding or averaging" (p. 68).

"The critical test between adding and averaging is obtained by comparing the dashed curve labeled 'none' with the solid curve labeled 'moderate.' For both curves, the judgment is based on the behavior information listed on the horizontal. The 'none' curve contains no more information; the 'moderate' curve contains the added information that the man is moderate. The test revolves on the effect of this added information.

"If an adding process was operative, then adding the mildly positive information that the man is moderate would cause the 'moderate' curve to lie above the 'none' curve every point. But the curves cross over, thereby eliminating the adding model. at This conclusion holds not only for the exact adding model, but also for any qualitative, directional adding model. This crossover eliminates an entire family of adding-type models.

"The averaging model provides a simple explanation of the crossover. If moderate is averaged in, that will lower the response to the very positive behavior, 'helps people.' Similarly, it will raise the response to the very negative behavior, 'hates people'" (p. 69). In other words, the relative importance, b_i/B, of a input variable, X_i, is indicated by the relative slope of the FUNCTION relating it to the output variable. If an averaging model applies, the addition of additional dimensions will increase B, decrease b_i/B, and decrease this slope, so that the new function will cross over the old one (Anderson, 1981, pp. 68ff.)

Anderson has found averaging processes to be far more common than adding processes. One attractive feature of the averaging model is that it provides an interpretation of the fact that attitudes based on more information are harder to change (Anderson, 1981, p. 72.) The averaging model is a CONFIGURAL MODEL.

Norman Anderson distinguishes between two variants of the averaging model: that in which the relative weights are constant across all levels of each variable (the EQUAL WEIGHTS model) and that in which the relative weights may vary across levels within any variable (the DIFFERENTIAL weights model). Both equal weights and differential weights are relative and exhibit the set-size effect. Only the equal weights model is a LINEAR MODEL.

SJT's "POLICY" AID AND BDT's SMART procedure both employ averaging models.

related terms: PARALLELISM, ADDING MODEL, LINEAR MODEL, INDEPENDENCE, FUNCTION FORM, WEIGHT.

AXIOM

definition: An axiom is an assertion about the relationship between or the existence of undefined primitive elements.

comment: There are two basic types of axioms. QUALITATIVE **AX**IOMS assert a relationship between elements. For example, the TRANSITIVITY axiom asserts "If a > b and b > c then a > c." **EXISTENTIAL AXIOMS** assert the existence of elements satisfying certain properties. For example, if $2a$ represents the concatenation of element a with itself, $3a$ the concatenation of a with $2a$, etc., then the ARCHIMEDEAN AXIOM asserts that "for any b, the set of integers n for which $b > na$ is finite" (Krantz, Luce, Suppes, & Tversky, 1971, p. 25); that is, if $b > a$ there exists an n large enough so that $na > b$. In general, qualitative axioms are empirically testable while existential axioms are not.

Axioms are usually grouped into axiom systems from which theorems and propositions are derived using the standard rules of logic and mathematics (these rules thereby become an implicit part of the axiom system). An axiom is INDEPENDENT from the other axioms in the system if it cannot be derived from the other axioms. An axiom system is consistent if there exists or can be constructed an example satisfying the axioms. Arrow (1951) shows that one particular set of "reasonable" axioms is actually inconsistent. The most common use of axiom systems in JUDGMENT and DECISION MAKING is for the derivation of representation theorems. A **REPRESENTATION THEOREM** asserts that if a given empirical relational structure satisfies certain axioms then that relational structure can be represented by a numerical system (e.g., a SCALE or scales). Important axiom systems and the representation theorems derived from them are described in von Neumann and Morgenstern (1947), Savage (1954), Luce and Raiffa (1957), Krantz, Luce, Suppes, and Tversky (1971), and Keeney and Raiffa (1976).

related terms: ARROW'S PARADOX, CONJOINT MEASUREMENT, MULTIATTRIBUTE UTILITY THEORY, SUBJECTIVELY EXPECTED UTILITY, SURE-THING PRINCIPLE, TRANSITIVITY, VON NEUMANN-MORGENSTERN UTILITY.

AXIOMATIC.

See AXIOM, CONJOINT MEASUREMENT.

AXIOMATIC CONJOINT MEASUREMENT.

See CONJOINT MEASUREMENT.

B WEIGHT.

See WEIGHT.

BALANCE SHEET

definition: A listing of the pros and cons of alternative courses of action, often arranged in the form of a cross-classification table in which either the row or column VARIABLE would be the alternative courses of action and the other variable would be the pros and cons of each. A balance sheet is an information display used to facilitate arriving at an overall evaluation of the alternatives.

example: Benjamin Franklin's (1956) suggestion was to make a column for each course of action and to list the arguments for and against each course of action in the appropriate column. More recently, Janis & Mann (1977, p. 138, 151) have suggested a cross classification of (a) courses of action by (b) utilitarian gains or losses for self, utilitarian gains or losses for significant others, (c) self-approval, and (d) social approval.

related terms: MULTIATTRIBUTE UTILITY, MULTIPLE OBJECTIVE DECISION MAKING, CONFLICT THEORY.

BASE RATE.

See PRIOR PROBABILITY, BASE-RATE FALLACY.

BASE-RATE FALLACY

definition: A term introduced by Kahneman & Tversky (1973) to indicate reliance on singular, or case, data (data that distinguish the particular case from other members of its class) without giving sufficient WEIGHT to distributional, or BASE-RATE data (data that apply to the class as a whole). Matching PROBABILITY estimates to sample proportions without taking PRIOR PROBABILITIES into account (Beach,Wise, & Barclay, 1970; Kriz, 1967; Shanteau, 1970.)

comment: The base-rate fallacy is illustrated by the taxi-cab problem (Tversky & Kahneman, 1977, p. 22.)

> A cab was involved in a hit-and-run accident at night: Two cab companies, the Green and the Blue, operate in the city. You are given the following data:
>
> a. 85% of the cabs in the city are Green and 15% are Blue.
>
> b. A witness identified the cab as a Blue cab. The court tested his ability to identify cabs under the appropriate visibility conditions. When presented with a sample of cabs (half of which were Blue and half of which were Green) the witness made correct identifications in 80% of the cases and erred in 20% of the cases.
>
> Question: What is the probability that the cab involved in the accident was Blue rather than Green?

The modal and median judgment of most subjects was 80%, which coincides with the credibility of the witness and ignores the base rate, that is, the relative frequency of Green and Blue cabs. (The correct probability is .41, which is considerably closer to the base rate. (See BAYES' THEOREM for the relevant calculations.)

comment: The base-rate fallacy is presumed to be produced by REPRESENTATIVENESS and leads to error that is non-CONSERVATIVE.

Nisbett, Borgida, Crandall, & Reed (1976, p. 128) attribute the base-rate fallacy to the fact that "case information is vivid, salient, and concrete", while "base-rate or consensus information is remote, pallid, and abstract." Borgida and Nisbett (1977) gave undergraduate subjects course-evaluation information and invited them to state their own CHOICES for future enrollment. Some students received summaries of the evaluations of previous course enrollees; others received the information through face-to-face contact with a small number of individuals. As anticipated by the investigators, abstract data-summary information had little IMPACT on course choices, whereas concrete information had a substantial impact.

See CAUSAL SCHEMA for an example where base-rate data that fit into a causal schema do tend to be taken into account.

related terms: CONSERVATISM, REPRESENTATIVENESS, CAUSAL SCHEMA.

BAYES' THEOREM

definition: A theorem, based on the work of Reverend Thomas Bayes (1763, reprinted 1958), for the revision of opinions, or BELIEFS, on the basis of evidence. If p(H) is the PRIOR PROBABILITY that hypothesis H is true, p(D) is the probability that datum D will be observed, p(D|H) is the CONDITIONAL PROBABILITY that datum D will be observed given that hypothesis H is true, and p(H|D) is the POSTERIOR PROBABILITY that hypothesis H is true given that datum D has been observed, then one form of Bayes' theorem states that

$$p(H|D) = \frac{p(D|H)p(H)}{p(D)}$$

provided p(D) and p(H) are not 0 (Edwards, Lindman, & Savage, 1963, p. 198). Bayes' theorem is a trivial consequence of the ADDITIVE property of probabilities and is noncontroversial (Edwards, 1968a, p. 19.)

comment: The use of Bayes' theorem assumes that data are CONDITIONALLY INDEPENDENT (Slovic & Lichtenstein, 1973, p. 32.) Bayes' theorem is employed by BAYESIANS (which see.)

related terms: BAYESIAN,   SUBJECTIVE   PROBABILITY,   CONDITIONAL
INDEPENDENCE.

BAYESIAN

definition: The school of thought, or an adherent to the school of
thought, which asserts (a) that SUBJECTIVE PROBABILITY is a MEASURE of
strength of BELIEF and (b) that BAYES' THEOREM is a formally optimal
rule for revising belief in the light of evidence (Edwards, Lindman, &
Savage, 1963; Edwards, 1968a; Savage, 1954.)

comment: The Bayesian school of thought derives from a paper by the
Reverend Thomas Bayes (1764, reprinted 1958) and has its modern
origins in works by von Neumann & Morgenstern (1947), Savage (1954),
Schlaifer (1959), and, in psychology, by Edwards (1962) (Edwards,
Lindman, & Savage, 1963, p. 194; Slovic & Lichtenstein, 1973, p.
30).

related terms: SUBJECTIVE PROBABILITY, BAYES' THEOREM.

B/C RATIO.

See BENEFIT-COST RATIO.

BDT.

See BEHAVIORAL DECISION THEORY.

BEHAVIORAL ACHIEVEMENT.

See LENS MODEL.

BEHAVIORAL DECISION THEORY

definition: A DESCRIPTIVE and NORMATIVE approach to JUDGMENT and
DECISION MAKING developed by Ward Edwards (1954, 1961).   Behavioral
Decision Theory (**BDT**) describes decision behavior in terms of
departures from the NORMATIVE MODELS of BAYES' THEOREM and UTILITY

theory, the same models that are used normatively by DT. This work has explored the SUBJECTIVE EXPECTED UTILITY (SEU) model and discovered CONSERVATISM in information processing. BDT has also developed the PIP DECISION AID for probabilistic information processing and the SMART decision aid for use in MULTIATTRIBUTE decision making.

synonym: BDT.

related terms: JUDGMENT vs. DECISION THEORIES, BAYESIAN, SUBJECTIVE EXPECTED UTILITY, PIP, SMART.

BELIEF.

See FACT JUDGMENT.

BELLMAN PRINCIPLE of OPTIMALITY.

See DYNAMIC PROGRAMMING.

BENEFIT-COST RATIO:

definition: The ratio of total present benefits (B) to total present costs (C), sometimes computed in COST-BENEFIT ANALYSIS as the summary criterion of the worthwhileness, or "economic feasibility," of an action option. If B/C > 1.0 the option is considered worthwhile (though perhaps less so than competing options); if B/C = 1.0, the option is considered marginal; and if B/C < 1.0, the option is considered *not* worthwhile (assuming all else equal in each case).

comment: The B/C ratio is *not* normally the appropriate criterion for choice of options in cost-benefit analysis, contrary to common belief and to common practice in some agencies such as the U.S. Army Corps of Engineers; the appropriate criterion is *net present benefit* (total present benefit minus total present cost) (Rothenberg, 1975, p. 77; Stokey & Zeckhauser, 1978, p. 146). Stokey and Zeckhauser state that the two criteria may indicate different choices in cases when options are mutually exclusive or when resources are constrained, although the criteria will often indicate the same choice in other situations. They further note in essence that the B/C ratio is less robust, being sensitive to arbitrary decisions about whether to define adverse consequences as costs or as negative benefits, while the net present benefit criterion is insensitive to such decisions.

> A municipal marina project costing $1 million might, for example, produce recreational benefits of $4 million and cause environmental damage of $2 million. Depending on whether that damage is regarded as a positive cost or a negative benefit, the benefit/cost ratio is 2 or 1.33. The maximize-net-benefits criterion is not susceptible to this ambiguity" (Stokey & Zeckhauser, 1978, p. 146).

More abstractly, defining F as favorable consequences, U as unfavorable consequences, and C as other costs:

$$[(F - U) - C] = [F - (C + U)]$$

while

$$\frac{(F - U)}{C} \neq \frac{F}{(C + U)}$$

synonym: **B/C RATIO.**

related terms: COST-BENEFIT ANALYSIS, VALUE, MARKET PRICE, SHADOW PRICE, NONMARKETED GOOD, PUBLIC GOOD, DECISION MAKING, TRADEOFF.

BETA WEIGHT

definition: A **STANDARD REGRESSION WEIGHT,** that is, a WEIGHT that relates a standardized predictor VARIABLE to the standardized criterion in REGRESSION ANALYSIS (Bock, 1975, p. 138.) The relative magnitudes of the beta weights generally reflect the relative importance of the predictor variables in "explaining" or "causing" variation in the criterion (McNemar, 1962, p. 176.)

comment: The interpretation placed on the beta weights depends on the correlations among the predictors. When the predictors are UNCORRELATED, the betas are equal to the simple correlations:

$$B_i = r_i$$

(Hursch, Hammond, & Hursch, 1964, p. 47.) When the predictors are correlated, very little reliance can be placed on beta weights as indicators of relative importance (Kendall, 1957, p. 74; Darlington, 1968). When the predictors are correlated and the emphasis is on cause and effect, the beta weight, which indicates the rate of change in the criterion as a function of the predictor, provides "the most useful form of a statement" (granting certain assumptions) (Darlington, 1968, p. 167). When the predictors are correlated and the emphasis is on prediction, **USEFULNESS** (the amount R^2 would drop if the variable were removed from the regression equation), which is closely related to the partial correlation coefficient, is "clearly the MEASURE of greatest interest" (Darlington, 1968, p. 167).

synonym: **STANDARD REGRESSION WEIGHT.**

related terms: WEIGHT, REGRESSION ANALYSIS.

BETWEENNESS PROPERTY.

See PORTFOLIO THEORY.

BIAS

definition: **SYSTEMATIC ERROR,** or **CONSTANT ERROR,** as opposed to unsystematic, or random, error. The difference between the mean of a (theoretical or empirical) distribution of MEASUREMENTS (statistical bias) or JUDGMENTS (judgmental bias) and the true VALUE. Departure from perfect CALIBRATION.

comment: A number of judgmental biases have been identified, including: error of leniency, error of central tendency, time order error, recency bias, round number bias, end effect, HINDSIGHT BIAS, NONREGRESSIVENESS BIAS. An important statistical bias is REGRESSION TOWARDS the MEAN.

synonyms: **CONSTANT ERROR, SYSTEMATIC ERROR.**

related terms: CALIBRATION, HEURISTICS, REGRESSION.

BIDDING GAME

definition: A technique for measuring the UTILITY (Definition 1), or
WORTH, to a person of changes on one descriptive dimension or set of
dimensions (X) in terms of changes on another descriptive dimension
(Y) which is used as a utility indicator, or NUMERAIRE. The numeraire
is often but not necessarily money. For given changes in X, the
analyst poses hypothetical exchanges in which the person either is
asked to specify maximum buying prices (WILLINGNESS TO PAY) or minimum
selling prices (WILLINGNESS TO ACCEPT PAYMENT) in units of Y
(noniterative variant), or is asked to accept or reject potential
buying or selling prices suggested by the analyst (iterative variant).
Responses yield the VALUE (Definition 2b) of any given change in X,
measured as the MARGINAL RATE OF SUBSTITUTION (MRS) between X and Y on
an. INDIFFERENCE CURVE relating the two.

examples: Examples involve both RISKY and RISKLESS situations.

Risky. Consider a lottery (STANDARD GAMBLE) in which the
respondent could receive a more desirable outcome M with probability P
and a less desirable outcome L with probability (1 - P). The
respondent is asked to specify his CERTAINTY EQUIVALENT for the
lottery, either (i) by assuming the analyst owns the lottery and
specifying the maximum amount he would bid to purchase it, or (ii) by
assuming he (the respondent) owns the lottery and specifying the
minimum amount he would demand to sell it.

Riskless. A coal-fired power plant is to be sited in a desert
area with presently pristine air. A major planning issue is the air
pollution and consequent degradation of visual air quality which the
plant would cause. The plant could be built with various levels of
pollution control with cost proportional to control level. Whether
the extra cost of maximal control would be justified by the resulting
higher visual air quality (relative to that expected with minimal
control) is a question appropriately addressed by COST-BENEFIT
ANALYSIS, but visual air quality is a NONMARKETED GOOD, so no MARKET
PRICE exists to indicate the VALUE (Definition 2b) of different levels
of it; a SHADOW PRICE must be estimated.

A bidding game is developed for use in a survey of people living
in or visiting the potentially affected region. Each survey
respondent is asked either the maximum yearly dollar sum he would be
willing to pay to maintain pristine air quality or the minimum yearly

sum he would demand to accept various extents of visual air quality degradation. (Whether respondents are asked for willingness to pay or willingness to accept payment depends on whether they are deemed to have property rights to the present pristine visual air quality level. See Hebert, Shikiar, & Perry, 1978, or Freeman, 1979, Ch. 3, for example.)

comment: Risky bidding games are used for assessment of subjective PROBABILITY and VON NEUMANN-MORGENSTERN UTILITY in STANDARD GAMBLES. (See, for example, Becker, 1962; Becker, DeGroot, & Marschak, 1964; Edwards, Lindman, & Phillips, 1965; Krantz & Tversky, 1965; Tversky, 1965.) Riskless bidding games are used for estimation of the monetary values of nonmarketed goods in COST-BENEFIT ANALYSIS and COST-EFFECTIVENESS ANALYSIS, as illustrated above. (See, for example, Bradford, 1970; Brookshire *et al.*, 1976, 1980; Freeman, 1979; Randall *et al.*, 1974; Sinden & Worrell, 1979, Ch. 4.)

Bidding games may be used with or without explicit budget constraints. Budget constraints can apply only to buying prices, not selling prices. In a budget-constrained game, a respondent is instructed to bid for the focal change only what he could actually afford to bid in a real-world exchange, even if he would bid more if his budget allowed. In a non-budget-constrained game, no such instruction is given: a legitimate response might be a bid of $1,000,000 ($1M) for restoration of the Taj Mahal (which is being severely damaged by pollution), say, indicating that *if* the respondent could afford to bid $1M he would be indifferent between the states (+ $1M Taj restoration, -$1M personal wealth) and ($0 Taj restoration, -$0 personal wealth), despite his present and probably future inability to pay $1M for Taj restoration or anything else. All applications in cost-benefit and cost-effectiveness analysis are budget-constrained because their aim is estimation of the bids which respondents *would* actually make in real-world markets for the focal (presently nonmarketed) goods if such markets could be created. A case could be made, in fact, that *all* bidding games are at least implicitly budget-constrained, including those where responses are selling rather than buying prices. The case would rest on the standard premise that the marginal utility of money (or any other numeraire, Y) decreases, and the MRS of Y for the focal good X therefore increases, as one's wealth in Y increases (see, for example, Baumol, 1977, Ch. 9; Samuelson, 1976, Ch. 22).

BILINEAR FAN.

See MULTIPLYING MODEL.

BILINEAR TERM.

See MULTILINEAR MODEL.

BOOTSTRAPPING

definition: Improving the quality of JUDGMENTS by basing decisions on a PARAMORPHIC MODEL that captures the judge's POLICY (Dawes & Corrigan, 1974, p. 101.) In bootstrapping, (a) a JUDGE attempts to make WHOLISTIC judgments of the VARIABLE of interest, (b) a PROPER LINEAR MODEL is constructed to predict the these judgments, and then (c) this same model is used as an IMPROPER LINEAR MODEL to predict the variable of interest (Dawes, 1979.) Dawes (1979) and Dawes & Corrigan (1974) have suggested that even an improper linear model of the judge's policy (VARIABLES and FUNCTION FORMS selected by the judge, WEIGHTS selected randomly or made equal) will perform as well as a proper one under certain fairly common conditions.

comment: The rationale behind bootstrapping is that, while the judge may be capable of arriving at a valid policy, he/she is not capable of applying that policy as consistently as a formula. Bootstrapping improves overall validity simply by improving reliability (Goldberg, 1970, p. 423; Hammond & Summers, 1972; Slovic & Lichtenstein, 1973, pp. 86f.) The work on bootstrapping is based on the LENS MODEL EQUATION. Bootstrapping can be used to reduce INTERPERSONAL CONFLICT, since even where "covert policy differences decrease markedly, inconsistency occurs in an amount sufficient to keep the overt judgments of the participants apart, and they continue to experience conflict" (Hammond & Brehmer, 1973, p. 386). SJT has used the "POLICY" AID for this purpose (Hammond & Brehmer, 1973).

related terms: POLICY CAPTURING, COGNITIVE CONTROL, LENS MODEL EQUATION, CONFLICT, "POLICY" AID.

BOUNDED RATIONALITY

definition: The notion that the capacity of the human mind for formulating and solving problems is so limited, compared with the complexity of the problems whose solution is required for objectively rational behavior in the real world, that we must construct a simplified (HEURISTIC) model of the real situation in order to deal with it. We behave rationally with respect to this model, but such bounded RATIONALITY is not even approximately optimal with respect to the real world (Simon, 1957, pp. 198f.; 1955; 1956). The picture is of "a creature of bounded rationality who copes with the complexity that confronts him by highly selective serial search of the environment, guided and interrupted by the demands of his motivational system, and regulated, in particular, by dynamically adjusting multidimensional levels of aspiration" (Simon, 1979b, p. 4).

comment: This conception of rationality is to be contrasted with the classical conception of rationality as MAXIMIZATION of EXPECTED UTILITY, which would require unlimited memory and computational capacity (Coombs, Dawes, & Tversky, 1970, p. 143.) It is also to be contrasted with the concept of QUASI-RATIONALITY which distinguishes between INTUITIVE and ANALYTIC mechanisms of information processing. Bounded rationality has been expressed in the form of two computer programs, the Logic Theorist, "which is based squarely on the idea of SATISFICING rather than MAXIMIZING" (Simon, 1957, p. 206), and the more recent General Problem Solver (Newell, Shaw, & Simon, 1962; Newell & Simon, 1972).

related terms: HEURISTIC, RATIONALITY, QUASI-RATIONALITY, SATISFICING.

BREAK-EVEN ANALYSIS

definition: Determination of that VALUE on an input VARIABLE (usually a PROBABILITY, a value, or a UTILITY) that would make the DECISION MAKER indifferent between two alternative courses of action.

comment: A break-even analysis helps the decision maker to JUDGE whether his/her CONFIDENCE INTERVAL for a given input variable is sufficiently narrow to provide an acceptable basis for the decision and thus whether more precise information is desirable. A limited form of SENSITIVITY ANALYSIS.

related terms: SENSITIVITY ANALYSIS, UNCERTAINTY, VALUE of INFORMATION.

BUYING PRICE.

See WILLINGNESS to PAY.

CALCULATED RATIONALITY.

See RATIONALITY.

CALIBRATION

definition : The extent to which the PROBABILITIES assigned to events are of the same magnitude as the corresponding empirical relative frequencies (Lichtenstein, Fischhoff, & Phillips, 1977; Lichtenstein & Fischhoff, 1980.)

> "If a person assesses the probability of a proposition being true as .7, and later finds that the proposition is false, that in itself does not invalidate the assessment. However, if a JUDGE assigns .7 to 10,000 independent propositions, only 25 of which subsequently are found to be true, there is something wrong with these assessments. The ATTRIBUTE which they lack we call calibration" (Lichtenstein, Fischhoff, & Phillips, 1977, p. 276).

In this sense of the term, a judge's calibration might be said to be poor.

related terms: OVERCONFIDENCE EFFECT, SUBECTIVE PROBABILITY, ACHIEVEMENT, BIAS.

CANCELLATION.

See ISOLATION EFFECT.

CANONICAL APPROACH to PROBABILITY.

See OBJECTIVE PROBABILITY.

CARDINAL UTILITY

definition: UTILITY measured on a METRIC SCALE.

comment: The definition of cardinal utility in terms of the various SCALES of MEASUREMENT varies widely, though all definitions include the requirement of some metric information. Samuelson (1947, p. 91, also p. 93) defines cardinal utility quite vaguely, contrasting it with "an *ORDINAL* PREFERENCE, involving 'more' or 'less' but not 'how much'...." Lange (1933; see Edwards, 1954, p. 385) and Edwards (1954, p. 384) define it as "measured on an INTERVAL scale." According to Stokey & Zeckhauser (1978, p. 264), cardinal utility was traditionally defined in terms of either a RATIO or INTERVAL scale: "In the past some economic theorists, following in the tradition of Jeremy Bentham, attempted to develop cardinal MEASURES of individual welfare, in other words, a measure of the absolute quantity of welfare an individual enjoys. A cardinal measure would convey two pieces of information--(1) how much better off the individual is in situation B than in situation A, and (2) how much better or worse off he is than someone else--just as a scale tells us how many pounds a man has gained and how much more or less he weighs than his neighbor. In fact, we would be happy to find a more restricted cardinal measure that would merely tell us about the magnitude of local changes; it would tell us whether John's gain in welfare when we undertake a particular POLICY is greater than Mary's loss." (The first scale Stokey & Zeckhauser seem to be trying to describe is a *ratio* scale, one with an absolute zero and a standard, though arbitrary, unit; it is comparable in its scale properties to the Kelvin scale of temperature. The second seems to be an *interval* scale, one with a relative zero (their example is a present-conditions zero), and a standard unit; it is comparable in its scale properties with the Fahrenheit and centigrade scales of temperature.)

Many current economists and others of the "ordinalist" viewpoint (e.g., Baumol, 1977, Ch. 9 & 17; Stigler, 1950; Savage, 1954) argue that the cardinal utility concept is not meaningful for evaluation of outcomes, or states of the world (the riskless case), as contrasted with evaluation of actions (the risky case), on the premise that riskless utility is measurable only on an ordinal, not an interval, scale. See UTILITY (Comment regarding Definition 1).

related terms: ORDINAL UTILITY, UTILITY, VALUE, SCALES OF MEASUREMENT, NUMERAIRE, MARGINAL RATE OF SUBSTITUTION, VON NEUMANN-MORGENSTERN UTILITY.

CASCADED INFERENCE

definition: A term introduced by Cameron Peterson (1973) to refer to multiple-step INFERENCE, in which the conclusion from an earlier step becomes a premise for a later step.

example: "...A physician who uses the condition of the patient's lungs as a CUE for diagnosis must infer that condition from unreliable data (e.g., the sound of a thumped chest)" (Slovic, Fischhoff, & Lichtenstein, 1977, p. 4).

comment: In cascaded inference tasks, subjects' judgments tend to be more extreme than those prescribed by the NORMATIVE MODEL because of NON-REGRESSIVENESS BIAS, "a result just the opposite of CONSERVATISM" (Slovic, Fischhoff, & Lichtenstein, 1977, p. 5).

related terms: INFERENCE, BAYES' THEOREM, CONSERVATISM, ANCHORING and ADJUSTMENT, RELEVANCE TREE.

CAUSAL.

See CAUSAL TEXTURE, CAUSAL SCHEMA.

CAUSAL AMBIGUITY

definition: UNCERTAINTY as to the correct causal INFERENCE, resulting from the fact that, in the CAUSAL TEXTURE of the environment, "any given type of GOAL will be capable of being causally reached by more than one type of means-object. And, vice-versa, any given type of means-object will be capable of leading to more than one type of goal. Similarly, any given type of means-object can cause more than one kind of sensory CUE and any one type of cue can be caused by more than one type of means-object" (Tolman & Brunswik, 1935, p. 75). Or, as Hammond and his associates have more recently put it, "(1) SURFACE data are less than perfectly related to DEPTH VARIABLES, (2) FUNCTIONAL RELATIONS between SURFACE and depth variables may assume a variety of forms (LINEAR, CURVILINEAR), and (3) the relations between surface and depth may be ORGANIZED (or combined) according to a variety of principles (for example, ADDITIVE or CONFIGURAL)" (Hammond, Stewart, Brehmer, & Steinmann, 1975, p. 275; see also Tolman & Brunswik, 1935, p. 44.)

comment: According to Hammond (Hammond, et al., 1975, p. 272) causal ambiguity is the very circumstance that requires human JUDGMENT and that leads to disputes when judgments differ. For studies of judgment to exhibit REPRESENTATIVE DESIGN, then, their task characteristics must reflect causal ambiguity. Hammond and his colleagues (e.g., Hammond, et al.., 1975, p. 275) describe causal ambiguity in terms of the same DIMENSIONS they apply to CAUSAL TEXTURE, generally, following the principle of PARALLEL CONCEPTS.

related terms: ZONE of AMBIGUITY, CAUSAL TEXTURE, DISCOUNTING, UNCERTAINTY, LENS MODEL.

CAUSAL DATA.

See CAUSAL SCHEMA.

CAUSAL SCHEMA

definition: A conceptual ORGANIZATION of events in which some are understood to be causes and others to be effects. One of the primary means by which individuals strive to achieve a coherent interpretation of the events that surround them (Heider, 1958.)

comment: The concept of causal schema is currently being elaborated in three major ways, exemplified by the work of Jones, of Kelley, and of Tversky and Kahneman.

Jones (Jones & Davis, 1965) is concerned with the fact that persons are perceived as causes more readily than are impersonal entities or events (the FUNDAMENTAL ATTRIBUTION ERROR.)

Kelley (1971) is concerned with the ways in which people act as INTUITIVE scientists to decide which of a variety of causal schemas best describes a situation. The principal methods Kelley attributes to the intuitive scientist are COVARIATION and DISCOUNTING. The kinds of causal schemas that he believes they most readily think in terms of are: multiple sufficient causes (see DISJUNCTIVE MODEL), multiple necessary causes (see CONJUNCTIVE MODEL), ADDITIVE effects (see ADDING MODEL), and person attibution (see FUNDAMENTAL ATTRIBUTION ERROR.)

Tversky and Kahneman (1977, pp. 24f) are concerned with the fact that we tend to comprehend the world only in terms of causal schemas and that events not so comprehended tend not to be taken into account in REASONING about the world. They distinguish among (a) **CAUSAL DATA,** which are seen as cause of the event of interest; (b) **DIAGNOSTIC DATA,** which are seen as consequence of the event of interest; and (c) **INCIDENTAL DATA,** which are seen as neither cause nor consequence of the event of interest. Though in a NORMATIVE analysis (in this case, a BAYESIAN analysis), the distinction among causal, diagnostic, and incidental data is immaterial, Tversky and Kahneman hypothesize that causal data have a greater IMPACT than diagnostic data of equal informativeness and that diagnostic data have a greater impact than incidental data of equal informativeness.

This is illustrated in the taxi cab problem (described under BASE RATE) in the fact that (a) when subjects are told that 85% of the cabs in the city are Green and 15% are Blue, 45% give the witness hit rate (80%), ignoring the base rate (15%) entirely, but (b) when subjects are told that 85% of the *accidents in the city involve*Green cabs and 15% *involve*Blue cabs, only 18% give the witness hit rate and ignore the base rate entirely (Tversky & Kahneman, 1977, pp. 24f.)

related terms: SCRIPT, COVARIATION PRINCIPLE, DISCOUNTING, FUNDAMENTAL ATTRIBUTION ERROR, CONJUNCTIVE and DISJUNCTIVE MODELS, ADDING MODEL.

CAUSAL TEXTURE

definition: The pattern of regular dependence of events in the environment upon one another (Tolman & Brunswik, 1935, p. 43.)

comment: One consequence of the dependence of environmental events on one another is that organisms come to use events as CUES for making INFERENCES about other events (Tolman & Brunswik, 1935, p. 43.) A consequence of the fact that this dependence tends to be ambiguous (see CAUSAL AMBIGUITY) is that such inferences tend to be QUASI-RATIONAL, as depicted in the LENS MODEL.

Hammond and his colleagues (e.g., Hammond, Stewart, Brehmer, & Steinmann, 1975, p. 275) have described causal texture in terms of the following DIMENSIONS:

- a. the correlations between PROXIMAL VARIABLES (cues) or SURFACE information) and DISTAL variables (criteria) or DEPTH information), see ECOLOGICAL VALIDITY;

- b. the FUNCTION FORMS relating proximal variables to distal variables;

- c. the correlations among the proximal variables (INTRA-ECOLOGICAL CUE CORRELATIONS);

- d. the ORGANIZING PRINCIPLE by which information from the different proximal variables combine to yield the best prediction (usually the best LINEAR prediction) of the distal variable; and

- e. the multiple correlation between (i) the best combination (usually linear combination) of the predictors of the distal variable and (ii) the distal variable, itself.

related terms: ZONE of AMBIGUITY, CAUSAL AMBIGUITY, CUE, PROBABILISTIC FUNCTIONALISM, LENS MODEL.

CAUSE.

See CAUSAL TEXTURE, CAUSAL SCHEMA, CAUSAL AMBIGUITY.

C/E RATIO.

See COST-EFFECTIVENESS RATIO.

CENTRAL.

See LENS MODEL.

CERTAINTY EFFECT

definition: The overweighting of OUTCOMES that are considered CERTAIN, relative to outcomes that are merely PROBABLE (Kahneman & Tversky, 1979b, p. 265.)

example: If people are asked to choose between (a) 2400 Israeli pounds with certainty and (b) 2500 pounds with PROBABILITY .33, 2400 pounds with probability .66, and 0 pounds with probability .01, about 80% choose (a). This CHOICE implies that

$$u(2400) > .33u(2500) + .66u(2400).$$

Combining terms by subtracting .66u(2400) from each side of the inequality yields:

$$.34u(2400) > .33u(2500).$$

Yet, if people are asked to choose between (a) a .34 chance at 2400 pounds and (b) a .33 chance at 2500 pounds, about 80% choose (b). Evidently, eliminating a .66 chance of winning 2400 pounds produces a greater reduction in desirability when it alters the character of the PROSPECT from a sure gain to a probable one, than when both the original and the reduced prospects are uncertain (Kahneman & Tversky, 1979b, p. 265.)

related terms: ALLAIS' PARADOX, PROSPECT THEORY, DECISION WEIGHT.

CERTAINTY EQUIVALENT.

See RISK PREMIUM.

CHANCE FORK.

See DECISION TREE.

CHANCE NODE.

See EVENT NODE.

CHOICE.

See DECISION MAKING.

CHOICE FORK.

See DECISION TREE.

CHOICE NODE.

See ACT NODE.

CLASSICAL APPROACH to PROBABILITY.

See OBJECTIVE PROBABILITY.

CLINICAL PREDICTION

definition: Prediction based on JUDGMENT. In clinical prediction, an impression (see IMPRESSION FORMATION) is formed on the basis of interview data, test scores, etc., and predictions are based on this impression (Meehl, 1954, pp. 3f.) What makes a prediction clinical is not the nature of the data, but how they are used to arrive at a judgment.

comment: Clinical prediction is frequently contrasted with ACTUARIAL PREDICTION. Actuarial predictions seem virtually always to be more accurate than clinical predictions (Sarbin, Taft, & Bailey, 1960; Goldberg, 1970; Meehl, 1954; Dawes, 1979.)

related terms: ACTUARIAL PREDICTION, JUDGMENT, INTUITIVE, IMPRESSION FORMATION, SUBJECTIVE PROBABILITY, ATTRIBUTION.

CLUSTER ANALYSIS

definition: A method of data reduction introduced by R. C. Tryon (1935) for the purpose of classifying objects into independent groups with common elements, thus producing "types." (To be distinguished from **FACTOR ANALYSIS,** a data reduction method which produces DIMENSIONS upon which persons receive "scores.") Types or groups produced by cluster analysis are usually based on common profiles of responses or elements thereof.

comment: In JUDGMENT and DECISION research cluster analysis is used to discover "factions" (persons with common judgment POLICIES) and/or persons whose policies are based on similar elements; for example, similar WEIGHTS on the same CUES, or similar FUNCTION FORMS between cue and response (see Hammond, Rohrbaugh, Mumpower & Adelman, 1977, p. 10, for an example). Various methods for clustering differ primarily in terms of the similarity measure (product-moment correlation coefficient, chi-square, etc.) and the clustering criterion (linkage, centroid, etc.; hierarchical, nonhierarchical) employed. See Anderberg, 1973; Wallace, 1968. of current procedures.

related terms: MULTIDIMENSIONAL SCALING, *N*-SYSTEM CASE.

COGNITIVE ALGEBRA

definition: A term coined by Norman H. Anderson (1974a,b,c) to refer to the fact that the processes by which humans accomplish INFORMATION INTEGRATION can be described PARAMORPHICALLY by simple algebraic models, such as ADDING, subtracting, AVERAGING, MULTIPLYING, and dividing. The standard against which FUNCTIONAL MEASUREMENT is validated.

examples: The value of a COMMODITY BUNDLE is the *sum* of the values of its components; the value of a LOTTERY is the *product* of the PAYOFF and its PROBABILITY; CHOICE behavior is a function of the *difference* between the values of the alternatives; one view of EQUITY is that benefits should be distributed in *proportion* to contributions; social compromise is usually thought of as an *average* of the initial positions.

related terms: INFORMATION INTEGRATION, ADDING MODEL, AVERAGING MODEL, MULTIPLYING MODEL, PARAMORPHIC MODEL.

COGNITIVE CONFLICT.

See CONFLICT.

COGNITIVE CONSISTENCY.

See COGNITIVE CONTROL.

COGNITIVE CONTINUUM.

See QUASI-RATIONALITY.

COGNITIVE CONTROL

definition: In terms of the LENS MODEL EQUATION (which see), G and C represent KNOWLEDGE, the extent to which the subject has learned the (LINEAR and NONLINEAR) properties of the task, and R_S represents cognitive control, the extent to which the subject performs in a manner that is consistent with this knowledge (Hammond & Summers, 1972.)

comment: Lack of cognitive control becomes increasingly important in accounting for poor performance as task complexity increases (Brehmer, 1969a; Deane, Hammond, & Summers, 1972.) The BOOTSTRAPPING technique achieves its effect by applying the individual's POLICY (knowledge) with perfect control (Goldberg, 1970.) Attempts to reduce INTERPERSONAL CONFLICT usually have the effect of decreasing dissimilarities in knowledge but, at the same time, reducing cognitive control (Brehmer, 1972; Hammond & Brehmer, 1973). Studies have found OUTCOME FEEDBACK to degrade cognitive control in complex probabilistic tasks, once JUDGES have obtained knowledge of task properties (Hammond & Summers, 1972). Certain drugs have been found to affect cognitive control (Gillis, 1975, 1980).

Recently (Hammond, et al., 1975, pp. 278ff), a distinction has been drawn between cognitive control and COGNITIVE CONSISTENCY. The distinction becomes important in those cases where the individual's judgments depart significantly from the model on which R_S is based. In such cases, R_S reflects systematic differences between the individual's policy and the model, as well as inconsistency in the application of his/her policy. A MEASURE that is sensitive only to the individual's inconsistency in the application of his/her policy is proposed.

synonyms: **RESPONSE LINEARITY.**

related terms: LENS MODEL EQUATION.

COGNITIVE FEEDBACK.

See FEEDBACK.

COGNITIVE SYSTEMS

definition: "A *cognitive system* is any minimally organized set of relationships between an individual's JUDGMENTS and the information ("CUES") on which the JUDGMENTS are based (Rappoport & Summers, 1973, p. 4). In judgment, both knower(s) and known(s) can be treated as systems interfaced with each other (Hammond, 1966). In the **SINGLE-SYSTEM CASE,** the only system under study is the judgment processes of an individual knower. The figure on the next page illustrates the single-system case. In the **DOUBLE-SYSTEM CASE,** the two systems under study are the task environment (situation or person about which judgments are made) and the judgment processes of an individual knower. The figure on page 43 illustrates the double-system case. In the **TRIPLE-SYSTEM** and **N-SYSTEM CASES,** multiple persons are *represented* as knowers of a common task environment, two persons in the triple-system case and more than two in the N-system case (Rappoport & Summers, 1973). The figure on page 44 illustrates the triple-system case.

These persons are parts of each other's task environments, as well as being knowers of each other and of the part of the task environment common to all.

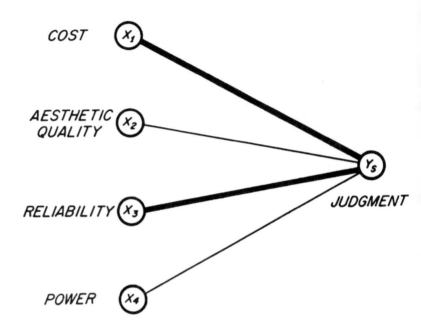

Single-System Case

examples: An example of a single-system case would be an individual
making judgments on the basis of uncertain information, that is, under
conditions in which the environmental system is largely unknown, such
as the foreign policy arena. Another would be value judgments.   An
example of a double-system case would be a person, such as a
laboratory scientist or a weather forecaster, making SUBJECTIVE
PROBABILITY judgments, where the OBJECTIVE PROBABILITIES are knowable,
though not known to the judge.

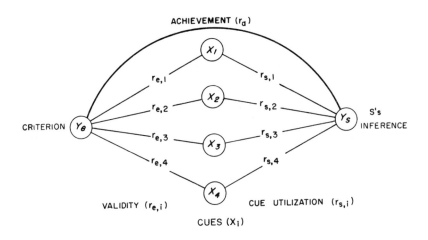

ACHIEVEMENT (r_a)

CRITERION Y_e

$r_{e,1}$ $r_{s,1}$

$r_{e,2}$ $r_{s,2}$

$r_{e,3}$ $r_{s,3}$

$r_{e,4}$ $r_{s,4}$

X_1 X_2 X_3 X_4

Y_s S's INFERENCE

VALIDITY ($r_{e,i}$)   CUE UTILIZATION ($r_{s,i}$)

CUES (X_i)

Double-System Case

Triple-system and n-system cases are those situations that constitute the subject matter of social psychology. An example of a triple-system or N-system case would be two or more people, perhaps members of a committee, trying to come to AGREEMENT on their POLICIES for dealing with a particular task environment.

comment: In the single-system case, the investigator is concerned only with describing an individual's policy. In the double-system case, because the task structure and task OUTCOMES are known, interest tends also to be directed towards ACHIEVEMENT and rate of learning. In the triple-system case, interpersonal AGREEMENT, interpersonal CONFLICT, and interpersonal learning become matters of additional interest. Finally, in the N-system case, it becomes possible to study factions (e.g., by means of CLUSTER ANALYSIS.) (See Hammond, Stewart, Brehmer, & Steinmann, 1975, pp. 291ff.)

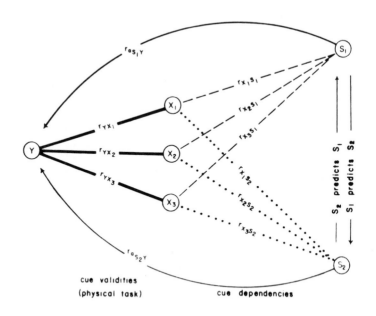

r_{as_1Y}

$r_{x_1s_1}$

$r_{x_2s_1}$

$r_{x_3s_1}$

r_{YX_1}

r_{YX_2}

r_{YX_3}

$r_{x_1s_2}$

$r_{x_2s_2}$

$r_{x_3s_2}$

r_{as_2Y}

S_2 predicts S_1

S_1 predicts S_2

cue validities
(physical task)

cue dependencies

Triple-System Case

related terms: VALUE JUDGMENT, FACT JUDGMENT, AGREEMENT.

COMBINING RULE.

  See AGGREGATION.

COMMENSURATION

definition: "The MEASURING of things in comparison with one another"
(Webster's, 1961, p.   456). The process of measuring in terms of a

single SCALE characteristics that are usually measured in terms of different scales.

comment: Commensuration is necessary in those MULTIATTRIBUTE DECISION situations in which TRADEOFFS are involved. In prediction situations, various predictor VARIABLES (e.g., grade-point average, Graduate Record Examination score) are commensurable in terms of a common scale of predictive usefulness (based on correlation with the criterion). In evaluation situations, various objective DIMENSIONS (e.g., cost, m.p.g., horsepower) are commensurable in terms of a common scale of VALUE. Commensuration across persons, or INTERPERSONAL COMPARISON, is also required when a SOCIAL WELFARE FUNCTION is desired.

related terms: TRADEOFF, WEIGHT, AGGREGATION.

COMMODITY BUNDLE.

  See INDIFFERENCE CURVE.

COMMONS DILEMMA.

  See SOCIAL DILEMMA.

COMPENSATORY MODEL

definition: A model for AGGREGATING information from different DIMENSIONS that permits a low VALUE on one dimension to be compensated for by a high value on another. LINEAR MODELS are generally thought of as compensatory models, though MULTIPLYING MODELS become NONCOMPENSATORY if a value on one dimension equals zero. BAYESIAN and SEU models are multiplying models.

related terms: NONCOMPENSATORY MODEL, ADDING MODEL, MULTIPLYING MODEL.

COMPOSITION.

  See AGGREGATION.

COMPOSITION RULE.

See AGGREGATION.

CONCEPT LEARNING

definition: Learning to classify two or more distinguishable objects or events (stimuli) together into a category (e.g., mammals, prime numbers) and to distinguish them from other objects or events on the basis of some common features or properties characteristic of each (Bourne, 1966, p. 1).

comment: Concept learning involves both **ATTRIBUTE LEARNING** and **RULE LEARNING**. Attribute learning involves learning to distinguish and label the different (abstract or concrete) DIMENSIONS, or VARIABLES, characterizing the focal objects and events, and to distinguish and label the different ATTRIBUTES, LEVELS, or VALUES of each dimension (see VALUE, Definition 1). (Note that "attribute" in this context means a level on a dimension, while elsewhere in this book it usually means a dimension itself.) Rule learning is learning the DECISION RULE (e.g., COMPENSATORY, CONJUNCTIVE, or DISJUNCTIVE) which specifies how to AGGREGATE the relevant attributes for classification of stimuli (Bourne, 1966, pp. 12-21).

Bourne distinguishes concept *learning* from concept *utilization*. "Learning" is the initial acquisition of the discriminations, labels, and rules, and "utilization" is the subsequent identification of circumstances in which a given concept is and is not appropriate as well as the application of the concept in (assumedly) appropriate circumstances (1966, p. 20).

comment: Uhl (1963, 1966) has used the term "learning of **INTERVAL CONCEPTS**" as a synonym for MULTIPLE-CUE PROBABILITY LEARNING (MCPL), equating the dimensions, attributes, rules, and concepts of concept learning with, respectively, the CUES or **PROXIMAL VARIABLES**, cue levels, **ORGANIZING PRINCIPLES**, and criteria or **DISTAL VARIABLES** of MCPL.

related terms: NONCOMPENSATORY MODEL, COMPENSATORY MODEL, INFERENCE, MULTIPLE CUE PROBABILITY LEARNING.

CONDITIONAL INDEPENDENCE

definition: In terms of BAYES' THEOREM, the condition that:

$$P(D_j/H_i) = P(D_j/H_i, D_k),$$

where $P(D_j/H_i)$ is the PROBABILITY of obtaining datum j given that hypothesis i is true, and $P(D_j/H_i, D_k)$ is the probability of obtaining datum j given both that hypothesis i is true and that datum k has been observed. (See INDEPENDENCE.)

A   rough translation of conditional independence in correlational terms would be that "residual   correlations   between   cues,   with   the criterion   DIMENSION   partialled   out,   must   be   zero" (Slovic & Lichtenstein, 1973, p.   38.)

Conditional independence involves independence in the sense of both Definition   1 and Definition 2 of INDEPENDENCE (which see). For two predictor variables to be conditionally independent, they must be UNCORRELATED (that   is,   independent in the sense of Definition 1) at *each* level of the criterion variable (that is, the lack of correlation must   itself exhibit independence as required by Definition 2). While conditional independence requires that independence, in the sense of Definition   1, hold at each level of the criterion it does not require that it hold across levels of the criterion; it is consistent with the existence of a non-zero correlation between each predictor and the criterion and thus with the existence of a non-zero correlation between the predictors *across* levels of the criterion. Conditional independence is the strongest kind of independence that is desirable in prediction situations, for any stronger kind of independence would require that the predictors be independent of the *criterion*.

example: Slovic and Lichtenstein (1973, p.   32) offer the following clarifying example: "Height and hair length are negatively correlated, and thus nonindependent, in the adult U.S. population... but within subgroups of males and females, height and hair length are, we might suppose, quite unrelated. Thus if the hypothesis of interest is the identification of a person as male or female, height and hair length data are *conditionally* independent.... In contrast, height and weight are related both across sexes and within sexes, and are thus both unconditionally and conditionally nonindependent.... One way of thinking about the difference between these two examples is that in the first case the correlation between the cues is mediated by the hypothesis: The person is tall and has short hair *because* he is male. In the case of conditional nonindependence, however, the correlation between the cues is mediated by something other than the hypothesis: The taller person tends to weigh more because of the structural properties of human bodies."

comment: "The use of BAYES' THEOREM assumes that data are conditionally independent.... If this assumption is not met, then the combination rule has to be expanded. For two data, the expanded version is:

$$P(H_i/D_1,D_2) \quad \alpha \quad P(D_2/H_i,D_1)P(D_1/H_i)P(H_i).$$

As more data are received, the equation requires further expansion and becomes difficult to implement" (Slovic & Lichtenstein, 1973, p. 320.)

related terms: INDEPENDENCE, BAYES' THEOREM.

CONDITIONAL MONOTONICITY.

See INDEPENDENCE.

CONDITIONAL PROBABILITY.

See BAYES' THEOREM.

CONFIDENCE INTERVAL

definition: A range of VALUES which is expected to include a true value with a specified PROBABILITY, or LEVEL of CONFIDENCE.

example: A .95 confidence interval of $10,000-$17,000 would indicate that the interval $10,000-$17,000 is expected to include the true value 95% of the time and to exclude it 5% of the time.

related terms: UNCERTAINTY, RISK, SENSITIVITY ANALYSIS.

CONFIGURAL MODEL

definition: A mode of INFORMATION INTEGRATION, or AGGREGATION, in whch the JUDGMENT of an item of information varies according to the nature of other available information (Meehl, 1954, p. 132; Slovic & Lichtenstein, 1973, p. 24.) "When DECISION MAKERS state that their judgments are associated with complex, sequential, and interrelated rules, it is likely that they are referring to some sort of configural process" (Slovic & Lichtenstein, 1973, p. 24).

comment: There are two rather different interpretations of the above definition. The first, historically, *includes* MULTIPLYING MODELS as configural. Meehl's original statement (1954, p. 133) was:

> "In the case of continuous predictive functions, what makes the system patterned is that the rate of change of the criterion estimate with respect to one of the predictor VARIABLES depends upon one or more of the other predictor variables. This is a stronger claim than mere nonlinearity, of which it is one, but not the only, form. A predictive function $y = \log \sin x_1 + x_2{}^3$ is not linear [in the sense of LINEAR RELATIONSHIP] and would be rather poorly approximated by the usual MULTIPLE REGRESSION methods. But neither is it patterned, because the mode of dependence of y upon x_1 is invariant with respect to the VALUES taken on by x_2, and conversely. On the other hand, a predictive function such as $y = x_1 + x_2 x_3$ [see MULTIPLYING MODEL, MULTILINEAR MODEL] is patterned, because the effect of an increment in x_2 depends upon the value of x_3. Similarly, $y = x_1 + x_2(1 - ax_3)$ is patterned, in a more complex manner. If the values of the x-variables are grouped and thus divided into discontinuous *levels*, what we have is simply a significant INTERACTION term in the analysis of variance."

This usage has been adopted by others (e.g., Hoffman, Slovic, & Rorer, 1968, pp. 340f).

The other interpretation of the above definition of "configural" *excludes* multiplying models as configural. This is the interpretation most consistent with DT, BDT, and CONJOINT MEASUREMENT. The argument is that multiplying models, like all LINEAR MODELS, exhibit INDEPENDENCE and can be DECOMPOSED for assessment purposes (Gardiner &

Edwards, 1975, p. 20; Keeney & Raiffa, 1976, Ch. 6). So long as all input variables are positively correlated (or all are negatively correlated) with the output variable, a logarithmic transformation on the input variables is all that is required to transform a multiplying model into an adding one. Truly configural models, on the other hand, are those that do not permit decomposition, those in which it is not possible "to say what individual stimuli mean because their meaning changes in the context of other stimuli" (Lopes, 1981, personal communication).

The AVERAGING MODEL is a configural model (Anderson, 1981, p. 72), but more in the sense of the first interpretation than the second. The CROSSOVER (see AVERAGING MODEL) indicates that the effect of a stimulus can change in *direction* from one context to another, yet the model is decomposable.

related terms: LINEAR RELATIONSHIP, LINEAR MODEL, INTERACTION, MULTIPLYING MODEL, INDEPENDENCE.

CONFLICT

definition: "...Clash, competition, or mutual interference of opposing or incompatible forces or qualities (as ideas, interests, wills)" (Webster's, 1976, pp. 476-477).

comment: A distinction is made between **INTERPERSONAL CONFLICT**, or conflict among persons, and **INTRAPERSONAL CONFLICT**, or conflict within a single individual.

Interpersonal conflict has been analyzed (e.g., Lord, et al., 1979) into **FACT CONFLICT**, or mutual interference in BELIEFS, **VALUE CONFLICT**, or mutual interference in preferences, and **INTEREST CONFLICT**, where the mutual interference is about, not what is achieved, but for whom it is achieved. GAME THEORY treats interpersonal conflict as interest conflict. SJT, on the other hand, points out (a) that interpersonal conflict can be caused by purely cognitive FACTORS and need not involve motivational differences, (b) that the persistence of interpersonal conflict in the face of attempts to reduce it can be caused by factors adversely affecting COGNITIVE CONSISTENCY and need not involve resistence to change, and (c) that the nature and course of conflict is strongly influenced by task VARIABLES (see Hammond, Stewart, Brehmer, & Steinmann, 1975, p. 302).

SJT treats fact conflict and value conflict together under the general rubric of **COGNITIVE CONFLICT**, or **POLICY CONFLICT** (Hammond, 1965; Hammond & Brehmer, 1973), but argues for FACT-VALUE SEPARATION in public POLICY formation.

Intrapersonal conflict is the focus of Janis & Mann's (1977) theory of "conflict, CHOICE, and commitment". According to this theory, the quality of information search and evaluation in DECISION MAKING increases as a function of intrapersonal conflict, so long as (a) it is realistic to hope to find a better alternative (otherwise the pattern is one of "defensive avoidance") and (b) there is sufficient time to search for and evaluate a better alternative (otherwise the pattern is one of "hypervigilance", or panic) (see Janis & Mann, 1977, espec. pp. 77 & 196). Like SJT theorists, Janis & Mann do not distinguish between fact conflict and value conflict.

Studies of **CUE CONSISTENCY** address questions about intrapersonal fact conflict, and various methods for dealing with TRADEOFFS among non-dominated (see DOMINANCE) alternatives deal with intrapersonal and interpersonal value conflict. The DELPHI technique provides a method for dealing with interpersonal fact conflict.

related terms: DIMENSION, ACT FORK, EVENT FORK, DECISION MAKING, CONFLICT THEORY, FACT-VALUE SEPARATION, POLICY CONFLICT, POLICY SIMILARITY, GAME THEORY, REDUNDANCY, CUE CONSISTENCY, DELPHI.

CONFLICT THEORY

definition: A DESCRIPTIVE and NORMATIVE approach to DECISION MAKING developed by Irving L. Janis and Leon Mann (1968, 1977). Conflict theory describes decision behavior in terms of the conditions that lead, and the decision behaviors that tend to occur in response, to varying levels of INTRAPERSONAL CONFLICT.

examples: Low conflict results when no serious RISKS are JUDGED to be contingent upon continuing with the present course of action, and this condition tends to lead to **UNCONFLICTED ADHERENCE**. Low conflict also results when serious risks are judged to be contingent upon continuing with the present course of action but no serious risks are judged to be contingent upon adopting a new course of action, and this condition tends to lead to **UNCONFLICTED CHANGE**.

Moderate to high conflict results when serious risks are judged to be contingent upon both continuing with the present course of action and changing to a new course of action. Any of three decision behaviors can occur in response to moderate to high conflict, depending on other factors. If the decision maker does not believe that there is a reasonable PROBABILITY of finding a better solution, the response tends to be one of **DEFENSIVE AVOIDANCE**, that is, the decision maker tends to engage in procrastination, shifting responsibility, or bolstering the preferred alternative. If the decision maker believes that there is a reasonable probability of finding a better solution yet doubts that there is sufficient time to search and deliberate, the response tends to be one of **HYPERVIGILANCE**, or panic. Only when (a) conflict is present, (b) there is hope of finding a better solution, and (c) there is believed to be sufficient time to search and deliberate does **VIGILANCE** or high-quality decision making, result. (See Janis & Mann, 1977, espec. pp. 70, 86, and 196.)

comment: Among the DECISION AIDS suggested by Conflict Theory (Janis, in press; Janis & Mann, 1977; Wheeler & Janis, 1980) are (a) use of a decisional BALANCE SHEET, (b) negative "outcome psychodrama", and (c) use of a Devil's Advocate (see also, Janis, 1972) to enlarge the decision maker's awareness of conflicting ATTRIBUTES of the decision problem.

related terms: CONFLICT, RISK, BALANCE SHEET.

CONJOINT ANALYSIS.

See CONJOINT MEASUREMENT.

CONJOINT MEASUREMENT

definition: An A POSTERIORI DECOMPOSITION approach, introduced by Luce & Tukey (1964), to "the construction of MEASUREMENT SCALES for composite objects which preserve their observed order with respect to the relevant ATTRIBUTE (e.g., PREFERENCE, comfort, momentum) and where the scale VALUE of each object is a FUNCTION of the scale values of its components. Since such theories lead to simultaneous measurement of the objects and their components, they are called conjoint measurement theories" (Krantz, Luce, Suppes, & Tversky, 1971, p.

245). "At its most general level, the purpose of conjoint measurement is to understand what sorts of numerical representations exist, if any, for orderings of Cartesian products of sets.... The problem is one of uncovering both SCALES of MEASUREMENT of the FACTORS and a law for combining these scales to form a composite or conjoint scale that recovers the qualitative ordering" (Luce, 1977, p. 148). "In conjoint measurement, as the name suggests, one tries to solve the MEASUREMENT and COMPOSITION problems *together* by finding scales that obey the stated composition rule to some suitable degree of approximation (Green & Wind, 1973, p. 54). "A close relation exists between conjoint measurement and the establishment of response measures in a two-way table, or other analysis-of-variance, situations, for which the 'effects of columns' and the 'effects of rows' are ADDITIVE" (Luce & Tukey, 1964, p. 1).

There are two complementary approaches to conjoint measurement: **AXIOMATIC CONJOINT MEASUREMENT** and **NUMERICAL CONJOINT MEASUREMENT.** The former "investigates qualitative properties of the set of data relations to determine if it is possible to scale the data set to a particular composition rule or model"; the latter "proceeds by assuming a *particular* composition rule and then SCALING the data set to that model" (Emery & Barron, 1979, p. 195; see also Green & Srinivasan, 1978, p. 103). Axiomatic conjoint measurement is represented by David Krantz, R. Duncan Luce, Patrick Suppes, and Amos Tversky (Krantz, Luce, Suppes, & Tversky, 1971). Numerical conjoint measurement (or **CONJOINT ANALYSIS,** as Green & Srinivasan (1978) now call it) is represented by Paul E. Green (Green & Wind, 1973) and J. B. Kruskal (1965). Conjoint analysis is one of the methods used for POLICY CAPTURING.

example: Axiomatic conjoint measurement might begin by presenting the JUDGE with multidimensional stimuli (e.g., 4-door sedan, 20 m.p.g., $4000; camper, 30 m.p.g., $3800; etc.) and obtaining WHOLISTIC ORDINAL-scale judgments (a ranking) of these stimuli, in terms of, for example, preference. Scale values on the stimulus DIMENSIONS, scale values on the response dimension, and the rule by which values on the stimulus scales are combined to yield values on the response scale can then be obtained by appropriate analyses of these judgments.

To determine the composition rule, the data are examined for properties that are required by the axioms of the various composition rules. If, for example, INDEPENDENCE holds for all stimulus VARIABLES, "double cancellation" is satisfied, and "joint independence" holds for all pairs of stimulus variables, the composition rule is presumed to be an additive one.

There are two procedures for scaling the stimulus dimensions. The first employs an algorithm (Kruskal, 1965) that iteratively adjusts trial INTERVAL-SCALE values for the stimulus variables until a set of values is obtained that, when combined by the composition rule, yield values that are monotonic with the ordering on the response scale. The second requires that all the axioms be satisfied and uses a variant of LINEAR PROGRAMMING to construct all possible numerical scale values consistent with the ordering of the data (McClelland & Coombs, 1975).

comment: Some controversy exists over the relationship between axiomatic conjoint measurement and FUNCTIONAL MEASUREMENT. On the side of axiomatic conjoint measurement is the argument that conjoint measurement's direct tests of axioms are more revealing than functional measurement's tests of overall goodness-of-fit to empirical data. On the side of functional measurement are the arguments that it has an error theory, that excellent fits to data have been obtained and that these data do not support the ADDING MODEL that has been so much the focus of conjoint measurement. (See Luce, 1977, p. 155.) In Luce's view, "the methods are largely complementary, not competitive" (Luce, 1977, p. 155).

related terms: AXIOM, MULTIVARIATE ANALYSIS.

CONJUNCTIVE and DISJUNCTIVE MODELS

definition: NONCOMPENSATORY **MULTIPLE-CUTTING-POINT MODELS** that classify alternatives into pass-fail categories, rather than order them. A conjunctive model classifies an alternative as acceptable if it reaches an acceptable LEVEL on DIMENSION A *and* dimension B *and* dimension C, etc. A disjunctive model classifies an alternative as acceptable if it reaches an acceptable level on dimension A *or* dimension B *or* dimension C, etc. (Coombs, 1964; Dawes, 1964; Einhorn, 1971.) The models are related in that, when the pass category is defined conjunctively, the fail category is defined disjunctively; and vice versa.

examples: Dawes (1964) described the evaluation of a potential inductee by a draft board physician as one example of a conjunctive process. The physician requires that the inductee meet an entire set of minimal criteria in order to be judged physically fit. A disjunctive evaluation, on the other hand, depends solely on the attribute with the highest value. For example, a scout for a professional football team may evaluate a player purely in terms of his best speciality, be it passing, running, or kicking (Dawes, 1964.)

comment: Einhorn (1971), employing REGRESSION ANALYSIS to identify conjunctive and disjunctive models, found that many subjects were fit better by the conjunctive model than by the LINEAR MODEL and that the conjunctive model provided a better fit where students ranked jobs according to their preferences than where faculty members ranked applicants for graduate school. (See SATISFICING.) Conjunctive and disjunctive models are commonly recommended only for preliminary screening decisions.

synonyms: MULTIPLE-CUTTING-POINT MODEL.

related terms: NONCOMPENSATORY, SATISFICING, CONCEPT LEARNING, MATHEMATICAL PROGRAMMING.

CONSERVATISM

definition 1: Revision of opinions (PROBABILITIES) on the basis of new information that is insufficient in comparison with the revision prescribed by BAYES' THEOREM (Edwards, 1968a).

comment with regard to definition 1: This effect was originally demonstrated by means of the bookbag-and-poker-chips task" (Phillips & Edwards, 1966.) For example, a subject might be shown two bookbags and told that one contains 70% red chips and 30% white chips and that the other contains 30% red chips and 70% white chips. Chips would then be drawn from one of the bags, and, after each chip was drawn, the subject would be asked to JUDGE the probability that it had been drawn from, say, the bag containing 70% red chips and 30% white chips. Revision of probabilities on the basis of such evidence is usually proportional to numbers calculated from Bayes' theorem, but it is insufficient in amount, that is, conservative. According to Edwards (1968a, pp. 18f), "it takes anywhere from two to five observations to do one observation's worth of work in inducing a subject to change his opinions."

Edwards (1968a) discusses three hypotheses to explain the conservatism effect: misperception, MISAGGREGATION, and artifact, the last asserting that people handle extreme probabilities and extreme ODDS poorly. Anderson (1974c, p. 270) comments: "Considerable effort has been made to 'explain' conservatism in terms of various psychological processes. But from the present view, conservatism is a noneffect. It has a purely nominal existence, by reference to a model that has no psychological content." Kahneman & Tversky (1972, p. 450) assert that "In his evaluation of evidence, man is apparently not a conservative BAYESIAN: he is not a Bayesian at all." (See BASE-RATE FALLACY.)

definition 2: Conservatism has been defined in correlational tasks in terms of (a) the dispersion of the judgments relative to the dispersion of the criterion values (Naylor & Clark, 1968), and (b) the standard error of estimate (Naylor & Clark, 1968). However, these two MEASURES "lead to opposite conclusions about conservatism" (Slovic & Lichtenstein, 1973, p. 73). Brehmer & Lindberg (1970) have defined conservatism in correlational tasks in terms of the relative slopes of the REGRESSIONS of the judged values and the criterion values on the CUE DIMENSION. By this measure, subjects are not conservative in this task.

related terms: SUBJECTIVE PROBABILITY, ODDS, FUNDAMENTAL ATTRIBUTION ERROR, BASE-RATE FALLACY, SUBCERTAINTY, NON-REGRESSIVENESS BIAS.

CONSISTENCY, LOGICAL.

See RATIONALITY.

CONSISTENCY, of CUES.

See REDUNDANCY.

CONSTANT.

See DIMENSION.

CONSTANT ERROR.

See BIAS.

CONSTANT SUBSTITUTION.

See UTILITY INDEPENDENCE.

CONSTANT TRADEOFF RATE.

See ADDING MODEL.

CORRESPONDENT INFERENCE

definition: Defined by Jones & Davis (1965), who originated the term, as the INFERENCE that behavior directly reflects underlying dispositions of the behaving person, in contrast to characteristics of his/her situation. A revised presentation (Jones & McGillis, 1976) places a greater emphasis on the information *gained* about dispositions as a function of observing behavior.

comment: CORRESPONDENT INFERENCE THEORY asserts that observers will assume behavior to be a direct reflection of underlying dispositions, thereby committing the FUNDAMENTAL ATTRIBUTION ERROR, to the extent that the effects of behavior are distinctive and depart from prior expectancy (Jones & Davis, 1965). (SEE ATTRIBUTION THEORY.)

related terms: ATTRIBUTION, AVAILABILITY, INFERENCE, FUNDAMENTAL ATTRIBUTION ERROR.

COST-BENEFIT ANALYSIS

definition: Cost-Benefit (**C-B**) analysis is a PRESCRIPTIVE approach, based in welfare economics, to prospective (*ex ante*) evaluation of public sector action options (projects, programs, policies), particularly investment (resource allocation) options. It is used as a basis for (i) JUDGING the desirability of each individual option, (ii) selecting one or more options from an initial set, and/or (iii) determining the optimal scale of operation of the option(s) selected (Mishan, 1976; Prest and Turvey, 1965; Quade, 1975; Rothenberg, 1975; Stokey and Zeckhauser, 1978). PROSPECTIVE (*EX ANTE*) EVALUATION is that undertaken before an option is chosen, based on its projected consequences; contrasted with RETROSPECTIVE (*EX POST*) EVALUATION, which is undertaken after an option is implemented and based on its actual observed consequences (Stokey & Zeckhauser, 1978, p. 134; Wolf, 1974, p. 14).

Each option is evaluated by (i) projection (FORECASTING) of its probable consequences over time, favorable (benefits) and unfavorable (costs); (ii) COMMENSURATION of each individual consequence onto a common scale of VALUE (Definition 2); (iii) DISCOUNTING of future benefits and costs to obtain corresponding present benefits and costs; (iv) determination of NET PRESENT VALUE or NET PRESENT WORTH (NPV, NPW) as total present benefits *minus* total present costs (Layard, 1972; Mishan, 1976; Prest & Turvey, 1965; Rothenberg, 1975; Stokey & Zeckhauser, 1978).

An option, or set of options, is *selected* according to the "Fundamental Rule: In any CHOICE situation, select the alternative that produces the greatest net benefit" (Stokey & Zeckhauser, 1978, p. 137), or equivalently, "MAXIMIZE the present value of all benefits less that of all costs, subject to specified constraints" (Prest & Turvey, 1965, p. 685).

comment: Most broadly, C-B analysis attempts to estimate and weigh the pros and cons of any public action option or set of options; it is thus a PRESCRIPTIVE MODEL (Stokey & Zeckhauser, 1978). Benefits and costs are ultimately MEASURES of change in UTILITY (Definition 1), or in sources thereof, which result from implementation of the action under consideration.

> Both benefits and costs are want-fulfillments: benefits are the want-fulfillment patterns made possible by the change: costs are the want-fulfillment patterns which were possible with the prior (or alternative) resource use configuration but no longer possible with the new one. Benefits are present opportunities, costs are opportunities presently foregone. This is the fundamental meaning. All definitions in terms of commodities or dollars are derivative and

> ultimately refer back to these notions of real
> fulfillment opportunities. (Rothenberg, 1975, p.
> 59)

C-B analysis, like most prescriptive models of DECISION MAKING, assumes actors to be intendedly RATIONAL ECONOMIC MEN (Rothenberg, 1975, pp. 55-58; Schulze & Kneese, 1980; Stokey & Zeckhauser, 1978). Several characteristics distinguish C-B analysis within the general class of such models.

First, admissible benefits and costs relate only to the direct and indirect OUTCOMES or consequences of the focal option(s). Outcomes may include both tangible commodities (e.g., water supply) and intangible commodities (e.g., scenic quality), privately or publically owned. Intrinsic characteristics of the alternatives (e.g., congruence with moral norms) or the process by which alternatives are generated or selected (e.g., extent of participation of affected publics) are not considered, however (Rothenberg, 1978, p. 56; Stokey & Zeckhauser, 1978, chs. 3, 9, 13).

Second, the analysis considers the benefits and costs which occur throughout the social system, not only direct benefits to intended beneficiaries and direct expenditures by the implementing agency. "The fundamental criterion is that the benefits of any alternative are the want-gratifications it makes possible anywhere in the system, the costs are the want gratification opportunities it removes anywhere in the system." This requires consideration of indirect as well as direct effects, since "each change, regardless of where it has its first direct impact, will typically lead to a variety of ramifying indirect impacts whose overall significance may far exceed that of the direct one" (Rothenberg, 1975, p.66).

Third, the value of any commodity (good or service, tangible or intangible) to any actor is conceptually defined (as in all economics) as his WILLINGNESS TO PAY to obtain it or prevent its loss, or similarly his WILLINGNESS TO ACCEPT PAYMENT (compensation) to accept its loss (Baumol, 1977; Stokey & Zeckhauser, 1978). A single NUMERAIRE good (composite good), normally money, is used as a common measure of value on the assumption that it can be traded for, and therefore used to represent, all other goods. Relative MARKET PRICES are used as the principal INDICATOR of the relative values which society as a whole places on different commodities, and therefore (i) the benefits of producing different commodities and (ii) the OPPORTUNITY COSTS (foregone utility) of shifting resources from production of some commodities to production of others. Real-world market prices are often imperfect indicators, however, and must be adjusted or supplemented. The resulting prices are termed SHADOW PRICES, or ACCOUNTING PRICES.

The value viewpoint applied in C-B analysis is that of *society as a whole*, not of any particular person or group within it or of the governmental entity responsible for an action option. Authority for VALUE JUDGMENT (expressed through market prices or BIDDING GAME results) is decentralized to all actors in the relevant social system. This societal perspective on value judgment is distinct from the societal scope of the consequences (benefits & costs) considered. A different sort of analysis might consider a society-wide consequence set, but from a more limited value perspective, possibly that of a single DECISION MAKER. (This would be an option within COST-EFFECTIVENESS ANALYSIS.) Conversely, it might consider consequences to a limited group within society but from the value perspective of society as a whole (market prices provide this perspective.) The latter might be considered a variant of C-B analysis, however, such as when consequences to each of several societal subgroups (e.g., different economic strata) are assessed separately, though all from a societal value perspective, to determine distributional effects (Stokey & Zeckhauser, 1978, pp. 155-158).

The SOCIAL WELFARE FUNCTION used to derive overall societal WELFARE from the welfare of individuals is simple addition (see ADDING MODEL). "Overall well-being is a matter of adding together the gains obtained by the totality of market participants. The 'general welfare' is a matter of AGGREGATING individual welfares, not of revealing a 'collective or corporate will'" (Rothenberg, 1975, p. 64).

The basic decision criterion of C-B analysis (as noted in the definition) is MAXIMIZATION of net present benefit (value, worth). This is measured as the *difference* between total present benefit and total present cost, *not* the *ratio* of present benefit to present cost. Contrary to common belief and to common practice in some agencies such as the U.S. Army Corps of Engineers, the BENEFIT-COST (B/C) RATIO is *not* normally the appropriate measure (Rothenberg, 1975, p. 77; Stokey & Zeckhauser, 1978, p. 146).

Several assumptions and other limitations of C-B analysis are important to note. Assumptions comprise one type of limitation in that they limit the appropriate applications of the method and the interpretability of its results. Those noted here concern only the nature of individual and societal preferences; others are discussed by the cited authors. The robustness of the method to violation of assumptions is beyond this discussion.

Two principal assumptions identified by most theorists are that monetary values (however ascertained) have a LINEAR RELATIONSHIP with utility (Definition 1), or welfare, and (ii) that this relationship is the same for different persons: "individuals' utility FUNCTIONS are linear with identical constant marginal utilities across individuals" (Schulze & Kneese, 1980, p. 3; see also Rothenberg, 1975, p. 65-71; Stokey & Zeckhauser, 1978, p. 278). Mishan (1976, p. 4040) asserts the contrary, but his rationale is unclear. (See INTERPERSONAL COMPARABILITY, IDIOGRAPHIC, NOMOTHETIC.)

Two further assumptions are that the PREFERENCE functions both of individuals and of society are well represented by COMPENSATORY MODELS. Regarding *individuals*, C-B analysis collapses multidimensional changes in the situation and opportunities of each individual into a single dimension of welfare, indicated by (though not conceptually identical to) market purchasing power in money. "In effect, 'human', 'nonmarket' values are translated into market value terms", implying the assumption that "individuals can feel as well off with greater command over marketable commodities but less of certain nonmarketable gratifications as in the reverse situation. Vulgarly, individuals can be bought off with money" (Rothenberg, 1975, p. 68-69). Regarding *society*, the preference model may be compensatory even if those of many individuals within society are not. Financial or resource constraints may be imposed at the societal level. But within those constraints, any adverse effect with a given monetary value (-$N) can be offset in net benefit calculation by any favorable effect with the same value (+$N), even if some citizens hold NONCOMPENSATORY preferences in which that adverse effect would be intolerable regardless of whatever favorable effects might accompany it. Society can be bought off with money. Effects which society deems *not* commensurable with money, possibly because of noncompensatory ethical views regarding them (see NONCOMPENSATORY MODEL), must be excluded from formal C-B analysis to be considered qualitatively as "incommensurables" or quantitatively in a separate COST-EFFECTIVENESS ANALYSIS. The insensitivity of the societal preference model to noncompensatoriness in individuals' preference models means that no individuals can veto societal decisions within a strict C-B analysis framework (Rothenberg, 1975, p. 65; also Mishan, 1976, ch. 59 and Stokey & Zeckhauser, 1978, ch. 13).

A fifth assumption is that the societal distribution of income is equitable. This is implied by the fact that both market prices and bidding game responses depend on actors' incomes as well as on their preferences. Incomes and preferences are jointly expressed through **DEMAND,** the relation between the price of a good facing consumers and the quantity consumers purchase of that good (Baumol, 1977, ch. 9; Sinden & Worrell, 1979, ch. 2). One's influence on prices (market or shadow) is proportional to one's income (Rothenberg, 1975, p. 73; Stokey & Zeckhauser, 1978, chs. 9 & 13).

Finally, reliance on the "maximize net present benefits decision criterion means that C-B analysis considers only *total* societal welfare (utility), not *distribution* of that welfare across people or groups within society; that is, it considers only economic *efficiency*, not *EQUITY* (Mishan, 1976, ch. 59; Rothenberg, 1975, pp. 71-74; Stokey & Zeckhauser, 1978, ch. 13, esp. pp. 277-280). In the language of welfare economics, which comprises the theoretical foundation of C-B analysis, this is the **KALDOR-HICKS CRITERION** which mandates maximization of *potential* Pareto improvement. It states in essence that "a change from the present social state should be undertaken if the gainers from the change *could* compensate the losers in such a way that everyone would be better off" (Stokey & Zeckhauser, 1978, p. 279). Such compensation need *not* actually be paid, however. Potential Pareto improvement contrasts with actual Pareto improvement, in which gainers must actually compensate losers such that, after payment of compensation, *no one* is worse off than initially, while at least one person is better off (Mishan, 1976, chs. 58 & 59; Stokey & Zeckhauser, 1978, ch. 13). (See PARETO FRONTIER). Reliance on the Kaldor-Hicks criterion means that strict C-B analysis could favorably evaluate redistribution of resources from the poor to the rich, as long as the rich gained more than the poor lost. On the premise that society is not and should not be indifferent to such inequities, analysts often suggest that C-B analysis be supplemented by analysis focusing on the societal distribution of benefits and costs. (See particularly Rothenberg, 1975, pp. 71-74; Stokey & Zeckhauser, 1978, pp. 155-158 and 280-284.)

Principal areas in which C-B analysis has been applied include evaluation of water resource development, transportation development (highway selection, airport siting), education, and urban development. The earliest and most extensive applications, as well as corresponding theoretical and methodological developments have concerned water resource development. Major sources include Eckstein, 1958; Hanke & Walker, 1974; Haveman & Margolis, 1970; Maass *et al.*, 1962; and *Benefit-Cost and Policy Analysis* Annual, 1971-present.

synonym: **BENEFIT-COST ANALYSIS, C-B ANALYSIS.**

related terms: BENEFIT-COST RATIO; BIDDING GAME; CARDINAL UTILITY; COMMENSURATION; COMPENSATORY MODEL; COST-EFFECTIVENESS ANALYSIS; DIRECT PRICE; DISCOUNTING; DOMINANCE; ECONOMIC MAN; EFFICIENT FRONTIER; EQUITY; INTERPERSONAL COMPARABILITY; MAXIMIZATION; PARETO FRONTIER; PRESCRIPTIVE MODEL; REVEALED PREFERENCE; TRADEOFF; UTILITY; NUMERAIRE; WILLINGNESS TO PAY; WILLINGNESS TO ACCEPT PAYMENT; MARKET PRICE; NONMARKETED GOODS; EXTERNALITIES; PUBLIC GOOD; SHADOW PRICE; IDIOGRAPHIC; NOMOTHETIC.

COST EFFECTIVENESS ANALYSIS

definition: A "truncated form of BENEFIT-COST ANALYSIS ... characterized by the MEASUREMENT of costs and benefits in different units, with no need to search for a common METRIC (Stokey & Zeckhauser, 1978, p. 153). Benefits are measured in their own natural units (e.g., disease rate, school achievement level, weapon effectiveness index) rather than COMMENSURATED into the same scale of VALUE (Definition 2) as costs. Costs are usually expressed in terms of monetary value, as in COST-BENEFIT ANALYSIS, but could also be expressed in natural units of the resources expended (e.g., person-months of staff time). (Levin, 1975, pp. 91-94; Rothenberg, 1975, pp. 59 & 78; Stokey & Zeckhauser, 1978, p. 138 & 153-155.) "Apart from not valuing benefits [in the same units as costs], the procedures are exactly the same as in cost-benefit analysis" (Layard, 1972, p. 29).

The term "effectiveness" is defined by Webster's (1976, p. 362) as "the power to produce an effect." It is a property of a means to an end, not the result of applying that means (the effects produced). The usage of Levin (1975), however, implies equation of "effectiveness" with "effects," i.e., benefits. This is exemplified by his use of the phrase "cost per unit of effectiveness" (pp. 108).

Webster's usage will be followed here; effectiveness is thus the power to *produce* benefits, not the benefits, themselves.

Three variants of cost-effectiveness (C-E) analysis can be distinguished. They differ in whether alternatives vary with respect to level of cost, level of benefits, or both.

> *Fixed benefit, variable cost.* All alternatives are assumed to yield identical benefits; only cost varies among them. The DECISION RULE applied in selecting an alternative is "minimize total cost" (Levin, 1975, p. 108), which is equivalent to minimizing cost per unit benefit.

> *Fixed cost, variable benefit.* All alternatives are assumed to have identical costs; only benefit varies among them. The decision rule is "MAXIMIZE total benefit" (Levin, 1975, p. 110; Stokey & Zeckhauser, 1978, p. 154), which is equivalent to maximizing benefits per unit cost.

> *Variable benefit & cost.* Alternatives may vary in both benefits and costs. Either of two approaches may be taken to selecting an alternative.

> One approach is to collapse the benefit and cost DIMENSIONS into either an "average" or a "marginal" **COST-EFFECTIVENESS** (**C-E**) **RATIO.** "Average" C-E is the average benefit per unit cost (to be maximized) or average cost per unit benefit (to be minimized), relative to a null base alternative with zero cost and benefit. "Marginal" C-E is the marginal benefit per unit cost--that is, change in effectiveness per change in cost--(to be maximized), or equivalently, marginal cost per unit benefit (to be minimized), relative to some *non*-null base alternative with *non*zero cost and (normally) benefit. (See Levin, 1975, pp. 94-110). These C-E ratios correspond to average and marginal cost-benefit (C-B ratios), with one exception: a C-E ratio is dimensional because its numerator and denominator are in different units, while a C-B ratio is

dimensionless because its numerator and denominator are in the same units which therefore cancel out.

The second approach is to present the benefit and cost levels of each alternative to the DECISION MAKER in multivariate (vector) form, casting the problem as one of MULTIATTRIBUTE DECISION MAKING. The decision maker then evaluates the alternatives subjectively, using any desired POLICY explicitly or implicitly to commensurate the dimensions into an overall judgment of VALUE (Definition 2); see COMMENSURATION (Stokey & Zeckhauser, 1978, p. 155).

comment: C-E analysis is used as a next-best substitute for C-B analysis when commensuration of benefits with costs on a monetary scale of VALUE (Definition 2b) is deemed infeasible, inappropriate, or (less often) unnecessary. Monetary valuation is infeasible when no empirical MARKET PRICE or SHADOW PRICE is available. It is inappropriate when there are ethical objections to it (e.g., often in the case of valuation of human life). It is unnecessary when either benefits or costs are essentially equal across alternatives and the decision to be made concerns only which alternative(s) to select, not whether any alternative is worth its cost.

No variant of C-E analysis can indicate directly whether the benefits of any alternative exceed its costs, and thus whether the alternative is worth undertaking. Any C-E variant yields a ranking of alternatives with respect to relative desirability, but even the top-ranked alternative might not be worthwhile.

Because benefits and costs are measured in different units, cost-effectiveness analysis provides no direct guidance when we are unsure whether the total benefit from an undertaking justifies the total cost, or when we are trying to select the optimal budget level for a project. But if we know what we have to achieve, or what we are allowed to spend, it is an appropriate criterion that reduces the complexity of CHOICE. (Stokey & Zeckhauser, 1978, p. 155)

The three variants of C-E analysis differ with respect to source of evaluative judgment, nature of implicit assumptions, and conditions of applicability.

Regarding source of value JUDGMENT, monetary valuation of costs relies on the value judgments of the full set of participants in society's economic markets, as indicated by market or shadow prices, while all other valuation of benefits and costs relies on the decision maker's own value judgments. Evaluation is thus more centralized in C-E than C-B analysis (Levin, 1975). More specifically, the decision maker determines the range of benefits or cost levels to be taken as value-equivalent in the Fixed Benefit or Fixed Cost variants, respectively; determines the evaluative ranking of benefit levels in the Fixed Cost variant and of cost levels (if not already valued monetarily) in the Fixed Benefit variant; and determines the value TRADEOFF between benefits and costs in the Variable Benefit and Cost variant.

Regarding assumptions, the Fixed Benefits and Fixed Cost variants assume that the decision maker's evaluative policy closely aproximates a step function in which all benefit or cost levels considered are indeed value-equivalent. The first approach within the *Variable Benefit and Cost* variant assumes (i) a fully compensatory policy for evaluating benefit and cost levels (see COMPENSATORY MODEL), though the policy applied to the derived C-E index may be compensatory or noncompensatory; (ii) LINEAR RELATIONSHIPS between VALUE (Definition 2) or UTILITY (Definition 1), and the MEASUREs of both benefits and costs. The second approach within this variant makes no assumptions about the decision maker's evaluative policy.

The applicability of all three variants is limited not only by the validity of their value assumptions (which depends on the particular decision makers involved) but also by variability in the technical relation between benefit and cost. Regarding the Fixed Benefits variant, Rothenberg (1975) notes that:

> The choice of alternative may well depend on the level of output selected to standardize the comparison. An alternative that wins at one output level need not win at a different one. The danger is that the cost-effectiveness test will be performed at a level other than what is actually

> intended in the project, and the results simply
> projected to the desired level. The choice may
> then be erroneous. (p. 78)

The equivalent point holds for the Fixed Cost approach.

Within the index-based approach of the Variable Effectiveness and Cost variant, average and marginal indices are apppropriate under different circumstances. An *average* index "has the very desirable quality of permitting cost-effectiveness comparisons among divergent programs with very different characteristics as long as the total costs of the program [alternative] are available and the OUTCOMES are measured in the same effectiveness units" (Levin, 1975, p. 108). However, use of such an index assumes either that the result is invariant over differing scales of program operation (i.e., that the effectiveness vs. cost function is linear) *or* that only one scale of operation (indicated by cost level) is decision-relevant for each alternative. If decision-relevant alternatives include change in the scale of one or more existing programs *and* if effectiveness is plausibly nonlinear with cost, a *marginal* index should be used (Levin, 1975, p. 110). The JUDGMENT-based approach of this variant does not appear subject to violation of these assumptions about value policies or technical benefit-cost relations, though it *is* subject to all the limitations of unaided judgment (see BOUNDED RATIONALITY, DECISION AIDS).

A problem common to all three variants is that of multiple objectives. The above discussion implicitly assumes concern with only a single benefit dimension and a single cost dimension, yet most programs have multiple objectives. Different alternatives will often have different patterns of outcome on different dimensions (Rothenberg, 1975, p. 78), and no alternative is likely to be most cost-effective for all dimensions (see DOMINANCE). The analyst could try to bypass this problem by commensurating the multiple benefit dimensions into a single dimension of "overall benefit" using methods of MULTIATTRIBUTE UTILITY THEORY, but would then confront the problem of placing WEIGHTS on the different dimensions or units on them. This is the problem that motivates recourse to C-E rather than C-B analysis in the first place, and is, in principle, as difficult for commensuration of multiple benefit dimensions as for commensuration of benefits with costs.

related terms: BENEFIT-COST RATIO; COMMENSURATION; COMPENSATORY

MODEL; COST-BENEFIT ANALYSIS; DOMINANCE; MAXIMIZATION; MULTIATTRIBUTE UTILITY THEORY; MULTIPLE OBJECTIVE DECISION MAKING; PRESCRIPTIVE MODEL; POLICY; RATIONALITY; SCALES of MEASUREMENT; TRADEOFF; VALUE; UTILITY; MARKET PRICE; SHADOW PRICE; BOUNDED RATIONALITY; DECISION AIDS.

COST-EFFECTIVENESS RATIO.

   See COST-EFFECTIVENESS ANALYSIS.

COSTING OUT.

   See WILLINGNESS to PAY.

COVARIATION PRINCIPLE

definition: ATTRIBUTION of an effect to the one of its possible causes with which, over time, it covaries (Kelley, 1967a,b, 1971).

example: A person who switches from cooperative to competitive behavior after his/her partner switches from cooperative to competitive behvior is perceived as more cooperative than a person who switches from cooperative to competitive behavior independently of his/her partner's actions (Kelley & Stahelski, 1970). In the former case, the partner's behavior is seen as the cause; in the latter, the person's internal disposition is seen as the cause.

related terms: ATTRIBUTION THEORY, DISCOUNTING, CAUSAL SCHEMA.

CROSS-IMPACT ANALYSIS

definition: A cross-impact model describes a system as a set of elements with pairwise relations linking some or all of the elements. In contrast to those in a STRUCTURAL MODEL, the relations are usually expressed quantitatively, either in terms of signed magnitudes (e.g., Kane, 1972) or PROBABLITIES (e.g., Turoff, 1972). Also in contrast to a structural model, a cross-impact model is used more to aid in FORECASTING the future than in preliminary PROBLEM STRUCTURING. Time is often explicitly represented. (Linstone, Hays, Rogers, & Lendaris,

1978, pp.   J-1ff.)

comment: "[Cross-impact   analysis] was first suggested by Helmer and Gordon with the game 'Futures' created for the Kaiser Corporation" (Dalkey, 1975, p.   327).

related terms: FORECASTING, STRUCTURAL MODELING, PROBABILITY TREE.

CROSSOVER.

See AVERAGING MODEL.

CUE

definition   1:   A stimulus DIMENSION; an aspect of an object or event to which an organism responds (e.g., Restle, 1955; Bourne & Restle, 1959).

example of definition 1: In cue-conditioning theory, aspects of geometric stimuli (such as size, shape, or color) serve as cues to which responses are conditioned.

definition 2:   An aspect of the PROXIMAL effects from an object or event to which an organism responds by making an INFERENCE about DISTAL   conditions   concerning   that or other objects or events (e.g., Hammond, Stewart, Brehmer, & Steinmann, 1975, p.   273.)

example of definition 2: Linear perspective is a cue to distance, and price is a cue to quality.

comment regarding definition 2:   "Cue" in this second sense is contrasted with "stimulus", which is conceived of as eliciting passive responses, rather than providing the basis for inferential activity.

synonym for definition 2: CLUE (Simon, 1957, p.   269).

terms related to definition 2: PROXY ATTRIBUTE, INFERENCE, LENS MODEL.

CUE CONSISTENCY.

See CONFLICT.

CUE INTERCORRELATION.

See ENVIRONMENTAL CORRELATION.

CUE UTILIZATION.

See LENS MODEL.

CURVILINEAR.

See FUNCTION FORM, ADDING MODEL.

CYBERNETICS

definition 1: Control (literally "steering") accomplished by the use of **NEGATIVE FEEDBACK,** that is, **FEEDBACK** that serves to change the behavior of the system in such a manner as to correct its course and keep it directed towards some GOAL (see Wiener, 1961; Ashby, 1956, 1960). "It is this study of messages, and in particular of the effective messages of control, which constitutes the science of *cybernetics*" (Wiener, 1950, pp. 8-9). ADAPTIVE behavior is usually cybernetic, or feedback controlled, behavior (Hinde, 1966).

comment on definition 1: The term, coined by Norbert Wiener, Arturo Rosenbluth, and others, comes from the Greek word for steersman, and "the steering engines of a ship are indeed one of the earliest and best-developed forms of feedback mechanisms" (Wiener, 1961, p. 12). "In choosing this term we wish to recognize that the first significant paper on feedback mechanisms is an article on governors, which was published by Clerk Maxwell in 1868, and that *governor* is derived from a Latin corruption of [the Greek word for steersman]" (Wiener, 1961, pp. 11-12).

related terms for definition 1: FEEDBACK.

definition 2: Mathematical techniques for analyzing the dynamic behavior of complex systems; now called DYNAMIC PROGRAMMING (Simon, 1977b, p. 56.)

synonym: DYNAMIC PROGRAMMING.

DEBIASING.

See DECISION AID.

DECISION.

See DECISION MAKING.

DECISION AID

definition: Any of a variety of methods for enhancing the RATIONALITY of DECISIONS, in particular, (a) DECOMPOSITION, (b) **DEBIASING**, (c) BOOTSTRAPPING, and (d) **GRAPHIC AIDS**.

comment: Bootstrapping attempts to reduce random error by extracting an "average" POLICY from repeated decisions. Decomposition seeks to "divide and conquer" complex decision problems by separating PROBABILITY JUDGMENT, UTILITY judgment, and AGGREGATION processes (see FACT-VALUE SEPARATION), and, further, by separating probability judgment into its components (see BAYES' THEOREM) and utility judgment into its components (see MULTIATTRIBUTE UTILITY THEORY). Debiasing attempts to reduce BIAS, or CONSTANT error, in the judgment of probabilities and utilities. (See Hammond, McClelland, & Mumpower, 1980, pp. 47, 168.) Hammond, McClelland, & Mumpower (1980, p. 106) observe that "Group I approaches [DT, BDT, and PDT] may aid the policy maker to explicate his probabilities and utilities and to organize these in a logical manner, thus avoiding the biases and fallibilities of unaided cognitive efforts, whereas Group II approaches [SJT, IIT, and AT] may aid the policy maker to see sources of these probabilities and utilities...." Graphic aids include TREE diagrams (notably DT's DECISION TREE diagrams), decisional BALANCE SHEETS (notably those employed by Conflict Theory), and FUNCTION FORM diagrams (notably those provided by SJT's "POLICY" AID), as well as the various graphic representations provided by STRUCTURAL MODELING and MULTIDIMENSIONAL

SCALING. For a comprehensive, non-technical treatment of decision aids, see Anderson (1980).

related terms: RATIONALITY, DECOMPOSITION, DEBIASING, BOOTSTRAPPING, JUDGMENT, PROBABILITY, UTILITY, AGGREGATION, TREE, FUNCTION FORM, STRUCTURAL MODELING.

DECISION ANALYSIS.

See DECISION THEORY.

DECISION DIAGRAM.

See DECISION TREE.

DECISION FLOW DIAGRAM.

See DECISION TREE.

DECISION FORK.

See DECISION TREE.

DECISION FRAME

definition: A term used by Tversky and Kahneman (1980) to refer to "the decision maker's conception of the acts, outcomes and contingencies associated with a particular CHOICE."

example: The following two problems (taken from Tversky & Kahneman, 1980) are actually the same problem framed in different ways. The different framings result in different choices.

> *Problem 1*
>
> Imagine that the U. S. is preparing for the outbreak of an unusual Asian disease, which is expected to kill 600 people. Two alternative

programs to combat the disease have been proposed. Assume that the consequences of the programs are as follows:

If Program A is adopted, 200 people will be saved.

If Program B is adopted, there is 1/3 PROBABILITY that 600 people will be saved, and 2/3 probability that no people will be saved.

Which of the two programs would you favor?

The majority choose Program A, a choice that is RISK AVERSE.

Problem 2

If Program C is adopted 400 people will die.

If Program D is adopted there is 1/3 probability that nobody will die, and 2/3 probability that 600 people will die.

The majority choose Program D, a choice that is RISK PRONE.

comment: The concept of decision frames raises important practical and theoretical questions. How do people tend to frame problems? How do different frames evoke different responses? How does one decide which frame to use in a DECISION ANALYSIS?

related terms: PROSPECT THEORY, BOUNDED RATIONALITY, RISK, GAINS and LOSSES.

DECISION MAKER.

See DECISION MAKING.

DECISION MAKING

suggested definition: Selecting and committing oneself to a course of action.

comment: Two terms that are closely related to "decision making" are JUDGMENT and CHOICE. There seems to be no consistent usage for any of these three terms. Webster's (1976) defines decision as "the act of forming an opinion or deciding upon a course of action" (p. 585) and judgment as "the mental or intellectual process of forming an opinion or evaluation by discerning or comparing" (p. 1223). Thus, according to Webster's, a judgment would seem to be a particular kind of decision. Webster's defines choice in a way that makes it difficult to distinguish from decision: "The voluntary and purposive or deliberate action of picking, singling out, or selecting from two or more that which is favored or superior" (p. 395).

The philosopher Lonergan (1970), on the other hand, treats judgment and decision as distinct. In discussing judgment, he writes, "A proposition may be the content of an act of judging; and then it is the content of an affirming or denying, an agreeing or disagreeing, an assenting or dissenting" (p. 271). In discussing decision, he writes, "The fundamental nature of decision is best revealed by comparing it with judgment. Decision, then, resembles judgment inasmuch as both select one member of a pair of contradictories [see CONFLICT, ACT FORK, EVENT FORK]; As judgment either affirms or denies, so decision either consents or refuses. Again, both decision and judgment are concerned with actuality; but judgment is concerned to complete one's KNOWLEDGE of an actuality that already exists; while decision is concerned to confer actuality upon a course of action that otherwise will not exist" (pp. 612-613).

Hammond, McClelland, & Mumpower (1980), Einhorn & Hogarth (1981), and Hogarth (1980) distinguish between judgment and choice, using the latter term in much the same way the Lonergan uses "decision". Hogarth (1980, p. 3) states that "choice reflects both evaluative and predictive judgments" (VALUE JUDGMENTS and FACT JUDGMENTS). Einhorn & Hogarth (1980, p. 31) point out that, in common parlance, "one can choose in spite of one's better judgment whereas the reverse makes little sense" and assert that "judgments serve to reduce the UNCERTAINTY and conflict in choice by processes of deliberative REASONING and evaluation of evidence" (p. 31). They give as an example of judgment clinical diagnosis and prognosis. Hammond, et al. (1980, p. 55ff), similarly, tie their discussion of judgment closely to the concept of knowing. They assert that "the study of knowing is...*propaedeutic* (that is, prior) to the study of choice" (p. 58). They add (p. 105) that "DECISION AIDS that deal with PROBABILITIES and UTILITIES address themselves to the *results* of inductive knowing...whereas judgment *aids* address themselves to the *sources* of those probabilities and utilities." They also point out (pp. 57f) that approaches to decision making that have their origins in psychology (Group II: SJT, IIT, and AT) are concerned primarily with judgment, whereas those that have their origins in economics (Group I: DT, BDT, and PDT) are concerned primarily with choice. "...There is a far greater use of the terms 'decision,' 'choice,' and 'PREFERENCE' in Group I and a much greater use of 'judgment' and 'INFERENCE' in Group II" (p. 55). Each of these theorists, however, clearly assumes that thought (judgment) does, as well as ought to, precede and guide action. Others (e.g., Langer, 1978) question this premise, arguing that much ostensibly thoughtful action is not based on thought.

Choice, while distinct from judgment, is used as an indicator of judgment in the method of REVEALED PREFERENCE.

related terms: INFERENCE, RATIONALITY, JUDGMENT vs. DECISION THEORIES, REVEALED PREFERENCE, CONFLICT.

DECISION NODE.

See DECISION TREE.

DECISION RULE.

See COMPENSATORY, NONCOMPENSATORY MODELS.

DECISION THEORY

definition: A NORMATIVE approach to JUDGMENT and DECISION MAKING developed by Howard Raiffa (1968), Robert O. Schlaifer (1969), Ralph L. Keeney (Keeney & Raiffa, 1976), Ronald A. Howard (1968), and Peter C. Fishburn (1970). Decision Theory (**DT**) seeks to aid decision behavior by providing normative models for taking RISK and UTILITY, which may be MULTIATTRIBUTE, into account in MAXIMIZING EXPECTED UTILITY. The methods of DT include BAYES' THEOREM for handling PROBABILITIES, STANDARD GAMBLE techniques for assessing von NEUMANN-MORGENSTERN UTILITY, techniques for assessing multiattribute utility, and the DYNAMIC PROGRAMMING algorithm for FOLDING BACK DECISION TREES.

synonym: **DECISION ANALYSIS, DT.**

related terms: JUDGMENT vs. DECISION THEORIES, DECISION TREE,
Von-NEUMANN-MORGENSTERN UTILITY, OBJECTIVE PROBABILITY, SUBJECTIVE
PROBABILITY, BAYESIAN, FOLDING BACK, EXPECTED UTILITY.

DECISION TREE

definition: A flow diagram of the sequence of significant CHOICES and
events in a DECISION problem (Brown, Kahr, & Peterson, 1974, pp. 9ff;
Raiffa, 1968, pp. 10ff; Schlaifer, 1969, pp. 7ff.) This flow diagram
has a TREE structure (which see).

   The diagram begins with a **DECISION FORK** (or **ACT NODE**, or **CHOICE
NODE**), usually designated by a square, as in the figure below.

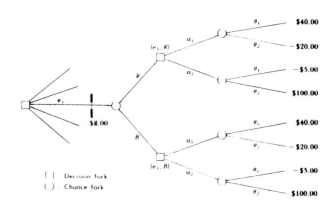

A Decision Tree

From Raiffa, 1968, p. 11. Copyright 1968 by Addison-Wesley Publishing
Company, Inc. Reprinted by permission.

This initial decision fork represents the choice currently confronting
the decision maker.   The branches emanating from any decision fork
represent the major courses of action open to the decision maker at

that point. These branches must represent courses of action that are mutually exclusive (see DIMENSION, CONFLICT) and exhaustive; that is, it must be the case that, eventually, the decision maker will proceed out one, and only one, of the branches. Although a decision tree must begin with a decision fork, decision forks may be located throughout the tree, for often complex decision problems require a sequence of choices, some of which are best not made until after additional information becomes available.

Decision trees are most frequently used for representing decisions under RISK or UNCERTAINTY. Risk or uncertainty is represented by **CHANCE FORKS,** or **EVENT FORKS,** or **EVENT NODES,** or usually designated by circles, as in the figure above. The branches emanating from a chance fork represent the major possible events at a particular point that would affect the ultimate consequences of a particular course of action. As in the case of a decision fork, the branches must represent possibilities that are mutually exclusive (see DIMENSION, CONFLICT) and exhaustive; that is, it must be the case that, eventually, chance will select one, and only one, of the branches at a chance fork. Because the selection of a branch at a chance fork is determined by forces beyond the control of the decision maker (otherwise the possibilities for control would have been represented by a decision fork), PROBABILITIES must be attached to the branches of every chance fork. And, because the events represented at a chance fork must be mutually exclusive and exhaustive, the probabilities at every chance fork must sum to 1.

The **ENDPOINTS** of the tree represent possible OUTCOMES of the decision process, possible future states. A VALUE must be attached to each of these.

A tree consisting only of chance forks is called a **PROBABILITY TREE.**

comment: A decision tree has been compared to a road map (Raiffa, 1968, p. 11). The current "location" of the decision maker is at the decision fork at the root of the tree. He/she chooses one of the "roads" leading out from this decision fork, then, at each chance fork, nature selects the "road", and, at each decision fork, the decision maker makes an additional choice. Each of the end points represents a "place" to which a particular sequence of choices and events leads.

Producing a tree to represent a decision problem is an important part of what is called PROBLEM STRUCTURING.

synonyms: **DECISION DIAGRAM, DECISION FLOW DIAGRAM.**

related terms: STRUCTURING the PROBLEM, RISK, UNCERTAINTY, TREE, FOLDING BACK.

DECISION VARIABLE.

See MATHEMATICAL PROGRAMMING.

DECISION WEIGHT

definition: A concept, which seems originally to have been suggested by Ward Edwards (1954, p. 398) and which has recently been elaborated by Kahneman & Tversky (1979b), to reflect "the IMPACT of events on the desirability of PROSPECTS, and not merely the perceived likelihood of these events" (p. 280). (The question of BIAS in the *perceived* likelihood of events is ruled out in the relevant studies, on the assumption that the subjects adopt the stated PROBABILITY values.) Decision weights are, in general, less than the corresponding probabilities, except in the case of low probabilities.

example: An example due to Zeckhauser (Kahneman & Tversky, 1979b) illustrates the difference between decision weights and probabilities. Suppose you are compelled to play Russian roulette, but are given the opportunity to purchase the removal of one bullet from the loaded gun. Would you pay as much to reduce the number of bullets from four to three as you would to reduce the number of bullets from one to zero? Though the difference in probability is the same in the two cases, 1/6, most people feel that they would be willing to pay much more to reduce the probability of death from 1/6 to zero.

related terms: PROSPECT THEORY, SUBCERTAINTY, CERTAINTY EFFECT, RISK PREMIUM, WEIGHT.

DECOMPOSITION

definition: Analyzing a problem into subproblems, so that the simpler subproblems can be solved and their solutions AGGREGATED to yield a solution to the original problem. "The spirit of decomposition is to DIVIDE and CONQUER: Decompose a complex problem into simpler problems, get one's thinking straight in these simpler problems [and] paste these analyses together with a logical glue..." (Raiffa, 1968, p. 271). The concept can be traced at least as far back as Jeremy Bentham. "Bentham's method may be shortly described as the method of detail; of treating wholes by separating them into their parts...and breaking every question into pieces before attempting to solve it..." (Mill, 1859-75).

example: In the DECISION ANALYSIS approach to MULTIATTRIBUTE DECISION MAKING, decomposition involves analyzing the entities of CHOICE into DIMENSIONS, obtaining judgments of VALUE (Definition 2) for the separate dimensions, and then aggregating these judgments to obtain evaluations of the multidimensional entities.

he BAYESIAN approach to PROBABILITY ESTIMATION is to decompose probability judgments into judgments of PRIOR PROBABILITIES and CONDITIONAL PROBABILITIES and then to aggregate these judgments into POSTERIOR PROBABILITIES by means of BAYES' THEOREM.

comment: The methods used for evaluating multidimensional entities (see MULTIATTRIBUTE DECISION MAKING, MULTIATTRIBUTE UTILITY THEORY) involve either A PRIORI DECOMPOSITION or A POSTERIORI DECOMPOSITION. In a priori decomposition, the stimuli are analyzed into dimensions before the judgments are obtained, and the judgments are obtained dimension by dimension. Examples of a priori decomposition are the methods of DT and BDT. In a posteriori decomposition, intact or schematic multidimensional stimuli are judged wholistically (see WHOLISTIC), and the judgments are then decomposed statistically, usually into subjective scale values or FUNCTION FORMS for the levels within each dimension and an importance WEIGHT for each dimension. Examples of a posteriori decomposition are the methods of SJT, IIT, and CONJOINT MEASUREMENT.

Shanteau & Phelps (1977, p. 259) remark: "Decomposition may well be the common foundation of judgment analysis."

synonyms: DIVIDE-and-CONQUER STRATEGY.

related terms: FACT-VALUE SEPARATION, AGGREGATION, WHOLISTIC, DECISION ANALYSIS, MULTIATTRIBUTE DECISION MAKING, DT, BDT, SJT, IIT, CONJOINT MEASUREMENT, FUNCTION FORM, WEIGHT.

DECREASING MARGINAL UTILITY.

See VALUE, FUNCTION FORM.

DEFENSIVE AVOIDANCE.

See CONFLICT THEORY.

DELPHI

definition: "...A method for structuring a group communication process so that the process is effective in allowing a group of individuals, as a whole, to deal with a complex problem. To accomplish this 'structured communication' there is provided: some FEEDBACK of individual contributions of information and knowledge; some assessment of the group JUDGMENT or view; some opportunity for individuals to revise views; and some degree of anonymity for the individual responses" (Linstone & Turoff, 1975, p. 3).

comment: "'Project Delphi' was the name given to an Air Force-sponsored Rand Corporation study, starting in the early 1950's, concerning the use of expert opinion. [See Dalkey & Helmer, 1963.] The objective of the original study was to 'obtain the most reliable consensus of opinion by a group of experts...by a series of intensive questionnaires interspersed with controlled opinion feedback" (Linstone & Turoff, 1975, p. 10). "While its principal area of application has remained that of technical FORECASTING, it has been used in many other contexts in which judgmental information is indispensible. These include normative forecasts; the ascertainment of VALUES and PREFERENCES; estimates concerning the quality of life; simulated and real DECISION MAKING; and what may be called 'inventive planning,' by which is meant the identification (including invention) of potential measures that might be taken to deal with a given problem situation and the assessment of such proposed measures with regard to their feasibility, desirability, and effectiveness" (Helmer, 1975, p.

xix).

related terms: SUBJECTIVE PROBABILITY, PROBLEM STRUCTURING, JUDGMENT.

DEMAND.

See COST-BENEFIT ANALYSIS.

DEPTH.

See LENS MODEL.

DESCRIPTIVE MODEL

definition: A set of statements describing what people actually do. Frequently contrasted with NORMATIVE MODEL. A descriptive model of DECISION MAKING thus tells what decision a person will make, given certain inputs (Edwards, Lindman, & Phillips, 1965, pp. 263f.) Descriptive models of JUDGMENT or CHOICE can be divided into PARAMORPHIC MODELS and PROCESS-TRACING MODELS.

related terms: PRESCRIPTIVE MODEL, NORMATIVE MODEL, PARAMORPHIC MODEL, PROCESS-TRACING MODEL.

DIAGNOSTIC DATA.

See CAUSAL SCHEMA.

DIAGNOSTIC IMPACT.

See DIAGNOSTICITY.

DIAGNOSTIC VALUE.

See DIAGNOSTICITY.

DIAGNOSTICITY

definition: A BAYESIAN term indicating the extent to which a datum provides information about a hypothesis, expressed as a LIKELIHOOD RATIO (ratio of the CONDITIONAL PROBABILITIES of the datum across alternative hypotheses, e.g., $p(D|H_1)/p(D|H_2)$) (Slovic & Lichtenstein, 1973, p. 93.) In correlational terms, the extent to which a predictor provides information about a criterion (ECOLOGICAL VALIDITY), usually expressed as a correlation coefficient or as a BETA WEIGHT.

comment: In BDT studies, "increased diagnosticity, no matter how produced, increases CONSERVATISM" (Slovic & Lichtenstein, 1973, p. 67). In PDT studies, it is found that "intuitive predictions are essentially unaffected by considerations of PRIOR PROBABILITY and expected predictive accuracy" (Kahneman & Tversky, 1973, p. 238). (See NON-REGRESSIVENESS BIAS, BASE RATE FALLACY.

synonyms: **DIAGNOSTIC IMPACT, DIAGNOSTIC VALUE** (Phillips & Edwards, 1966, p. 347).

related terms: ECOLOGICAL VALIDITY, WEIGHT, LIKELIHOOD RATIO, NON-REGRESSIVENESS BIAS, BASE-RATE FALLACY.

DIFFERENTIAL WEIGHT.

See WEIGHT.

DIMENSION

definition: In its broadest sense, a set of mutually exclusive characteristics or properties. Often, however, more narrowly understood to imply a degree of quantification, as in Webster's (1976) definition: "...a MEASURE in a single line...magnitude, size...the range over which or the degree to which something extends" (p. 634).

examples: "...Red, orange, yellow, and so forth are clearly different values within the dimension of color..." (Bourne, 1966, p. 4). "These stimuli are either circles or squares, so form is one dimension; they are open on the left or on the right, so position of the opening is a second dimension; each has a center line which is either vertical or horizontal, so position of the center line is a third dimension..." (Garner, 1974, pp. 5-6). Dimensions commonly employed in JUDGMENT and DECISION MAKING include CUES, PROBABILITIES, and UTILITIES.

comment: The characteristics or properties that constitute a dimension are called LEVELS, or VALUES. A dimension that takes on different levels for different objects or events under consideration is called a **VARIABLE**, while one that has the same level for all objects or events under consideration is called a **CONSTANT**. However, the term "variable" is often used interchangeably with "dimension."

FACTOR is also often used interchangeably with dimension; however, it frequently carries the sense of UNCORRELATED dimension, as in "FACTOR ANALYSIS", "factorial design", and "factorial plot". **ATTRIBUTE** is often used interchangeably with dimension, or even with value ("A dimension has, by definition, at least two and usually many more discriminably different *values* or *attributes*." Bourne, 1966, p. 4.); yet it is used in a more restricted sense by Keeney & Raiffa (1976, p. 40) to refer to a quantifiable dimension. Dimensions may be quantified in terms of any of a number of SCALES of MEASUREMENT.

synonyms: **VARIABLE, ATTRIBUTE, FACTOR.**

related terms: SCALES of MEASUREMENT, ACT FORK, EVENT FORK, CONFLICT, DECISION MAKING.

DIMINISHING MARGINAL UTILITY.

See VALUE, UTILITY, FUNCTION FORM.

DIRECT ASSESSMENT.

See DIRECT PREFERENCE MEASUREMENT, WEIGHT.

DIRECT PREFERENCE MEASUREMENT

definition: Direct estimation by a DECISION MAKER of the UTILITY (Definition 2) of an action alternative on a given OUTCOME ATTRIBUTE (Keeney & Raiffa, 1976, p. 62).

comment: The theoretically appropriate approach to estimating the utility of an alternative on an outcome attribute is a three-step process involving FACT-VALUE SEPARATION:

      a. estimate a PROBABILITY distribution over the various possible LEVELS of the attribute (FACT JUDGMENT).

      b. assess a utility function over those levels (VALUE JUDGMENT).

      c. calculate expected utility (analytic integration, or AGGREGATION, of FACT and VALUE JUDGMENTS).

Direct preference measurement collapses these three steps into one, so that the three are performed implicitly rather than explicitly.

Direct preference measurement is one of three options for estimating the utility of an alternative on a SUBJECTIVE ATTRIBUTE. The others are use of a SUBJECTIVE INDEX or a PROXY ATTRIBUTE, either of which requires the full three-step process (Keeney & Raiffa, 1976, pp. 61-62).

related terms: UTILITY (Definition 2), VALUE (Definition 2), AGGREGATION, DECOMPOSITION, DECISION THEORY, PRESCRIPTIVE MODEL, SUBJECTIVE ATTRIBUTE, SUBJECTIVE INDEX, PROXY ATTRIBUTE, REVEALED PREFERENCE, FACT-VALUE SEPARATION.

DIRECT PRICE.

    See MARKET PRICE.

DISCOUNT RATE.

    See DISCOUNTING.

DISCOUNTING

definition 1: Reducing the estimated WORTH of a quantity, for example, of future benefits.

comment regarding definition 1: Future benefits are generally discounted to take account of **OPPORTUNITY COSTS**, the benefits (e.g., interest) that could be realized from alternative forms of investment. The **DISCOUNT RATE** might be taken to be some standard interest rate. A second reason sometimes given for discounting future benefits is that they are less certain than present benefits.

terms related to definition 1: COST-BENEFIT ANALYSIS.

definition 2: Attributing an effect less to any one cause, the greater the plausibility of alternative possible causes (Kelley, 1967a, p. 8.)

comment regarding definition 2: A person is seen as less a cause of his/her behavior if both external conditions (e.g., obligation, coercion) and internal conditions (e.g., traits, motives) are plausible explanations for the behavior.

terms related to definition 2: ATTRIBUTION.

DISCRIMINATION REDUNDANCY.

See REDUNDANCY.

DISJUNCTIVE MODEL.

See CONJUNCTIVE and DISJUNCTIVE MODELS.

DISTAL.

See LENS MODEL.

DIVIDE-AND-CONQUER STRATEGY.

See DECOMPOSITION.

DOMINANCE

definition: One alternative, X, dominates another, Y, when it is at least as good as Y on all DIMENSIONS and better on at least one (Keeney & Raiffa, 1976, p. 70.)

comment: Determination of dominance requires only ORDINAL information.

related terms: ADMISSABLE SET, EFFICIENT FRONTIER, PARETO FRONTIER.

DOMINATED ALTERNATIVE.

See DOMINANCE.

DOUBLE COUNTING

definition: Counting the same thing twice.

comment: A problem frequently encountered in MULTIATTRIBUTE DECISION MAKING. If the GOAL set is not properly structured, the same VALUE dimension may be counted in more than one OBJECTIVE.

example : Including both cause and effect may produce double counting. For example, income and status, as objectives for choosing among jobs, may double count, to the extent that status is dependent on the clothes, house, car, and activities that a greater income can make possible. If an alternative is given a plus for income and a plus for status, income will be counted twice.

related terms: REDUNDANCY.

DOUBLE-SYSTEM CASE.

See COGNITIVE SYSTEM.

DT.

See DECISION THEORY.

DYNAMIC PROGRAMMING

definition: A decision rule for optimizing a process "that consists of several stages, where the result from previous stages affects later stages. The method is based on the **BELLMAN PRINCIPLE of OPTIMALITY,** stated by Kim (1976) as follows: 'an optimal POLICY has the property that, whatever the initial environment and initial decisions are, the remaining decisions must constitute an optimal policy with regard to the environment resulting from the initial decision. Put another way, one starts from the last stage and, for each possible environment that could result, optimizes it. Then one optimizes the last two stages together, and so on, until one gets to the first stage" (quoted in Kim & Roush, 1980, p. 208).

comment: The technique of FOLDING BACK, or ROLLING BACK, a DECISION TREE is an application of the Bellman principle of dynamic programming.

related terms: FOLDING BACK.

ECOLOGICAL FALLACY.

See NOMOTHETIC.

ECOLOGICAL INFERENCE.

See NOMOTHETIC.

ECOLOGICAL RELIABILITY.

See ENVIRONMENTAL CORRELATION.

ECOLOGICAL VALIDITY.

See ENVIRONMENTAL CORRELATION.

ECONOMIC MAN

definition: The economist's concept, originating with philosophers Jeremy Bentham and James Mill, of an ideal person who MAXIMIZES EXPECTED UTILITY in all his/her CHOICES (Coombs, Dawes, & Tversky, 1970, p. 122.) An economic man is assumed (a) to have complete information, (b) to be infinitely sensitive, and (c) to be RATIONAL (Edwards, 1954, p. 381). The complete information assumption is that economic man knows "not only what all the courses of action open to him are, but also what the outcomes of any action will be" (Edwards, 1954, p. 381). The infinite sensitivity assumption is only to make the relevant functions continuous and differentiable; it seems to have no important behavioral implications (Edwards, 1954, p. 381). The crucial assumption is that economic man is rational. In this context, "this means two things: He can weakly order [in terms of preference] the states into which he can get, and he makes his choices so as to maximize something" (Edwards, 1954, pp. 381, 403). (See RATIONALITY.)

Note again that economic man maximizes *expected utility*, not necessarily money, despite the reliance of economics on money as a primary indicator of VALUE (Definition 2) or UTILITY (Definition 1); that is, as a NUMERAIRE, money (income, wealth) is viewed as a means toward attainment of utility, or as a fallible indicator of it, not as the ultimate end in itself. Maximization of expected utility involves OPTIMIZATION of monetary income or wealth. (See, for example, Becker, 1976.) COST-BENEFIT ANALYSIS, however, assumes a LINEAR RELATION between monetary income or wealth and utility.

related terms: MAXIMIZATION, EXPECTED UTILITY, RATIONALITY, BOUNDED RATIONALITY, QUASI-RATIONALITY.

EFFICIENT FRONTIER

definition: The set of alternatives no one of which is DOMINATED by any other alternative or by any LINEAR combination of other alternatives (see, e.g., Coombs & Avrunin, 1977, p. 220). In the figure below (which is drawn so that the most desirable region is in the southeast portion), point B lies on the PARETO FRONTIER, but not on the efficient frontier. Points on the line between A and C (linear combinations of A and C) lie on the efficient frontier and dominate B.

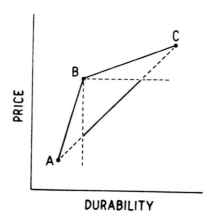

Efficient and Pareto Frontiers

From Coombs & Avrunin, 1977, p. 220. Copyright 1977 by the American Psychological Association. Reprinted by permission.

See PARETO FRONTIER. The figure below represents an efficient frontier and an INDIFFERENCE CURVE on the same graph.

comment: The rationale for taking linear combinations of alternatives into account (whereas the concept of a Pareto frontier does not) is that any point on a straight line connecting two points can be arrived at by adjusting the probabilities in a LOTTERY on those points.

synonyms: One possible meaning for **ADMISSABLE SET, NON-DOMINATED**

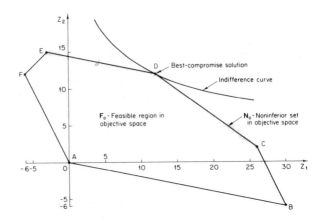

Efficient Frontier and Indifference Curve

From Cohon, 1978, p. 74.   Copyright 1978 by Academic Press.   Reprinted by permission.

SET, NON-INFERIOR SET, **POSSIBILITY FRONTIER**, or **PRODUCTION POSSIBILITY FRONTIER**.   Sometimes (e.g., Keeney & Raiffa, 1976, p.   71) also used synonymously   with PARETO FRONTIER.

related   terms: DOMINANCE,   PARETO   FRONTIER,   LINEAR MODEL, EXPECTED UTILITY.

EIA.

See ENVIRONMENTAL IMPACT ASSESSMENT.

EIS.

See ENVIRONMENTAL IMPACT ASSESSMENT.

ELIMINATION by ASPECTS

definition: A theory developed by Amos Tversky (1972) in which decisions are made according to a LEXICOGRAPHIC MODEL in which the ordering of DIMENSIONS is not fixed but probabilistic, with the probabilities being proportional to the importance WEIGHTS of the dimensions.

example: Tversky (1972) uses the following television commercial as an example of elimination by aspects:

> "There are more than two dozen companies in the San Francisco area which offer training in computer programming." (Announcer puts two dozen eggs and a walnut on the table.)

> "Let us examine the facts. How many of these schools have on-line computer facilities for training?" (Removes several eggs.)

> "How many of these schools have placement services that would help find you a job?" (Removes more eggs.)

> "How many of these schools are approved for veterans' benefits?" (Removes more eggs.)

> This continues until the walnut alone remains, at which point the announcer cracks the nutshell, which reveals the name of the company, and concludes: "This is all you need to know, in a nutshell."

related terms: LEXICOGRAPHIC ORDERING.

ELLSBERG PARADOX

definition: A paradox pointed out by Daniel Ellsberg (1961.) Individuals are asked to imagine that they are confronted with two urns containing red and black balls, from which one will be drawn at random. Urn I contains 100 red and black balls but in an unknown ratio; Urn II contains exactly 50 red balls and exactly 50 black balls. Urn I, thus, presents the decision maker with UNCERTAINTY, whereas Urn II presents the decision maker with RISK.

Most individuals (a) are indifferent between betting on a red ball from Urn I and betting on a black ball from Urn I and (b) are indifferent between betting on a red ball from Urn II and betting on a black ball from Urn II, but (c) prefer betting on a red ball from Urn II to betting on a red ball from Urn I and (d) prefer betting on a black ball from Urn II to betting on a black ball from Urn I (Ellsberg, 1961; MacCrimmon, 1968; Becker & Brownson, 1964.)

According to the principle of REVEALED PREFERENCE, Choice A indicates that $p(R_i) = p(B_i)$, and Choice B indicates that $p(R_{ii}) = p(B_{ii})$. Similarly, Choice C indicates that $p(R_{ii}) > p(R_i)$, and Choice D indicates that $p(B_{ii}) > p(B_i)$. Yet, if $p(R_i) + p(B_i) = 1.00$, to say that $p(R_{ii}) > p(R_i)$ and $p(B_{ii}) > p(B_i)$ is to say that $p(R_{ii}) + p(B_{ii}) > 1.00$, which contradicts certain axioms of probability theory (Savage, 1954.) Whence, the paradox. Choices, in this case, are clearly not in any simple way revealing beliefs about probabilities.

comment: Ellsberg's suggestion is that many decision makers maximize expected utility in situations involving risk, maximize minimum utility (MAXIMIN strategy) in situations involving uncertainty, and adopt compromise strategies in situations in which their degree of confidence in their estimates of probabilities are intermediate between risk (high confidence) and uncertainty (low confidence.) Letting ρ denote the decision maker's degree of confidence in the estimated probability distribution, est(x) the expected payoff, and min(x) the minimum expected payoff, the decision rule becomes: "*Associate with each x the index*:

$$\rho \cdot \text{est}(x) + (r - \rho) \cdot \text{min}(x)$$

Choose that act with the highest index" (Ellsberg, 1961, p. 664). Thus, the von-Neumann-Morgenstern technique for measuring UTILITY would be appropriate only in situations involving risk, and revealed preference methods for obtaining SUBJECTIVE PROBABILITIES would be more nearly appropriate, the more closely uncertainty approximated risk.

related terms: RISK, UNCERTAINTY, REVEALED PREFERENCE, SUBJECTIVE PROBABILITY, UTILITY.

EMPIRICAL FREQUENCY.

See OBJECTIVE PROBABILITY.

ENDPOINT.

See DECISION TREE.

ENVIRONMENTAL CORRELATION

definition: Correlation among environmental VARIABLES.

examples: Several kinds of environmental correlation have been regarded as sufficiently important to have been given labels. **ECOLOGICAL RELIABILITY** is the correlation between successive MEASUREMENTS of an environmental variable. **ECOLOGICAL VALIDITY,** on the perceptual side, is the degree of relationship between an PROXIMAL stimulus, or CUE, and a DISTAL stimulus, or object. On the response side, it is the degree of relationship between proximal responses and distal effects. **CUE INTERCORRELATIONS,** or **INTRAECOLOGICAL CUE CORRELATIONS,** are correlations among those aspects of the environment to which the organism is responding.

comment: Positive environmental correlations make it difficult to assess WEIGHTS (Darlington, 1968); however, by the same token, they contribute to the robustness of LINEAR MODELS (Yntema & Torgerson, 1961; Dawes & Corrigan, 1974). Negative environmental correlations exist at the EFFICIENT FRONTIER and require TRADEOFFS; they also require more precise estimates of weights (McClelland, 1978). SYSTEMATIC DESIGN employs UNCORRELATED independent variables so as to estimate weights more precisely; REPRESENTATIVE DESIGN employs independent values that are correlated in the same way they are correlated in the environment so as not to disturb the judgment process under study (Brunswik 1955, pp. 204-205).

synonym: INTRAECOLOGICAL CORRELATION.

related terms: REDUNDANCY, VICARIOUS MEDIATION, INDEPENDENCE, LENS MODEL, MARGINAL RATE of TRANSFORMATION.

ENVIRONMENTAL IMPACT ASSESSMENT

definition: The assessment of the IMPACT of human activities, "particularly the profound influences of population growth, high-density urbanization, industrial expansion, resource exploitation, and new and expanding technological advances", on all components of the natural environment (National Environmental POLICY Act, or "NEPA", - Public Law 91-190, Sec. 101(a)) in order to determine the extent to which such activities:

"(1) fulfill the responsibilities of each generation as trustee of the environment for succeeding generations;

(2) assure for all Americans safe, healthful, productive, and esthetically and culturally pleasing surroundings;

(3) attain the widest range of beneficial uses of the environment without degradation, RISK to health or safety, or other undesirable and unintended consequences;

(4) preserve important historic, cultural, and natural aspects of our national heritage, and maintain, wherever possible, an environment which supports diversity and variety of individual CHOICE;

(5) achieve a balance between population and resource use which will permit high standards of living and a wide sharing of life's amenities; and

(6) enhance the quality of renewable resources and approach the maximum attainable recycling of depletable resources" (NEPA, Sec. 101(b)).

The aim of NEPA and of related laws and regulations is to "ensure that balanced DECISION MAKING occurs in the total public interest" through planning which involves "the integrated consideration of technical, economic, environmental, social, and other FACTORS" rather than domination of the decision-making process by technical and economic factors (Canter, 1977, p. 1).

Environmental impact assessment involves three essential elements:

(1) Prediction [FORECASTING] of the anticipated change in an environmental descriptor;

(2) Determination of the magnitude or scale of the particular change;

(3) Application of an importance or significance factor to the change (Canter, 1977, p. 2).

These elements embody a FACT-VALUE SEPARATION: the first two involve FACT JUDGMENT, while the third involves VALUE JUDGMENT.

comment: **IMPACT ASSESSMENT** is to be distinguished from **EVALUATION RESEARCH,** "which gauges the effectiveness of programs already in operation" (Wolf, 1980). The distinction between impact assessment and evaluation research is basically the distinction between prediction of possible future effects (for PROSPECTIVE EVALUATION) and description of actual past or present effects (for RETROSPECTIVE EVALUATION).

An environmental impact assessment (Jain, Urban, & Stacey, 1977; Jain & Hutchings, 1978) may involve **TECHNOLOGY ASSESSMENT** (**TA**) (Coates, 1976a, 1976b), the assessment of the potential impacts of technological innovations on the human and non-human environment; **SOCIAL IMPACT ASSESSMENT** (**SIA**) (Finsterbusch & Wolf, 1977), the assessment of the potential impacts of various plans or policies on the human environment; and **RISK ASSESSMENT** (Kates, 1977), the identification, estimation, and evaluation of risks.

Environmental impact assessment can result in various types of documents,, depending on the governmental level of authority (federal or state), scope of activity assessed (major or minor), and magnitude and significance of impacts predicted. Principal documents are the **ENVIRONMENTAL IMPACT STATEMENT** (**EIS**), required by NEPA for all "major Federal actions significantly affecting the quality of the human environment " (Section 102C), and the corresponding Environment Impact Report (EIR), required by the "little NEPA" laws which some states (e.g., California) have passed since the passage of NEPA to establish state-level policies similar to those stated by NEPA.

synonym: **EIA.**

related terms: FACT-VALUE SEPARATION, FORECASTING, EVALUATION RESEARCH, TECHNOLOGY ASSESSMENT, RISK ASSESSMENT, DECISION MAKING, POLICY.

ENVIRONMENTAL IMPACT STATEMENT.

  See EIS.

ENVIRONMENTAL PREDICTABILITY.

  See LENS MODEL EQUATION.

EQUAL WEIGHTS.

  See IMPROPER LINEAR MODEL, AVERAGING MODEL.

EQUIFINALITY.

  See LENS MODEL.

EQUIPOTENTIALITY.

  See VICARIOUS FUNCTIONING, LENS MODEL.

EQUITY

definition: The fairness with which UTILITY (Definition 1; synonym, WELFARE) or material wealth (taken as a means toward and surrogate for utility) is distributed among persons. One interpretation of fairness is uniformity of distribution (Rawls, 1971; Sen, 1973); another is that each should receive in proportion to what he/she contributes (Aristotle; see Anderson & Farkas, 1975); still another is "from each according to his abilities, to each according to his needs" (Marx; see Berlin, 1978). Principles of equity are distinguished from the principle of MAXIMIZING AGGREGATE UTILITY across persons.

comment: The relative importance to be placed on equity (often measured as equality) and aggregate utility is a central problem in choice of a SOCIAL WELFARE FUNCTION.

The social welfare function implicit in BENEFIT-COST ANALYSIS (the "KALDOR-HICKS" or "potential Pareto improvement" criterion), for example, considers only aggregate utility; it equates maximization of social welfare with unconstrained maximization of aggregate utility. The PARETO PRINCIPLE equates a social optimum with a constrained maximum of aggregate utility, stating that "situation Q is preferred to situation R [i.e., is "Pareto superior" to R] if at least one person is better off on situation Q and no one is worse off" (Stokey & Zeckhauser, 1978, p. 270). This implies that the greater the aggregate utility the better, subject to the constraint that no one be made worse off in absolute terms. Reduction in total utility is always social deterioration, since this can occur only if at least one person becomes worse off, but reduction in equality is *not* necessarily deterioration: a change that increased aggregate utility yet decreased equality by making the rich richer while leaving the poor as poor as before would be judged to be a "Pareto improvement".

Harsanyi (1975) argues from a different point of view against taking separate account of equity. Moral preferences are based on impersonal and impartial criteria; moral choices are made in ignorance, or at least voluntary disregard, of what the decision maker's personal position would be in either situation. "Thus, according to BAYESIAN decision theory, he would have to choose the social situation yielding him a higher EXPECTED UTILITY..." (1975, p. 314). This is "equivalent to expressing a preference based on the arithmetic mean of all individual utilities as one's SOCIAL WELFARE FUNCTION" (p. 314).

McClelland and Rohrbaugh (1978) have found that people place more weight on equity than these principles prescribe. Experimental subjects acting as arbitrators of two-person conflicts in two studies "showed a willingness to accept reduced total utility in order to obtain a more nearly equal [interpreted as equitable] distribution of utility" (p. 453) between the conflicting parties.

Measurement of equity requires INTERPERSONAL COMPARABILITY of utility (as does measurement of aggregate utility).

related terms: UTILITY,   WELFARE, SOCIAL WELFARE FUNCTION, BENEFIT-
COST ANALYSIS, PARETO PRINCIPLE, INTERPERSONAL COMPARABILITY.

EU.

See EXPECTED UTILITY.

EV.

See EXPECTED VALUE.

EVALUATION RESEARCH.

See ENVIRONMENTAL IMPACT ASSESSMENT.

EVENT FORK.

See DECISION TREE.

EVENT NODE.

See DECISION TREE.

EX ANTE EVALUATION.

See COST-BENEFIT ANALYSIS.

EX POST EVALUATION.

See COST-BENEFIT ANALYSIS.

EXISTENTIAL AXIOM.

See AXIOM.

EXPECTED UTILITY

definition: The expected utility of an alternative with uncertain consequences is the sum of the UTILITIES of its possible OUTCOMES, each weighted by its PROBABILITY of occurrence (Coombs, Dawes, & Tversky, 1970, p. 119.) Expected utility (*EU*) is expressed by:

$$EU = p_1 U_1 + p_2 U_2 + \cdots + p_k U_k,$$

where p_i is the probability of a given outcome and U_i is the utility of that outcome. Initiated by Bernoulli (1738, reprinted 1954) and significantly developed by von Neumann & Morgenstern (1947).

comment: Expected utility, in contrast to EXPECTED VALUE, takes account of the value of RISK. Consider the CHOICE between betting $10,000 on the toss of a coin and not betting at all. The expected *value* of not betting is, of course, $0. The expected *value* of betting is .50 ($10,000) + .50 (-$10,000) = $0. Though both of these alternatives have the same expected value, few people would be indifferent between them. Because most people are RISK AVERSE, most would prefer not to bet in this situation. A decreasing UTILITY CURVE, which reflects risk aversion, would yield a utility for -$10,000 that is farther below the utility for $0 than that for +$10,000 is above the utility for $0. Thus, while the expected *value* of gambling would be equal to the expected value of not gambling, the expected *utility* of gambling would be lower than the expected utility of not gambling. The rationale for basing decisions on expected, or average, utility is different from that for basing decisions on expected, or average, value (see EXPECTED VALUE) and is given in connection with the definition of von NEUMANN-MORGENSTERN UTILITY.

synonym: **EU.**

related terms: EXPECTED VALUE, MAXIMIZATION, RISK, St. PETERSBURG PARADOX, SUBJECTIVE EXPECTED UTILITY, von NEUMANN-MORGENSTERN UTILITY, DECISION THEORY.

EXPECTED VALUE

definition: The expected value of an alternative with uncertain consequences is the sum of the VALUES (definitions 1, 2, or 3 of VALUE) of its possible OUTCOMES, each weighted by its PROBABILITY of occurrence (Coombs, Dawes, & Tversky, 1970, p. 118.) Expected value (EV) is expressed by:

$$EV = p_1 v_1 + p_2 v_2 + \cdots + p_k v_k,$$

where p_i is the probability of a given outcome and v_i is the value of that outcome.

comment: "The rationale generally given for using expected value involves an argument as to what will happen in the long run when the gamble is repeated many times (Luce & Raiffa, 1957, p. 20). Expected value, in contrast to EXPECTED UTILITY, does not take account of the value of RISK.

synonym: **EV.**

related terms: EXPECTED UTILITY, MAXIMIZATION, RISK PREMIUM, VALUE, PROBABILITY.

EXTERNALITY

definition: An adverse or beneficial effect of action that (i) affects parties other than the actor; (ii) occurs through a direct change in those parties' consumption or production opportunities, and thus WELFARE, rather than through the market prices those parties face; (iii) is not intended by the actor; and (iv) is not taken into account by the actor in determining the production (including pricing) or consumption decisions he makes based on his self-interest. Point (iv) implies that the actor does not compensate the affected parties for adverse effects or receive payment from them for beneficial effects. (Mishan, 1976, Ch. 16; Prest & Turvey, 1965; Rothenberg, 1975; Stokey & Zeckhauser, 1978, Ch. 14).

synonym: Spillover, external economy or diseconomy, side effect.

examples: Classic adverse externalities involve pollution and the depletion of commonly held resources. The former class includes pollution of waterways and water tables caused by the waste effluents of industries which do not pay to offset it (e.g., contamination of the Love Canal area by Hooker Chemical Co. wastes) and pollution of downwind air by upwind cigar smokers. The latter includes the TRAGEDY of the COMMONS (Hardin, 1968). Favorable externalities include development by one municipality of facilities that are available without cost to residents of a neighboring municipality, and development by a private party of an attractive building or garden that can be viewed without cost by passersby. PUBLIC GOODS are a major category of favorable externalities. Some externalities (e.g., music emanating from an outdoor concert) may be judged adverse by some affected parties but favorable by others. Most externalities cited in the literature are adverse, but whether most actual ones are so is unclear.

comment: Externalities are important for at least three related reasons. First, they lead to societally suboptimal economic equilibria. Rational self-interested market behavior based on incomplete accounting of consequences "produces too little of activities that generate positive externalities [because benefits are underestimated]" and too much of those that generate external costs [because costs are underestimated]"; (Stokey & Zeckhauser, 1978, p. 305). Second, they distort the results of COST-BENEFIT ANALYSIS and COST-EFFECTIVENESS ANALYSIS for the same reason. Adverse externalities cause overestimation of benefits and underestimation of costs, while favorable externalities have the opposite effect (Mishan, 1976, Chs. 16-19; Layard, 1972; Schultze & Kneese, 1980). Third, adverse externalities are inequitable, or unjust (see EQUITY), as they involve imposition of uncompensated costs by some parties on others (Mishan, 1976; Rothenberg, 1975).

Mishan (1976, Ch. 16) notes that the number of externalities in the world is virtually unlimited, but that society normally distinguishes those that are sources of "legitimate" grievance from those that are not. The former include all the pollution examples cited above, while the latter include "the resentment or envy felt by some people at the achievement or possessions of others" (p. 116).

Mishan also notes that many externalities can be eliminated, at least in principle, by creation of markets in which the adverse or favorable effects involved are exchanged and priced along with all other marketed commodities. Creation of such markets would cause the former externalities to be "internalized" into the decision making of the responsible actors. Actors responsible for adverse effects would now be financially accountable for them; this might lead either to elimination of the effect (e.g., through installation of pollution control devices at the plant) or to compensation of those adversely affected by it (e.g., through purchase from them of "pollution rights"). Actors responsible for beneficial effects could now (somehow) recoup payment from those who formerly enjoyed them free. Elimination of the effect itself would violate condition (i), and thus (ii) and (iii) of the definition of "externality," while payment or collection of payment for a continuing effect would violate condition (iv).

Valuation of those externalities not internalized by the responsible actors is no different, in principle, from valuation of any other marketed or nonmarketed commodities. "Any particular spillover effect associated with a given project is but one among any number of consequences affecting the welfare of different people in the community" (Mishan, 1976, p. 122). Effects with MARKET PRICES can be valued in terms of those prices. Air pollution, for instance, can be "costed out" at least in part by reference to the market values of the extra expenditures required (e.g., on medical services, air filtration devices, and cleaning or replacement of pollution-damaged materials) and the income reductions imposed (e.g., due to ill health, loss of agricultural productivity, loss of tourism, and reduction in property values); see, for example, Freeman, 1979; Mishan, 1976, Ch. 18; Seskin, 1977. Effects without market prices are valued by the usual methods used for NONMARKETED GOODS.

related terms: PUBLIC GOOD, NONMARKETED GOOD, MARKET PRICE, SHADOW PRICE, COST-BENEFIT ANALYSIS, COST-EFFECTIVENESS ANALYSIS, EQUITY, TRAGEDY OF THE COMMONS.

FACT CONFLICT.

See CONFLICT.

FACT JUDGMENT.

See FACT-VALUE SEPARATION.

FACT-VALUE SEPARATION

definition: DECOMPOSITION of DECISIONS into (a) FACT JUDGMENTS (often expressed in terms of PROBABILITIES) about the elements of various alternatives or their OUTCOMES and (b) VALUE JUDGMENTS about the desirability (often expressed as UTILITIES) of these alternatives or outcomes. (Values may be further decomposed into hedonistic and moral values.) It is generally assumed that, although fact judgments can be checked for correctness and consistency, value judgments can be checked only for consistency.

comment: This topic has a long history and carries deep and pervasive moral and ethical implications. For example, the notion that reasoning can not be applied to questions of ethics and that ethical disputes therefore resolve into contests for power was put forward by Plato's Thrasymachus, who, in the first book of *The Republic* proclaims that "Justice is nothing else than the interests of the stronger" (see Russell, 1945, pp. 116-117).

The strongest claim among modern philosophers for the necessity of the separation of fact and value was made by David Hume (1711-1776, see 1888):

> "Nor does this reasoning only prove, that morality consists not in any relations, that are the objects of science; but if examin'd, will prove with equal certainty, that it consists not in any *matter of fact*, which can be discover'd by the understanding" (p. 468). It "seems altogether inconceivable, how this new relation [*ought* and *ought not*] can be a deduction from others [*is* and *is not*], which are entirely different from it" (p. 469, 1888 edition).

Marxists take the opposite view. In a definitive biography of Marx, Isaiah Berlin (1978) observes:

> "Marx does not explicitly draw this distinction, which has been brought to the forefront of philosophical attention by Hume and Kant, but it seems clear that for him (he follows Hegel on this) judgments of fact cannot be sharply distinguished from those of value: all one's judgments are conditioned by practical activity in a given social milieu which, in its turn, are functions of the stage reached by one's class in its historical evolution: one's views as to what one believes to exist and what one wishes to do

with it, modify each other. If ethical judgments
claim objective validity, they must be definable
in terms of empirical activities and be verifiable
by reference to them. He does not recognise the
existence of a non-empirical, purely contemplative
or specifically moral intuition or moral reason.
The only sense in which it is posssible to show
that something is good or bad, right or wrong, is
by demonstrating that it accords or discords with
the historical process--the collective progressive
activity of men--that it assists it or thwarts it,
will survive or will inevitably perish. All
causes permanently lost or doomed to fail, in the
complex but historically determined ascent of
mankind, are, by that very fact, made bad and
wrong, and indeed this is what constitutes the
meaning of such terms. But this is a dangerous
empirical criterion, since causes which may appear
lost may, in fact, have suffered only a temporary
setback, and will in the end prevail" (p. 113).

In the twentieth century, the separation of fact and value was
insisted upon by the well-known sociologist and student of
bureaucracy, Max Weber (transl. 1949):

"The establishment of empirical facts" and
"evaluation of these facts" are "logically
different and to deal with them as though they
were the same represents a confusion of entirely
heterogenous problems" (p. 11).

"We can also offer the person, who makes a
CHOICE, insight into the significance of the
desired object. We can teach him to think in
terms of the context and the meaning of the ends
he desires, and among which he chooses. We do
this through making explicit and developing in a
logically consistent manner the 'ideas' which
actually do or which can underlie the concrete
end" (p. 53)....the ultimate standards of value
which he does not make explicit to himself or,
which he must presuppose in order to be
logical".... "As to whether the person expressing

these value-judgments *should* adhere to these ultimate standards is his personal affair; it involves will and conscience, not empirical KNOWLEDGE.

"An empirical science cannot tell anyone what he *should* do--but rather what he *can* do--and under certain circumstances--what he wishes to do" (p. 54).

For further philosophical discussion, see W. D. Hudson, Editor, *The Is/Ought Question* (1969).

Among contemporary writers in the area of JUDGMENT and DECISION MAKING, Pearl (1977) rejects the fact-value distinction altogether, arguing that "value judgments and probability statements are one and the same thing", that, for example, "the statement 'I prefer outcome A to outcome B' may be interpreted to mean 'I estimate the probability of reaching a certain state of satisfaction conditioned upon A to be higher than that conditioned upon B'" (p. 350). He goes on to show how BAYESIAN techniques can be applied to the processing of value judgments.

Simon (1976) seems to agree that, in practice at least, it is difficult to distinguish facts from values:

"...The further the means-end chain is followed, i.e., the greater the ethical element, the more doubtful are the steps in the chain, and the greater is the element of judgment involved in determining what means will contribute to what ends" (p. 51).

He adds that, while analysis of the first portion "could be pretty well restricted to factual problems", analysis of the second would "involve both ethical and factual considerations" (p. 53). However, contrary to Pearl, Simon (1977a, Ch. 3.1) insists that there is a sharp *logical* distinction between "is" and "ought" statements, that "ought" statements have nothing to do with probabilities.

Hammond & Adelman (1976) urge that, in public policy decisions, fact judgments about the probabilities of the various outcomes be made by appropriate experts, without their knowing how the public evaluates these outcomes, and value judgments about the desirability of the various outcomes be made by representatives of the public, without their knowing which outcomes the experts judge to be likely consequences of which alternatives, and finally that fact judgments and value judgments be AGGREGATED by analytical, RETRACEABLE means. In this way, a "veil of ignorance" (Rawls, 1971, p. 136) will be maintained between those making judgments of fact and those making judgments of value, with the presumed consequence that distortions will be reduced in both kinds of judgment.

Hammond, McClelland, & Mumpower (1980, p. 179) point out that "The three approaches actively involved in applications, DT, BDT, and SJT, all seem to agree that (a) POLICY makers should make judgments about values or preferences and (b) substantive experts should make judgments about facts or INFERENCES about environmental ATTRIBUTES."

related terms: DECOMPOSITION, PROBABILITY, UTILITY.

FACTOR.

See DIMENSION.

FACTOR ANALYSIS.

See MULTIDIMENSIONAL SCALING.

FAULT TREE

definition: A hierarchical representation of possibilities for failure in terms of "functional categories" (Fischhoff, Slovic, & Lichtenstein, 1978.)

examples: A fault tree for reasons why a car will not start could begin with the categories: battery charge insufficient, starting system defective, fuel system defective, etc. Battery charge insufficient (B) could then be further divided into: faulty ground connections (c), terminals loose or corroded (t), and battery weak (w). Similarly, each of the other categories could be further detailed (Fischhoff, et al., 1978.)

comment: A fault tree differs from a PROBABILITY TREE or a DECISION TREE in that its levels represent different levels of abstraction (in the example, the abstract category *B* includes the more specific possibilities *c*, *t*, and *w*). Perhaps more important, whereas the set of endpoints in a probability tree or a decision tree represents all possible *combinations* of the events under consideration (in the example, *c*, *t*, *w*, *ct*, *cw*, *tw*, and *ctw*), the set of endpoints in a fault tree represents all of the events under consideration, *taken one at a time* (in the example, *c*, *t*, and *w*). A fault tree is thus similar in structure to a GOAL TREE.

Fault trees are used to estimate probabilities of failure both in designing trouble-free systems and in trouble shooting existing systems (Fischhoff, et al., 1978).

related terms: TREE, PROBABILITY TREE, DECISION TREE, PROBABILITY.

FEEDBACK

definition: Information received by a system (e.g., an organism) about its responses or their consequences. "The organism affects the environment, and the environment affects the organism: such a system is said to have 'feedback'" (Ashby, 1960, p. 37). "The control of a machine on the basis of its *actual* performance rather than its *expected* performance is known as *feedback*..." (Wiener, 1950, p. 12). "Learning is a most complicated form of feedback, and influences not merely the individual action, but the pattern of action" (Wiener, 1950, p. 69).

comment: **FEEDBACK CONTROL** is control of the systems subsequent response(s) by feedback from previous response(s). Feedback control in ADAPTIVE systems tends to be **NEGATIVE FEEDBACK CONTROL**; that is, it is such as to reduce discrepancies from an ideal condition, GOAL, or target. **POSITIVE FEEDBACK CONTROL** is such as to increase such discrepancies. The first produces stability; the second, instability.

The feedback provided to subjects in studies of learning (see MULTIPLE-CUE PROBABILITY LEARNING, DOUBLE-SYSTEM CASE) can be either **OUTCOME FEEDBACK** or **COGNITIVE FEEDBACK** (the latter sometimes termed **COGNITIVELY-ORIENTED FEEDBACK**). Outcome feedback is information about the consequences of responses (e.g., discrepancy between response and correct answer). Cognitive feedback is information about the statistical relations both between the PROXIMAL variables (cues) and DISTAL variable (criterion) in the task, and between the proximal variables and the subject's JUDGMENTS; that is, about both the optimal judgment POLICY and the subject's actual judgment policy. (See LENS MODEL, LENS MODEL EQUATION.) Learning is generally more effective (reaches a higher ACHIEVEMENT level) and more efficient (reaches a given achievement level more quickly) with cognitive than with outcome feedback, particularly when FUNCTION FORMS and AGGREGATION rules are NONLINEAR, cues are intercorrelated (see ENVIRONMENTAL CORRELATION) or differentially valid as predictors of the criterion, and cue-criterion relations are probabilistic (Adelman, 1977; Hammond, Summers, & Deane, 1973; Lindell, 1974; Todd & Hammond, 1965). Feedback solely about the subject's judgment policy (cue-response relations) without accompanying information about the optimal judgment policy (cue-criterion relations) does not aid learning in the double-system case, however (Schmitt, Coyle, & King, 1976).

The "POLICY" AID uses POLICY CAPTURING (which see) as a basis for providing cognitive feedback in the form of graphically depicted WEIGHTS and FUNCTION FORMS, among other functions.

related terms: CYBERNETICS, GOAL, INFERENCE, MULTIPLE-CUE PROBABILITY LEARNING, DOUBLE-SYSTEM CASE, LENS MODEL, LENS MODEL EQUATION, ACHIEVEMENT, WEIGHT, FUNCTION FORM, AGGREGATION, LINEAR MODEL, ENVIRONMENTAL CORRELATION, "POLICY" AID, POLICY CAPTURING, POLICY, DECISION AID.

FEEDBACK CONTROL.

See FEEDBACK.

FLIPPING a TREE

definition: Applying BAYES' THEOREM to derive POSTERIOR PROBABILITIES from PRIOR PROBABILITIES and CONDITIONAL PROBABILITIES (Raiffa, 1968, p. 17).

example: Consider the taxicab problem discussed in connection with the BASE-RATE FALLACY. The original, "unflipped" PROBABILITY TREE for this situation is as shown in the figure on the left below:

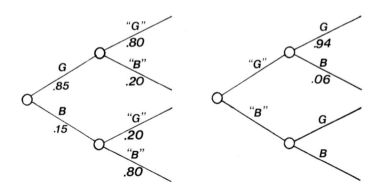

Unflipped and Flipped Trees

G and B stand, respectively for the possibility that the cab was Green and the possibility that the cab was Blue. "G" and "B" stand, respectively, for a report by the witness that the cab was Green and a report by the witness that the cab was Blue. The prior probability, $p(H)$, that the cab was Green is .85, and the conditional probability, $p(D|H)$, that the witness said the cab was Green given that it was Green is .80. And the unconditional probability, $p(D)$, that the witness would, under any conditions, say it was Green is

$$(.85 \times .80) + (.15 \times .20) = .71.$$

What one would like to know is the posterior probability, $p(H|D)$, that the cab was, in fact, Green given that the witness said that it was Green. This is given by Bayes' Theorem:

$$p(H|D) = \frac{p(D|H)\,p(H)}{p(D)}$$

$$p(G|"G") = \frac{.80 \times .85}{.71} = .94$$

This result can be represented in the form of a TREE that has been "flipped" end for end, as in the figure on the right above. This tree begins with the two data posibilities, "*G*" and "*B*". Since the datum is known to be "*G*", it is necessary to pursue only this branch. The calculated posterior probability, $p(G|"G")$, indicates that, on this branch, the probability that the cab was, in fact, Green, is .94.

related terms: BAYES' THEOREM, BASE-RATE FALLACY.

FLOW DIAGRAM.

   See DECISION TREE.

FOCUS.

   See LENS MODEL.

FOLDING BACK

definition: Evaluating a DECISION TREE by beginning with VALUES or UTILITIES at the ENDPOINTS, computing EXPECTED VALUE or UTILITY at each EVENT FORK and selecting the highest expected value or utility at each ACT FORK (MAXIMIZING expected value or utility) , until the initial act fork is reached.

example: A simple example is shown on the next page. The first step in folding back the tree is to compute expected value or utility at the event fork, for example:

$$.8(\$40) + .2(\$20) = \$28$$

The expected utility of this event fork is, thus, $28. The next step is to is to maximize the expected utility at the act fork, that is, to

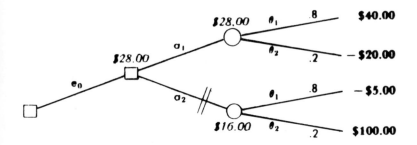

Folding Back a Tree

From Raiffa, 1968, p. 22. Copyright 1968 by Addison-Wesley Publishing Company, Inc. Reprinted by permission.

select $28 in preference to $16. The expected utility of this act fork is, thus, $28.

synonym: **ROLLING BACK.**

related terms: DECISION TREE, EXPECTED UTILITY, MAXIMIZATION, DYNAMIC PROGRAMMING.

FORECASTING

definition: The use of analytical or JUDGMENTAL techniques (a) to detect a pattern in past data and (b) to generate predictions of future data on the basis of this pattern. The pattern is generally assumed to take one of two forms. **TIME SERIES FORECASTING** techniques assume that it is a function simply of time, while **MULTIPLE REGRESSION FORECASTING** techniques assume that it is a function of two or more VARIABLES (Makridakis & Wheelwright, 1977, p. 14, 363)

comment: Among analytic techniques, the particular type of forecasting method that is appropriate depends on the kind of pattern

that is present in the data. This can usually be determined by an
AUTOCORRELATION analysis.

If the data are stationary (show no pattern), a mean, a single
moving average, or exponential smoothing is appropriate for
forecasting. If the data show a LINEAR trend, a linear moving average
or linear exponential smoothing are appropriate. If the data show a
NONLINEAR trend, quadratic exponential smoothing or S-curve fitting
are appropriate; and, if the data show a cyclical pattern,
DECOMPOSITION and MULTIPLE REGRESSION techniques are appropriate. In
all of these cases, the Box-Jenkins technique is appropriate, though
it is more complicated and costly than the others.

If forecasting is to be made on the basis of two or more
variables, only multiple regression is appropriate. And, if the time
horizon of forecasting is long, only S-curve fitting is appropriate
(Makridakis & Wheelwright, 1977, pp. 8, 191-198.)

Among judgmental techniques, the appropriate relations among
techniques, problem, and data are less well defined. The most
prominent judgmental forecasting technique is DELPHI (Linstone &
Turoff, 1975). Judgmental techniques are also discussed by Miller
(1977) and Ben-Dak (1977).

related terms: PROBABILITY ESTIMATION, AUTOCORRELATION, LINEAR,
NONLINEAR, MULTIPLE REGRESSION, FACT JUDGMENT.

FRACTILE ESTIMATION.

See ANCHORING and ADJUSTMENT.

FRAME.

See DECISION FRAME, PROSPECT THEORY.

FREQUENTISTIC PROBABILITY.

See OBJECTIVE PROBABILITY.

FUNCTION.

See FUNCTION FORM.

FUNCTION FORM

definition: The form, or shape, of the functional relationship between two VARIABLES (usually a predictor and a criterion or an objective MEASURE and a corresponding subjective measure of VALUE).

examples: The most common distinctions among function forms are the following.

    a. **MONOTONIC.** One-directional; the output variable increases but never decreases, or decreases but never increases, as the input variable increases.

        1. **LINEAR.** The output variable is a linear function of the input variable (see LINEAR RELATIONSHIP).

        2. **NEGATIVELY ACCELERATED.** The change in the output variable that is associated with a given change in the input variable decreases with increasing values on the input variable. Where the output variable is UTILITY, this function form is typical and is referred to as DECREASING MARGINAL UTILITY. A logarithmic function is an example of a negatively accelerated function.

        3. **POSITIVELY ACCELERATED.** The change in the output variable that is associated with a given change in the input variable increases with increasing values on the input variable. An exponential function is an example of a positively accelerated function.

    b. **NONMONOTONIC.** Not one-directional; the output variable both increases and decreases as the input variable increases. (A common example is an optimum, for example, desirability increasing as population increases to a certain point and then decreasing beyond that point.) See SINGLE-PEAKED PREFERENCE FUNCTION.

Some examples are shown in the following figure:

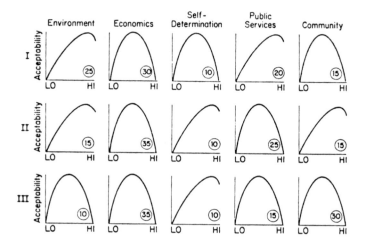

Examples of Function Forms

From Rohrbaugh & Wehr, 1978, p. 529. Copyright 1978 by Public Opinion Quarterly. Reprinted by permission.

comment: Used by nearly all approaches to JUDGMENT and DECISION ANALYSIS, but perhaps most frequently by SJT (see Hammond, McClelland, & Mumpower, 1980, pp. 21-112), to describe relations between CUES and JUDGMENTS or between cues and OUTCOMES. SJT has investigated the learning of function forms (Hammond & Summers, 1965; Brehmer, 1971b, 1974, 1975, 1976b) and the role of function forms in contributing to INTERPERSONAL CONFLICT (see Brehmer & Hammond, 1977).

synonym: **VALUE FUNCTION, FUNCTIONAL FORM, VALUE CURVE.**

related terms: LINEAR, NONLINEAR, WEIGHT, GRAPHIC AIDS.

FUNCTIONAL ACHIEVEMENT.

See LENS MODEL.

FUNCTIONAL MEASUREMENT

definition: Simultaneous validation of INTERVAL stimulus and response scales in terms of the goodness-of-fit of an assumed algebraic model of INFORMATION INTEGRATION, using analysis-of-variance techniques. (Anderson, 1974c, p. 238; Klitzner & Anderson, 1977, pp. 349-51).

comment: Some controversy exists over the relative merits of functional measurement and CONJOINT MEASUREMENT. On the side of functional measurement are the arguments that it has an error theory, that excellent fits to data have been obtained, and that these data do not support the ADDING MODEL that has been so much the focus of conjoint measurement. On the side of conjoint measurement is the argument that direct tests of AXIOMS are more revealing than overall goodness-of-fit to empirical data. (See Luce, 1977, p. 155.) In Luce's view, however, "the methods are largely complementary, not competitive" (Luce, 1977, p. 155).

related terms: INFORMATION INTEGRATION THEORY, COGNITIVE ALGEBRA, CONJOINT MEASUREMENT, MULTIVARIATE ANALYSIS.

FUNCTIONAL RELATIONS.

See FUNCTION FORM.

FUNDAMENTAL ATTRIBUTION ERROR

definition: The tendency for JUDGES to overestimate the role of personal (dispositional) FACTORS, and to underestimate the role of contextual factors, in INFERRING the CAUSES of behavior (Heider, 1944, 1958; Jones, 1979; Ross, 1977.)

example: Jones & Harris (1967) found that listeners assumed some correspondence between communicators' pro-Castro remarks and private opinions even when these listeners knew that the communicators were obeying the experimenter's explicit request in making these remarks.

comment: The fundamental attribution error is presumed to be a consequence of the actor and his act forming a natural cognitive unit (Jones, 1979, p. 115.) (See CAUSAL SCHEMA, SCRIPT.) Presumably, a CORRESPONDENT INFERENCE "becomes the ANCHOR for an adjustment process" (see ANCHORING and ADJUSTMENT), insufficient adjustment in the processing of sequentially presented information resulting in a CONSERVATIVE judgment (Jones, 1979, p. 115.)

The reader's surprise over Milgram's (1963) demonstrations of obedience and Asch's (1955) demonstrations of conformity is seen by Ross (1978, p. 377) to reflect a common underestimation of the power of situational influences.

Similarly, the forced-compliance effect in dissonance research is thought (Ross, 1977, pp. 349f) to be based on the tendency of subjects to fall victim to the fundamental attribution error when appraising their own actions. Otherwise, they would be aware that the contextual arrangements provided a perfectly sufficient explanation for their compliant behavior. (The forced-compliance effect is the tendency of people's attitudes to change toward increased consistency with counterattitudinal behavior they have performed under external inducement, the tendency being greatest when inducement was least [Kiesler, Collins, & Miller, 1969].)

related terms: INFERENCE, CORRESPONDENT INFERENCE, ANCHORING and ADJUSTMENT, CONSERVATISM, CAUSAL SCHEMA, SCRIPT.

FUZZY SET

definition: A concept developed by Zadeh (1965). "A fuzzy set is a class of objects with a continuum of grades of membership. Such a set, A, is characterized by a membership (characteristic) function, f_a, which assigns to each object a grade of membership ranging from zero to one" (Zadeh, 1965, p. 338). The nearer the value of $f_a(x)$, the membership function, to unity, the higher the grade of membership of x in A. When A is a set in the ordinary sense of the term, its membership function can take on only the two values 0 and 1. Although the membership function of a fuzzy set has some resemblance to a PROBABILITY function, the notion of a fuzzy set is "completely nonstatistical in nature" (Zadeh, 1965, p. 340.) Fuzzy set theory can be used to model the imprecision inherent in probability and UTILITY assessments, providing an "automatic SENSITIVITY ANALYSIS" (Freeling, 1979). In MULTIPLE-OBJECTIVE DECISION MAKING, it can be used to measure an ordering of the alternatives "which is at some minimal overall distance from the ATTRIBUTE-wise orderings" (Blin, 1977, p. 144).

examples: The class of "all real numbers which are much greater than 1" or the class of "beautiful women" or the class of "tall men" do not constitute classes or sets in the usual mathematical sense of these terms, yet such imprecisely defined "classes" play an important role in human thinking (Zadeh, 1965, p. 338.)

"Let X be the real line R and let A be a fuzzy set of numbers which are much greater than 1. Then, one can give a precise, albeit subjective, characterization of A by specifying $f_a(x)$ as a function of R. Representative values of such a function might be: $f_a(0) = 0$, $f_a(1) = 0$, $f_a(5) = .01$, $f_a(10) = .2$, $f_a(100) = .95$, $f_a(500) = 1$" (Zadeh, 1965, p. 340).

The notions of complement, inclusion, union, intersection, etc. are defined for the case of fuzzy sets. The *complement* of a fuzzy set A is denoted by A' and is defined by

$$f_a' = 1 - f_a.$$

A is *contained in* (is a subset of, is smaller than or equal to) B if and only if $f_a < f_b$. The *union* of two fuzzy sets A and B is a fuzzy set C whose membership function is related to those of A and B by

$$f_c(x) = \text{Max}[f_a(x), f_b(x)].$$

The *intersection* of two fuzzy sets A and B is a fuzzy set C whose membership function is related to those of A and B by

$$f_c(x) = \text{Min}[f_a(x), f_b(x)].$$

comment: Because of certain computational anomalies, for example, the fact that it is not possible to "evaluate a TREE node-by-node if any probability appears more than once in it" (Freeling, 1980, p. 350), fuzzy DECISION ANALYSIS "lacks much of the conceptual clarity that decisionmakers so often find appealing" (p. 353).

GAINS and LOSSES

definition: Increases or decreases in VALUE or UTILITY with respect to the status quo. Kahneman & Tversky (1979b, p. 277) suggest that "the carriers of value are changes in wealth or welfare, rather than final states." More specifically, they have proposed that "the value FUNCTION is (i) defined on deviations from the reference point; (ii) generally concave for gains and commonly convex for losses; (iii) steeper for losses than for gains" (Kahneman & Tversky, 1979b, p. 279). A value function that satisfies these properties is shown in the figure below:

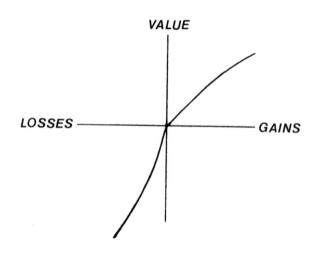

Value Function for Gains and Losses

From Kahneman & Tversky, 1979, p. 279. Copyright 1979 by Econometrica. Reprinted by permission.

example: Kahneman & Tversky (1979b, p. 273) describe the following problems. In one problem, people are told that they have been given 1000 Israeli pounds and are asked to choose between 500 pounds for sure and a .50 chance at 1000 pounds. Some 80% choose the 500 pounds for sure. In a second problem, people are told that they have been given 2000 pounds and are asked to choose between losing 500 pounds for sure and a .50 chance on losing 1000 pounds. Some 70% choose the .50 chance on losing 1000 pounds.

Yet these are the same problem. The second is derived from the first by adding 1000 pounds to the initial bonus and subtracting 1000 pounds from all outcomes. In both cases, the overall CHOICE is between 1500 pounds for sure and a .50 chance on 2000 pounds or 1000 pounds. The problems seem different because different bonuses common to the alternatives are cancelled out in the two cases. "The apparent neglect of a bonus that was common to both options...implies that the carriers of value or utility are changes of wealth, rather than final asset positions that include current wealth" (Kahneman & Tversky, 1979b, p. 273).

related terms: PROSPECT THEORY, ISOLATION EFFECT.

GAMBLER'S FALLACY

definition: The fallacious BELIEF that events in a random sequence are dependent on preceding events in such a manner as to make extended runs of the same event unlikely, for example, the belief that a boy is more likely than a girl following a sequence of girls (see Coombs, Dawes, & Tversky, 1970, p. 236; McClelland & Hackenberg, 1978.)

related terms: BIAS, INDEPENDENCE, SUBJECTIVE PROBABILITY, ILLUSORY CORRELATION.

GAME THEORY

definition: An abstract, usually mathematical, analysis of CONFLICT of interests among parties who interact according to rules. Game theory probably originated in the work of Borel (1921, 1924, 1927) but did not become important until the publication of von Neumann & Morgenstern's *Theory of Games and Economic Behavior* (1947). (See Edwards, 1954, p. 406; see also Luce & Raiffa, 1957). Game theory deals with DECISION problems whose OUTCOME is determined by the courses of action taken by each of the parties involved. Because it deals with the effectiveness of various action strategies for achieving the ends of the interacting parties, it is a branch of NORMATIVE, or PRESCRIPTIVE, DECISION THEORY (Coombs, Dawes, & Tversky,

1970, p. 202).

related terms: CONFLICT, MINIMAX REGRET CRITERION, SOCIAL DILEMMA, DECISION THEORY, NORMATIVE MODEL, PRESCRIPTIVE MODEL.

GLOBAL.

  See WHOLISTIC.

GOAL

definition 1: A desired state toward which one strives; a target level on a dimension (Cohon, 1978, p. 188; Keeney & Raiffa, 1976, pp. 32-34; Wickelgren, 1974). To be contrasted with an **OBJECTIVE** (see below).

discussion on definition 1: An **OBJECTIVE** involves both a descriptive DIMENSION on which one strives to improve and specification of the direction of variation defined as improvement (Keeney & Raiffa, 1976, p. 33). A goal is simply achieved or not, while attainment of an objective is a matter of degree which involves MAXIMIZING, minimizing, or OPTIMIZING the level of the corresponding descriptive dimension. *definition 2*: An OBJECTIVE.

comment on definition 2: In GOAL PROGRAMMING, a form of MATHEMATICAL PROGRAMMING used for MULTIPLE-OBJECTIVE DECISION MAKING, achievement of a goal (target) is a matter of degree rather than all-or-nothing; the optimal solution is that which minimizes deviations from goal (target) levels on the multiple outcome dimensions of interest (Cohon, 1978, pp. 187-196).

related terms: OBJECTIVE FUNCTION, DIMENSION, MAXIMIZATION, OPTIMIZATION, GOAL PROGRAMMING, MATHEMATICAL PROGRAMMING, MULTIPLE-OBJECTIVE DECISION MAKING.

GOAL PROGRAMMING.

  See MATHEMATICAL PROGRAMMING.

GOAL SET.

See RELEVANCE TREE.

GOAL TREE.

See RELEVANCE TREE.

GRAPHIC AIDS.

See DECISION AIDS.

HEURISTIC

definition: A rule of thumb for simplifying complex problems in a way that increases the PROBABILITY that a solution will be found within a "reasonable" amount of time. To be contrasted with an ALGORITHM. While algorithmic search is based on calculation or on exhaustive consideration of all possibilities and is guaranteed to find a solution if there is one, heuristic search is based on "educated guesses" as to where in the search space the solution is likely to be found and merely increases the chances of finding a solution within a "reasonable" amount of time.

examples: Examples of heuristics suggested by Newell, Shaw, and Simon (1958) as ones used in problem-solving tasks are: means-ends analysis, planning, and working backwards. Examples of heuristics suggested by Kahneman and Tversky (1972, 1973, 1979b; Tversky & Kahneman, 1974) as ones used in JUDGMENT tasks are: AVAILABILITY, REPRESENTATIVENESS, ANCHORING and ADJUSTMENT, and CANCELLATION.

comment: Simon (1957, pp. 198f) sees heuristics as necessitated by the limited information processing capacity of humans and resulting in a BOUNDED RATIONALITY.

related terms: BOUNDED RATIONALITY, AVAILABILITY, REPRESENTATIVENESS, ANCHORING and ADJUSTMENT, CANCELLATION, SATISFICING.

HICKS-KALDOR CRITERION.

See COST-BENEFIT ANALYSIS.

HIERARCHICAL.

See TREE.

HINDSIGHT BIAS

definition: The tendency for postdicted PROBABILITIES of events that are known or believed to have occurred to be higher than predicted probabilities for the same events. "...In hindsight, we systematically underestimate the surprises which the past held and holds for us..." (Fischhoff, 1975, p. 298).

comment: KNOWLEDGE of which event occurred also changes the perceived relevance of event-descriptive data. "For example, the fact that 'the British officers learned caution only after sharp reverses'...was judged most relevant by subjects told of a British victory, and rather irrelevant by subjects told of a Gurka victory" (Fischhoff, 1975, p. 292).

related terms: BIAS, SUBJECTIVE PROBABILITY.

HURWICZ CRITERION.

See MINIMAX REGRET CRITERION.

HYPERVIGILANCE.

See CONFLICT THEORY.

IDIOGRAPHIC

definition: A term coined by the philosopher Windelband (1904) to refer to the study of the individual case. A method of data analysis that assumes that JUDGES differ from one another systematically and

that consequently looks for patterns of behavior within judges before
AGGREGATING across judges (Hammond, McClelland, & Mumpower, 1980, pp.
115ff.)

comment: The advantage of the idiographic method is that it avoids
aggregating over systematic differences and thus obtaining a result
for the aggregate that may not apply to any individual.   To be
contrasted with the NOMOTHETIC method, although Allport (1937, p. 22)
objects that "the dichotomy, however, is too sharp; it requires a
psychology divided against itself.... It is more helpful to regard
the two methods as overlapping and as contributing to one another."

related terms: NOMOTHETIC, AGGREGATION.

IIT.

See INFORMATION INTEGRATION THEORY.

ILLUSORY CORRELATION

definition: An error of judgment in which a relationship between two
VARIABLES is reported when in fact none exists (Chapman & Chapman,
1967; Jenkins & Ward, 1965; Einhorn & Hogarth, 1978; Nisbett & Ross,
1980, pp. 90-112; Tversky & Kahneman, 1974).

synonym: **SPURIOUS CORRELATION.**

related terms: COVARIATION PRINCIPLE, DIAGNOSTICITY, WEIGHT, BIAS.

IMPACT.

See VALUE.

IMPACT ASSESSMENT.

See ENVIRONMENTAL IMPACT ASSESSMENT.

IMPLICATION.

See INFERENCE.

IMPRESSION FORMATION

definition: The rapid arrival at a unified concept, or understanding, of "something of the character of another person" on the basis of "a large number of diverse characteristics" (Asch, 1946, p. 258).

comment: A major question in research on impression formation has been whether the process of forming impressions is best described by an ADDITIVE or a CONFIGURAL MODEL (Asch, 1946; Anderson, 1962, 1965.) The study of impression formation was an early and major topic within the broader study of person perception (Taguiri, 1968, pp. 414, 423-5, 431-5), which has now evolved into the study of ATTRIBUTION: "in both approach and method, ATTRIBUTION THEORY has developed out of the area of social psychology known as person perception" (Shaver, 1975, p. 9).

related terms: JUDGMENT, INFERENCE, AGGREGATION, ADDING MODEL, CONFIGURAL MODEL, ATTRIBUTION, ATTRIBUTION THEORY.

IMPROPER LINEAR MODEL

definition: A term coined by Dawes (1979) to refer to a LINEAR MODEL in which the WEIGHTS are chosen by some non-optimal method. Examples are random choice, intuition, BOOTSTRAPPING, and equal weights.

comment: Dawes & Corrigan (1974) and Wainer (1976) have argued that equal weights are often preferable to differential weights, because they entail little loss in accuracy and are simpler to use. Einhorn & Hogarth (1975) and Newman (1977), on the other hand, believe that, while equal weights are preferable for some cases, differential weights are preferable for others. Einhorn & Hogarth (1975) provide guidelines to follow in deciding which to use in any particular case.

related terms: PROPER LINEAR MODEL, BOOTSTRAPPING, POLICY CAPTURING.

INCIDENTAL DATA.

See CAUSAL SCHEMA.

INDEPENDENCE

definition 1: VARIABLE A is said to be independent of variable B if A is not systematically different at different LEVELS of B. Definition 1 refers to *individual* FUNCTION FORMS. Independence, in this sense, means UNCORRELATED.

example for definition 1: Performing arts may be independent of professional sports in that the level of performing arts in different cities is not systematically different at different levels of professional sports. This concept of independence is not usually applied to values, though it could be. Value independence in this sense would simply be irrelevance to one's value system.

definition 2. Variable A is said to be independent of variable B if the relationship between A and some other variable, X, is not systematically different at different levels of B. Definition 2 refers to the *relationships among* function forms at different levels of a third variable. (See PARALLELISM, LINEAR FAN, INTERACTION.)

example for definition 2: Performing arts may be *factually* independent of professional sports in that the relationship between quality of performing arts and some other variable of interest, for example, number of institutions of higher education, is not systematically different at different levels of quality of professional sports. Or performing arts may be *value* independent of professional sports in that the relationship between quality of performing arts and judged value of performing arts is not systematically different at different levels of quality of professional sports.

example for both definitions 1 and 2: See CONDITIONAL INDEPENDENCE.

general comment: To say that the relationship between A and X is "not systematically different" at different levels of B can mean that, apart from random error, (a) the predicted X values are identical (identity transformation), (b) the ratios among differences between predicted X values are identical (LINEAR transformation), or (c) the

ORDINAL relationships among the predicted X values are identical (MONOTONIC transformation).

While Definition 1 is usually intended to exclude systematic differences of any kind, an important distinction is made within Definition 2 between those cases where the relationship between A and X is the same at different levels of B only up to an order-preserving, or monotonic, transformation, and those cases where it is the same up to an interval-preserving, or linear, transformation. The ordinal version of Definition 2 is sufficient only for eliminating DOMINATED ALTERNATIVES. The interval version of Definition 2 is required where TRADEOFFS must be made, including the special case of trading PROBABILITY off against value in RISKY decision making. It is important to add that, if it is the order of *pairs* of attributes that is preserved, then *intervals* are preserved on the individual attributes. See PREFERENTIAL INDEPENDENCE, UTILITY INDEPENDENCE. No stronger form of independence than the interval version of Definition 2 is required for DECISION MAKING, because in comparing alternatives, only differences among them, and not ABSOLUTE values of each, need be taken into account. The general value of independence is that it permits DECOMPOSITION. It permits PROBABILITIES to be assessed EVENT by event and VALUES to be assessed ATTRIBUTE by attribute and then AGGREGATED.

synonyms: UNCORRELATED (in the case of Definition 1), **DECOMPOSABLE** (in the case of the interval version of Definition 2).

related terms: PREFERENTIAL INDEPENDENCE, UTILITY INDEPENDENCE, DECOMPOSITION, CONDITIONAL INDEPENDENCE, FUNCTION FORM, PARALLELISM, REDUNDANCY, CONFIGURAL MODEL.

INDICATOR

definition: An objective VARIABLE (e.g., number of hospital beds, number of arrests) that indicates the LEVEL of some environmental or social system on a descriptive or evaluative DIMENSION (e.g., health care, social stability).

synonym: PROXY ATTRIBUTE. The term "indicator" tends to be used in connection with public POLICY analysis and impact assessment; the term "proxy attribute" tends to be used in connection with individual and corporate DECISION MAKING.

related terms: ENVIRONMENTAL IMPACT ASSESSMENT, SOCIAL IMPACT ASSESSMENT, PROXY ATTRIBUTE, NUMERAIRE, MULTIATTRIBUTE DECISION MAKING.

INDIFFERENCE CURVE

definition: A curve connecting a set of points (each of which represents a combination of DIMENSION LEVELS) among which the respondent is indifferent. "A constant-UTILITY [Definition 1] curve" (Edwards, 1954, p. 384). The concept was introduced by Edgeworth (1881) to deal with goods whose utilities are not independent (see Edwards, 1954, p. 383), though it can deal with independent utilities as well.

example: (From Samuelson, 1976, p. 444) Consider two commodities, food (F) and clothing (C). To plot an indifference curve between them, the analyst begins with a reference point (here, a **"COMMODITY BUNDLE,"** defined as a set of distinct entities as contrasted with a sed of characteristics of a given entity or process), say, 3 units of food and 2 of clothing (3F, 2C), then asks (using any of several procedures), how many clothing units a consumer would require in a new bundle having only 2F units in order to be indifferent between the reference bundle and that new one. If this were, say, 3C units, then the bundles (3F, 2C) and (2F, 3C) would be indifferent to each other and so would fall on the same indifference curve. The bundles (4F, 1.5C) and (1F, 6C) might also fall on the same curve, as shown in the figure on the next page.

Different reference points may be used and may yield different curves. If the reference point were (4F, 3C) for instance, other bundles indifferent to it might be (3F, 4C), tracing out the curve U4 in the figure on page 129. But if the reference were (2F, .75C), other bundles indifferent to it might be (4F, .25C) and (1F, 1.5C), tracing the curve U1 in this figure, where the curve from the first figure is shown as U3 for comparison. A set, or family, of indifference curves as shown is called an **INDIFFERENCE MAP.**

comment: An indifference map is analogous to a segment of a topographic map of land terrain; any indifference curve on that map is analogous to a contour line on the topographic map. A contour line

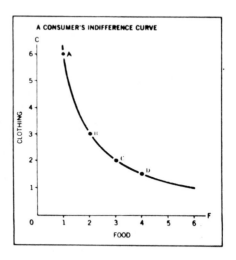

An Indifference Curve

From Samuelson, 1980, p. 417. Copyright 1980 by McGraw-Hill Book Company. Used with the permission of McGraw-Hill Book Company.

represents a locus of points at a constant altitude (isoaltitude line), just as an indifference curve represents a locus of points at a constant utility level (isopreference or isoutility line). Indifference maps are typically drawn, as in the two figures, so that utility increases toward an imaginary hilltop beyond the upper right corner; dimension levels increase or decrease upward and rightward from the origin, depending on whether higher levels are deemed more or less desirable (i.e., whether the dimension's UTILITY (Definition 1) function has positive or negative slope), respectively. Curves U1 to U4 in the indifference map thus represent increasing utility levels. This convention assumes monotonic utility functions ("nonsatiety"), however. Nonmonotonic functions (which entail placement of utility peaks within the map) and nonstandard orientations (e.g., where utility decreases rightward) can be accommodated but complicate the development and interpretation of maps. (See Baumol, 1977, pp. 198-201.) One important difference between indifference and

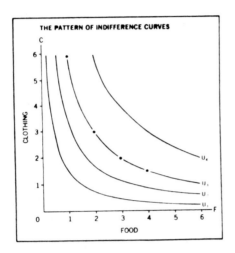

An Indifference Map

From Samuelson, 1980, p. 419. Copyright 1980 by McGraw-Hill Book Company. Used with the permission of McGraw-Hill Book Company.

topographic maps is that the latter have known and constant altitude intervals (e.g., 40 feet) between contour lines, while the latter generally (though not always) have unknown utility intervals between indifference curves; that is, altitude is measured on an interval SCALE of MEASUREMENT while utility is generally (some believe necessarily) measured on only an ordinal scale. (See CARDINAL UTILITY.)

The slope of an indifference curve at any point is the MARGINAL RATE OF SUBSTITUTION (MRS), or VALUE (Definition 2b) TRADEOFF, between the two dimensions at that point, which indicates the ratio of the marginal utilities (UTILITY in the sense of Definition 1) of the dimensions at that point (Samuelson, 1976, p. 443). A normally oriented indifference curve that is convex to the origin (as are all those here) reflects decreasing MRS with more desirable dimension levels (e.g., the greater the Food level, the less Clothes one will trade for still more Food), while a linear "curve" reflects constant MRS. Indifference curves should not cross, as crossing indicates intransitivity (see TRANSITIVITY). Techniques for empirical generation of indifference maps are discussed under TRADEOFF.

Indifference curves (maps) are the conceptual basis for the "ordinalist revolution" in economics, starting with Pareto (1906) who "saw that the same conclusions [with respect to RISKLESS CHOICE] which had been drawn from marginal utilities could be drawn from "indifference curves" (Edwards, 1954, p. 384). (See CARDINAL UTILITY, ORDINAL UTILITY.) However, von Neumann and Morgenstern (1947, pp. 19-20) comment: "...We hope we have shown that the treatment of indifference curves implies either too much or too little: if the preferences of the individual are not all comparable, then the indifference curves do not exist. If the individual's preferences are all comparable, then we can even obtain a (uniquely) defined) numerical utility which renders the indifference curves superfluous." What Von Neumann and Morgenstern seem to be saying is that, if one can compare the value (in the sense of definition 2a) of a change on dimension A with that of a change on dimension B (which is what an indifference curve requires), then one should be able to compare the value of a change on dimension A with that of a different change on the same dimension A (which is all that cardinal utility requires).

synonym: ISOPREFERENCE CURVE.

related terms: DIMENSION, UTILITY, TRADEOFF, CARDINAL UTILITY, ORDINAL UTILITY, TRANSITIVITY, RISKLESS CHOICE.

INDIFFERENCE MAP.

See INDIFFERENCE CURVE.

INDIFFERENCE TRADEOFF METHOD.

See TRADEOFF.

INDIRECT ASSESSMENT.

See REVEALED PREFERENCE, WEIGHT.

INFERENCE

definition: Reasoning from observations or premises to a conclusion. "We *infer* one proposition from another *validly* only if there is an objective relation of **IMPLICATION** ["necessary conjunction"] between the first proposition and the second.   Hence, it is essential to distinguish *inference*, which is a temporal process, from *implication*, which is an objective relation between propositions " (Cohen & Nagel, 1934, pp. 7-8).   **PROBABLE INFERENCE** is inference "which from true premises gives us conclusions which are true in most cases" (Cohen & Nagel, 1934, p. 13).

comment: "Strictly speaking, all our knowledge outside mathematics and demonstrative logic (which is, in fact, a branch of mathematics) consists of conjectures.... We secure our mathematical knowledge by *demonstrative reasoning*, but we support our conjectures by **PLAUSIBLE REASONING**....   The difference between the two kinds of reasoning is great and manifold. Demonstrative reasoning is safe, beyond controversy, and final.   Plausible reasoning is hazardous, controversial, and provisional.   Demonstrative reasoning penetrates the sciences just as far as mathematics does, but it is in itself (as mathematics is in itself) incapable of yielding essentially new knowledge about the world around us. Anything new that we learn about the world involves plausible reasoning, which is the only kind of reasoning for which we care in everyday affairs" (Polya, 1954, p. v).

Hammond, McClelland, & Mumpower (1980, p. 180) point out that "five of the six approaches are frequently involved with *inferences* about states of affairs in the world; these are BDT, PDT, SJT, IIT, and AT.... Paradigmatically, such inferences are instances of the DOUBLE-SYSTEM CASE, since in principle there exists an environmental criterion or 'correct answer.' Such judgments constitute instances of the SINGLE-SYSTEM CASE, however, in those frequent cases in which the value of the environmental criterion or correct answer is intrinsically unknown or unknowable".

related terms: JUDGMENT,   CUE,   RATIONALITY,   BAYES' THEOREM,

ATTRIBUTION, ILLUSORY CORRELATION, CASCADED INFERENCE.

INFORMATION INTEGRATION.

See AGGREGATION.

INFORMATION INTEGRATION THEORY

definition: A DESCRIPTIVE approach to JUDGMENT and DECISION MAKING developed by Norman Anderson (1974a, b, c). Information Integration Theory (**IIT**) simultaneously accomplishes FUNCTIONAL MEASUREMENT on subjective METRICS and identification of the COGNITIVE ALGEBRA (e.g., ADDING MODEL, MULTIPLYING MODEL, or AVERAGING MODEL), by which information on these metrics is integrated, or AGGREGATED.

synonyms: INTEGRATION THEORY, IIT.

related terms: JUDGMENT vs. DECISION THEORIES, COGNITIVE ALGEBRA, INTEGRATION RULE, FUNCTIONAL MEASUREMENT, CONJOINT MEASUREMENT, AGGREGATION.

INFORMATION-PROCESSING MODEL.

See PROCESS-TRACING MODEL.

INITIAL FOCUS.

See LENS MODEL.

INSUFFICIENT REASON

definition: The principle, attributed to Bernoulli, of assigning equal SUBJECTIVE PROBABILITIES to all states of nature when there is no reason to believe that any one is more likely to occur than any other (Coombs, Dawes, & Tversky, 1970, p. 142.)

comment: The principle of insufficient reason is a principle for reducing UNCERTAINTY to RISK (Coombs, Dawes, & Tversky, 1970, p. 142.)

synonym: **La PLACE CRITERION** (La Place, 1814).

related terms: UNCERTAINTY, RISK.

INSURANCE PREMIUM.

See RISK PREMIUM.

INTEGER PROGRAMMING.

See MATHEMATICAL PROGRAMMING.

INTEGRATION RULE.

See AGGREGATION.

INTEGRATION THEORY.

See INFORMATION INTEGRATION THEORY.

INTERACTION.

See ADDING MODEL.

INTEREST CONFLICT.

See CONFLICT.

INTERPERSONAL COMPARABILITY

definition: Comparability from person to person of some MEASURE of subjective states, "either a COMMENSURATION unit, or a base of reference, or both" (Luce & Raiffa, 1957, p. 345; see also Sen, 1970, p. 393). The subjective states of interest are usually degrees of PREFERENCE, though they may also be degrees of BELIEF.

comment: Interpersonal comparability is important where one is concerned with measuring social VALUE AGGREGATED across individuals; that is, with arriving at a SOCIAL WELFARE FUNCTION. Goodman & Markowitz (1952) have suggested the just-noticeable-difference as an interpersonally comparable unit, and Nash (1950) has suggested the status quo as an interpersonally comparable base of reference. Others (e.g., Harsanyi, 1955; Keeney & Raiffa, 1976, Ch. 10) have considered the possibility that a third-party DECISION MAKER, whom Keeney & Raiffa call a "Supra Decision Maker", is able to make interpersonal comparisons of preference. Pareto (1927, reprinted 1971) and Arrow (1951, 1963), however, have explored the possibility of making social decisions on the basis of ORDINAL measures of value, on the premise that meaningful interpersonal comparisons on METRIC scales are impossible, or at least have not been proved to be possible.

related terms: SOCIAL WELFARE FUNCTION, CARDINAL UTILITY, ARROW's PARADOX, PARETO FRONTIER, SCALES of MEASUREMENT.

INTERPERSONAL CONFLICT.

See CONFLICT.

INTERVAL.

See SCALES of MEASUREMENT.

INTERVAL CONCEPT.

See CONCEPT LEARNING.

INTRAECOLOGICAL CORRELATION.

See ENVIRONMENTAL CORRELATION.

INTRAPERSONAL CONFLICT.

See CONFLICT.

INTUITIVE PROBABILITY.

See SUBJECTIVE PROBABILITY.

INTUITIVE PROCESSES.

See QUASI-RATIONALITY.

INTUITIVE THOUGHT.

See QUASI-RATIONALITY.

IRRELEVANT ALTERNATIVES.

See ARROW'S PARADOX, MINIMAX REGRET.

ISOLATION EFFECT

definition: The fact that DECOMPOSING (FRAMING) a pair of PROSPECTS into common and distinctive components in different ways can lead to different PREFERENCES (Kahneman & Tversky, 1979b, P. 271). Attributed to **CANCELLATION**, a HEURISTIC that involves "the discarding of components that are shared by the offered prospects" (Kahneman & Tversky, 1979b, p. 274).

example: Consider the following two-stage game. In the first stage, there is a PROBABILITY of .75 to end the game without winning anything and a probability of .25 to move into the second stage. If you reach the second stage, you have a CHOICE between 3000 Israeli pounds for sure and a .80 chance at 4000 pounds. The choice for the second stage must be made before the outcome of the first stage is known. The two alternatives are thus: (a) a .75 chance at nothing vs. a .25 chance at 3000 pounds, and (b) a .75 chance at nothing vs. a .25 chance at a .80 chance at 4000 pounds.

What people seem to do is ignore the first stage, which is common to both alternatives and choose on the basis of the second stage alone. About 80% choose the 3000 pounds for sure, treating this as a certain outcome (see CERTAINTY EFFECT). Yet the overall prospects are a .25 x 1.00 = .25 chance at 3000 pounds versus a .25 x .80 = .20 chance at 4000 pounds. When the choice is presented this way, 65% choose the .20 chance at 4000 pounds (Kahneman & Tversky, 1979b, p. 271).

As a practical example, "one may invest money in a venture with some probability of losing one's capital if the venture fails, and with a choice between a fixed agreed return and a percentage of earnings if it succeeds. The isolation effect implies that the contingent certainty of the fixed return enhances the attractiveness of this option, relative to a RISKY venture with the same probabilities and outcomes" (Kahneman & Tversky, 1979b, p. 272.)

comment: The isolation effect applies to OUTCOMES, as well as to probabilities. See GAINS and LOSSES.

related terms: HEURISTIC, PROSPECT THEORY, GAINS and LOSSES, CERTAINTY EFFECT, FRAME.

ISOPREFERENCE CURVE.

See INDIFFERENCE CURVE.

JUDGE.

See JUDGMENT.

JUDGMENT.

See DECISION MAKING.

JUDGMENT vs. DECISION THEORIES

definition: In comparing the major approaches to human judgment and decision making, Hammond, McClelland, & Mumpower (1980) draw a number of contrasts between "decision theorists", or Group I approaches, (DT, BDT, and PDT) and "judgment theorists", or Group II approaches, (SJT, IIT, and AT)--two slopes of a "conceptual watershed".

"...The work of researchers on both sides of the conceptual watershed may very well be complementary .... DT, BDT, and PDT aim at describing and explaining decisions to select, choose or to prefer one alternative (an object, an action, etc.) rather than another as a function of one's interests or goals" (p. 57) "...Judgment theorists see problems of choice, action, and preferences for various outcomes of the world as subproblems of the more general theory of knowing" (p. 58). "...There is a far greater use of the terms 'DECISION,' 'CHOICE,' and 'PREFERENCE' in Group I and a much greater use of 'JUDGMENT' and 'INFERENCE' in Group II" (p. 55).

"In Group I, evaluation of the subjects' decision behavior is carried out with reference to the decision behavior of a mathematical model of RATIONALITY; the model is used to evaluate logical correctness.... BAYESIAN research and PDT research move one step closer to empirical, as against logical, evaluation of the subjects' performance by calculating the correct answer to a decision problem through the use of a statistical model.... In contrast, on the other side of the conceptual watershed, when SJT and AT evaluate subjects' performance in judgment tasks they do so in terms of the subjects' achievement of an empirical criterion" (pp. 58-59).

"...DT, BDT, and PDT are ordinarily concerned with...'RISKY' decision making, or decision making under conditions of UNCERTAINTY, although DT and BDT are increasingly also concerned with 'riskless' decision making, or decision making under conditions of certainty. SJT, IIT, and AT, on the other hand, are ordinarily concerned with riskless decision making..." (p. 181).

"...Group I approaches may aid the policy maker to explicate his

PROBABILITIES and UTILITIES and to organize these in a logical manner, thus avoiding the BIASES and fallibilities of unaided cognitive efforts, whereas Group II approaches may aid the policy maker to see sources of these probabilities and utilities" (p. 106).

related terms: JUDGMENT, DECISION MAKING, DT, BDT, PDT, SJT, IIT, AT.

JUDGMENTAL PREDICTABILITY.

See LENS MODEL EQUATION.

KALDOR-HICKS CRITERION.

See COST-BENEFIT ANALYSIS.

KNOWLEDGE.

See LENS MODEL EQUATION.

La PLACE CRITERION.

See INSUFFICIENT REASON.

LAW of SMALL NUMBERS

definition: Belief that small random samples will be highly representative of the population from which they have been drawn. The law of *large* numbers guarantees that very large random samples will be highly representative of the population from which they have been drawn. "People's intuitions about random sampling appear to satisfy the law of small numbers, which asserts that the law of large numbers applies to small numbers as well" (Tversky & Kahneman, 1971, p. 106).

example: Kahneman & Tversky (1972, p. 443) told subjects that a town was served by a large hospital, in which 45 babies are born each day, and a small hospital, in which 15 babies are born each day, and asked them which hospital recorded more days on which (more/less) than 60%

of the babies born were boys. Though an extreme proportion of boys is more probable in a smaller sample (15) than in a larger sample (45), the modal response was "same", and there was no systematic preference for either the large or the small hospital.

comment: Kahneman & Tversky (1972, p. 437) explain belief in the law of small numbers in terms of the REPRESENTATIVENESS HEURISTIC. The degree to which the sample is judged to be representative of the population is determined by the similarity of the sample statistic (e.g., the proportion or the mean) to the corresponding population parameter. "Since the size of the sample does not reflect any property of the parent population, it does not affect representativeness" (p. 437).

Tversky & Kahneman (1971, p. 109) list four characteristics of the scientist who believes in the law of small numbers: (a) he gambles his research hypotheses on small samples; (b) he has undue confidence in early trends; (c) he has unreasonably high expectations about the replicability of significant results; and (d) he rarely attributes a deviation of results from expectation to sampling variability, looking instead for a CAUSAL explanation.

Tversky & Kahneman (1971, p. 109, footnote) contrast the belief in the law of small numbers with CONSERVATISM.

related terms: REPRESENTATIVENESS, CONSERVATISM, SUBJECTIVE PROBABILITY, BAYESIAN, BIAS.

LENS MODEL

definition: A model of the mediation of relatively stable ADAPTIVE relationships between environmental events (**DISTAL VARIABLES**) and mental events (**CENTRAL VARIABLES**) on the basis of relatively unstable events (see CAUSAL AMBIGUITY) at the **SURFACES** of the environment (**PROXIMAL VARIABLES**) and the organism (**PERIPHERAL VARIABLES**) (Brunswik, 1952, 1956, pp. 16ff; Hammond, 1966, pp. 17ff, 37ff; Postman & Tolman, 1959, pp. 511ff.) Usually represented graphically, as in the figure on the next page. The lens model applies to stabilized ACHIEVEMENT in perception, JUDGMENT, and motor behavior.

examples: In the case of perception, the lens model represents stabilized **PERCEPTUAL ACHIEVEMENT** (**EQUIPOTENTIALITY**, object constancy) on the basis of unstable proximal stimuli. For example, size judgments are more closely related to actual size than are the cues of retinal size, linear perspective, etc. on which they are based. The rays in the lens model diverge from an object in the environment (**INITIAL FOCUS, DISTAL FOCUS, DISTAL STIMULUS**) to produce events at the sensory surface (**PROXIMAL STIMULI**) that are only imperfectly related to the object (have imperfect ECOLOGICAL VALIDITIES.) These proximal stimuli produce physiological responses in

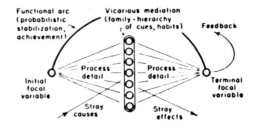

Lens Model Diagram

From Brunswik, 1952, p. 201. Copyright 1952 by the University of Chicago Press. Reprinted by permission.

the organism (**PERIPHERAL CUES.**) The peripheral cues are then taken into account by the organism to varying degrees (that is, there are varying degrees of **CUE UTILIZATION**) and "focussed" to yield an internal representation (**TERMINAL FOCUS, CENTRAL FOCUS**) whose relationship to the distal object (**FUNCTIONAL ACHIEVEMENT**) is generally greater than either (a) its relationship to any one peripheral CUE (**CUE UTILIZATION**) or (b) that of any one proximal stimulus to the object (COLOGICAL VALIDITY.) By accumulating and AGGREGATING cues, the organism has thus improved its "cognitive wager."

The case of judgment is similar to that of perception. Many different cues can, by VICARIOUS FUNCTIONING, lead to the same judgment, for example, of honesty (or of a high PROBABILITY of honest behavior.) Such judgments are often difficult to justify, because they are QUASIRATIONAL.

In the case of motor responses, the lens model similarly represents stabilized **BEHAVIORAL ACHIEVEMENT** (**EQUIFINALITY**, purposive behavior) on the basis of unstable proximal responses.

comment: The lens model represents the basic concepts of **PROBABILISTIC FUNCTIONALISM**: (a) that the organism is adapted to the (distal) world about it (functionalism), and (b) that this adaptation is achieved despite the fact that the predictors (**SURFACE VARIABLES**) on which it is based are only imperfectly related to those environmental variables (**DEPTH** variables) that are important to the survival of the organism.

The emphasis in the lens model is on the improvement of prediction by combining REDUNDANT probabilistic data. Two NORMATIVE MODELS for accomplishing this are REGRESSION analysis and BAYESIAN ANALYSIS.

related terms: ENVIRONMENTAL CORRELATION, CAUSAL AMBIGUITY, VICARIOUS FUNCTIONING, QUASI-RATIONALITY, REDUNDANCY, REGRESSION ANALYSIS, BAYESIAN ANALYSIS.

LENS MODEL EQUATION

definition: A DESCRIPTIVE MODEL of JUDGMENT behavior, in the form of an equation that expresses ACHIEVEMENT, in the DOUBLE-SYSTEM CASE, and AGREEMENT, in the TRIPLE-SYSTEM CASE, in terms of various LINEAR and NONLINEAR components. First proposed by Hursch, Hammond, & Hursch (1964) and later modified by Tucker (1964) and by A. L. Dudycha & Naylor (1966). The Tucker modification is as follows. (Reference to the Hursch, Hammond, & Hursch (1964, p. 43) quantification of the LENS MODEL diagram, shown below, clarifies the meanings of the terms.)

Where:

r_a = ACHIEVEMENT, the correlation between Y_e, the DISTAL VARIABLE, and Y_s, the JUDGE's estimate of the distal variable,

R_e = ENVIRONMENTAL (linear) PREDICTABILITY, the

multiple correlation between the CUE variables and the distal variable,

R_S = **JUDGMENTAL** (linear) **PREDICTABBILITY**, the multiple correlation between the cue variables and the judge's estimate of the distal variable (sometimes termed COGNITIVE CONTROL),

G = (linear) **KNOWLEDGE**, the correlation between Y_e', the linearly predicted component of

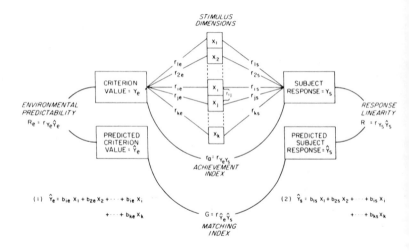

Quantified Lens Model Diagram

From L. W. Dudycha & Naylor, 1966. Copyright 1966 by Academic Press. Reprinted by permission.

Y_e, and Y_S', the linearly predicted component of Y_S',

C = (nonlinear knowledge), the correlation between Z_e', the residual about the linear prediction of Y_e, and Z_S', the residual about the linear prediction of Y_s,

$$r_a = GR_eR_s + C \sqrt{1 - R_e^2} \; \sqrt{1 - R_s^2}.$$

comment: The lens equation indicates that total achievement equals linear achievement plus nonlinear achievement. Further, it indicates that linear achievement (GR_eR_s) is the product of (a) the correlation (R_e) between the distal variable and the linearly predictable component of the distal variable, (b) the correlation (R_s) between the judge's estimate of the distal variable and the linearly predictable component of the judge's estimate of the distal variable, and (c) the correlation (G) between the linearly predictable component of the judge's estimate of the distal variable and the linearly predictable component of the distal variable. Nonlinear achievement is analyzed similarly. The equation exemplifies the principle of PARALLEL CONCEPTS (Hammond, Stewart, Brehmer, & Steinmann, 1975).

When the equation is used to analyze agreement between two people (1 and 2): r_a is the **AGREEMENT** between their judgments; R_e and R_s become R_1 and R_2, the linear predictability of their respective judgments; G becomes linear POLICY SIMILARITY; and C becomes nonlinear POLICY SIMILARITY.

The lens equation has been extended by Stewart (1976) to make possible the separation of nonlinear effects from error and the comparison of systems based on different sets of cues.

related terms: LENS MODEL, KNOWLEDGE, COGNITIVE CONTROL, COGNITIVE CONSISTENCY, POLICY SIMILARITY, CAUSAL TEXTURE, INFERENCE, PARALLEL CONCEPTS, DOUBLE-SYSTEM CASE, TRIPLE-SYSTEM CASE.

LEVEL.
——————

See VALUE.

LEVEL of CONFIDENCE.

See CONFIDENCE INTERVAL.

LEXICOGRAPHIC MODEL

definition: A NONCOMPENSATORY MODEL in which the DIMENSIONS are ordered according to importance and the alternatives are ordered with respect to their VALUES on the most important dimension, the next most important dimension being taken into account only in the case of ties on the most important dimension. Similarly, the third most important dimension is taken into account only in the case of ties on the second most important dimension, and so forth for even less important dimensions (Coombs, 1964; Green & Wind, 1973, p. 42; Keeney & Raiffa, 1976, p. 78.) The model is noncompensatory in that differences on more important dimensions cannot be compensated for by differences on less important dimensions. The term "lexicographic" comes from the fact that this is the way words are alphabetized; they are ordered according to the position of initial letter in the alphabet, without regard to subsequent letters; and, only if their initial letters are identical, is attention turned to subsequent letters. (Keeney & Raiffa, 1976, p. 78).

related terms: NONCOMPENSATORY, ELIMINATION by ASPECTS, PREFERENCE TREES.

LIKELIHOOD RATIO

definition: The ratio between (a) the PROBABILITY of some datum conditional on one hypothesis and (b) the probability of the same datum conditional on an alternative hypothesis (Edwards, Lindman, & Savage, 1963, p. 218; Slovic & Lichtenstein, 1973, p. 31):

$$\frac{p(D|H_1)}{p(D|H_2)}.$$

related terms: ODDS, ECOLOGICAL VALIDITY, DIAGNOSTICITY, BAYES' THEOREM.

LINEAR.

See LINEAR SCALE, LINEAR RELATIONSHIP, LINEAR MODEL.

LINEAR FAN.

See MULTIPLYING MODEL.

LINEAR INTERACTION.

See MULTILINEAR MODEL.

LINEAR MODEL

definition: A model for AGGREGATING information from different VARIABLES in such a way that the relationship between each input variable and the output variable is linear (see LINEAR RELATIONSHIP). It is important to note that the transformation of variables (for example, by VALUE or UTILITY FUNCTIONS) is a separate matter from their aggregation. Linear aggregation rules can take as inputs the outputs of either linear or nonlinear transformations. A linear model exhibits ADDITIVE INDEPENDENCE.

examples: ADDING MODEL, AVERAGING MODEL (in the case of EQUAL WEIGHTS only), MULTIPLYING MODEL, MULTILINEAR MODEL.

comment: **NONLINEAR MODELS**, that is, models for aggregating information that fail to satisfy this condition, are referred to as CONFIGURAL MODELS.

related terms: FUNCTION FORM, LINEAR RELATIONSHIP, AGGREGATION, INDEPENDENCE, ADDING MODEL, AVERAGING MODEL, MULTIPLYING MODEL, MULTILINEAR MODEL, CONFIGURAL MODEL.

LINEAR PROGRAMMING.

See MATHEMATICAL PROGRAMMING.

LINEAR RELATIONSHIP

definition: A relationship, or FUNCTION FORM, in which VALUES on the output variable (Y) can be derived from corresponding values on the input variable (X) by (a) multiplying the input variable by a constant (which may be 1) and (b) adding a constant (which may be 0) to the product. Thus,

$$Y = a + bX.$$

Linear, roughly speaking, means that, if two variables are plotted one against another, the plot tends to follow a straight line (Kerlinger, 1967, p. 204.) (For the case of multiple input variables, see LINEAR MODEL.)

comment: **NONLINEAR RELATIONSHIPS** include, for example, those in which the input variable is raised to a power (quadratic relationships, cubic relationships), and certain NONMONOTONIC relationships. For example,

$$Y = a + bX^c$$

where c is not equal to 0 or 1, and

$$Y = a + b(X - c)^2.$$

A linear relationship preserves the INTERVAL properties of the input scale.

related terms: MULTILINEAR MODEL, FUNCTION FORM, LINEAR PROGRAMMING, NONMONOTONIC, DECREASING MARGINAL UTILITY, INTERVAL SCALE.

LINEAR SCALE.

See INTERVAL SCALE.

LOTTERY.

See STANDARD GAMBLE.

LP.

See LINEAR PROGRAMMING.

LR.

See LIKELIHOOD RATIO.

MAJORITY PREFERENCE CYCLE.

See AGENDA PROBLEM.

MAJORITY RULE CYCLE.

See AGENDA PROBLEM.

MANAGEMENT SCIENCE.

See OPERATIONS RESEARCH.

MARGINAL RATE of SUBSTITUTION.

See TRADEOFF.

MARGINAL RATE of TRANSFORMATION.

See TRADEOFF.

MARGINAL UTILITY.

See UTILITY.

MARKET.

See COST-BENEFIT ANALYSIS.

MARKET PRICE

definition: The monetary price prevailing for a commodity (good or service) in economic markets.

example: The prices of apples and oranges are $.39/lb. and $.49/lb., respectively. The prices of the services of professors and plumbers are $10/hour and $20/hour, respectively.

comment: Economic markets are formal or informal arrangements for bringing together potential buyers and sellers of any commodity to allow exchange among them (Sinden & Worrell, 1979, Ch. 2; Stokey & Zeckhauser, 1978, Ch. 14). Prices serve in markets simultaneously as indicators to consumers of the relative opportunity costs of purchasing different kinds and amounts of commodities, indicators to suppliers of the relative profits to be gained by producing different kinds and amounts of commodities, and thereby, regulators of demand and supply which tend to bring the two into balance, or equilibrium. In perfectly competitive markets at equilibrium, the relative prices of any two goods A and B equal both (i) consumers' MARGINAL RATE of SUBSTITUTION (MRS) between A and B, the relative marginal utilities of the two (see UTILITY, Definition 1), and (ii) producers' MARGINAL RATE of TRANSFORMATION (MRT), the relative marginal costs of producing the two (and thus the relative opportunities foregone by producing one or the other); (see TRADEOFF). This is the basis for the reliance of COST-BENEFIT ANALYSIS on market prices as the primary indicator of both the *benefits* and the *OPPORTUNITY COSTS* of producing different commodities. (See Baumol, 1977, Chs. 20 & 21; McKean, 1968; Sinden & Worrell, 1979, Ch. 2; Stigler, 1966; and Stokey & Zeckhauser, 1978, Ch. 14, for example, for explanation of price theory, the perfect competition concept, and market imperfections and their consequences. Stokey & Zeckhauser are particularly clear at an introductory level.)

Real markets are normally incomplete or imperfect in various respects, so market prices normally must be supplemented or adjusted to obtain valid indicators of relative benefit and cost. Market prices are incomplete when relevant commodities include NONMARKETED GOODS (UNPRICED GOODS), particularly PUBLIC GOODS. Market prices are biased when markets are imperfect, for instance due to EXTERNALITIES. Any supplementary or adjusted price developed in these circumstances is termed a SHADOW PRICE, or ACCOUNTING PRICE (Definition 1). McKean (1968), however, while skeptical about market prices, is even more skeptical about shadow prices.

> There are enough things wrong with observed [market] prices to make one's hair stand on end. Most of the time they are defective representations of the appropriate substitution ratios. The only good thing one can say about market prices is that they are usually better than the alternatives--prices that are derived rather than observed (p. 143).

synonym: **DIRECT PRICE.**

related terms: TRADEOFF, UTILITY, COST-BENEFIT ANALYSIS, COST-EFFECTIVENESS ANALYSIS, OPPORTUNITY COST, NONMARKETED GOOD (UNPRICED GOOD), SHADOW PRICE.

MATHEMATICAL PROGRAMMING

definition: A set of mathematical procedures for MAXIMIZING or OPTIMIZING an OBJECTIVE FUNCTION, given (a) a set of **DECISION VARIABLES,** or control variables, bearing specified direct or indirect relationships to the objective function and (b) a set of constraints on the levels that may be taken by decision variables and by the input and output variables driven by them (Bell, Keeney, & Raiffa, 1976, p. 6; Cohon, 1978; Taha, 1976). Decision variables are those that characterize the decision maker's action alternatives and whose levels are solved for in the programming. Mathematical programming selects the combination of levels of the decision variables, within the constraints, that maximizes the objective function and thus comprises an optimal action plan.

comment: In LINEAR PROGRAMMING, each decision variable is LINEARLY related to the objective function directly or indirectly. In NONLINEAR PROGRAMMING, these relations may be nonlinear. In INTEGER PROGRAMMING, decision variables may assume only discrete values. In GOAL PROGRAMMING, the objective function is multivariate, with each variable in it being a discrepancy from a prespecified GOAL, or target point, on an output variable representing an OBJECTIVE rather than on a decision variable (Bell *et al.*, 1976, p. 6; Cohon, 1978, pp. 187-190).

It is instructive to compare MULTIPLE-CUTTING-POINT MODELS, linear programming, and goal programming as approaches to MULTIOBJECTIVE DECISION MAKING. The principal forms of the three differ with respect to the use of dichotomous and continuous VALUE FUNCTIONS. The *multiple cutoffs* procedure relies solely on constraints. A constraint (cutoff level), based on a GOAL, or ASPIRATION LEVEL, is set on each objective, and then either: (i) the constraints are iteratively adjusted (if necessary) until only one alternative in the full set emerges as acceptable (satisfying all constraints); or (ii) the alternatives are sequentially searched until one satisfying all original or revised constraints is found and is chosen without search through the remaining alternatives (this is SATISFICING). The process involves no analytic optimization; any optimization is done implicitly through judgmental adjustment of constraints. *Linear programming* involves constrained optimization of a *single* objective. The objective function is defined to represent just one objective, e.g., profit. Constraints are set on some or all decision, input, and output variables, except for the objective function. This objective function, and thus attainment of the single objective it represents, is then maximized and the corresponding alternative(s) chosen as optimal. *Goal programming* involves constrained optimization of *multiple* objectives. Multiple objective functions are defined on the decision variables, each function representing a different objective; a goal (target) level is specified on each objective; and an overall (meta-) objective function specifying a rule for AGGREGATING goal-outcome discrepancies across the individual objectives is defined. (The rule can involve a LEXICOGRAPHIC ORDERING, a COMPENSATORY MODEL, or a combination of the two.) Constraints are set on some or all decision, input, and output variables, as in linear programming. The objective function, and thus attainment of the multiple objectives it represents, is then minimized and the corresponding alternative(s) chosen as optimal.

These three approaches do not always differ as sharply as indicated--for instance, a linear programming objective function can be defined as a weightd sum of two or more objective functions in order to represent multiple objectives jointly, while a goal programming (meta-) objective function can be defined to consider just a single objective. However, the three do generally represent progressively greater sophistication with respect to number of objectives effectively considered and sensitivity to variation in attainment of each.

Conventional mathematical programming addresses UNCERTAINTY only through SENSITIVITY ANALYSIS, but recent advances in "stochastic programming" allow consideration of uncertainty explicitly in the programming model (Taha, 1976, Ch. 16).

related terms: OPERATIONS RESEARCH, MULTIATTRIBUTE DECISION MAKING, MULTIOBJECTIVE DECISION MAKING.

MAXIMAX STRATEGY.

See MINIMAX REGRET CRITERION.

MAXIMAX UTILITY CRITERION.

See MINIMAX REGRET CRITERION.

MAXIMIN GAIN CRITERION.

See MINIMAX REGRET CRITERION.

MAXIMIN STRATEGY.

See MINIMAX REGRET CRITERION.

MAXIMIN UTILITY CRITERION.

See MINIMAX REGRET CRITERION.

MAXIMIZATION

definition: A DECISION rule that prescribes selection of that course of action that results in the maximum value on some descriptive or evaluative DIMENSION (for example, size of wildlife herd in habitat, amount of some product produced, amount of financial profit earned, amount of UTILITY (Definition 1) obtained).

comment: Maximization is to be contrasted with optimization and minimax regret. **OPTIMIZATION** is selection of that course of action that results in the optimum, or most favorable, value on some dimension, where this optimum need not be the maximum value on that dimension. Thus, one might prefer a POLICY that led to an intermediate number of deer, rather than as many deer as possible, in a given habitat. MINIMAX REGRET is a competing decision rule for dealing with GAMES or with UNCERTAINTY.

related terms: VALUE, UTILITY, EXPECTED VALUE, EXPECTED UTILITY, MINIMAX REGRET CRITERION.

MCPL.

See MULTIPLE-CUE PROBABILITY LEARNING.

MEASURE.

See MEASUREMENT, SCALES of MEASUREMENT.

MEASUREMENT

definition: "In its broadest sense measurement is the assignment of numerals to objects or events according to rules. And the fact that numerals can be assigned under different rules leads to different kinds of scales and different kinds of measurement" (see SCALES of MEASUREMENT) (Stevens, 1951, p. 1; a paraphrase of Campbell, 1940). "Measurement of magnitude is, in its most general sense, any method by which a unique and reciprocal correspondence is established between all or some of the magnitudes of a kind and all or some of the numbers...." (Russell, 1937, p. 176).

comment: "Scales are possible in the first place only because there exists an isomorphism between the properties of the numeral series and the empirical operations that we can perform with the aspects of objects. This isomorphism, of course, is only partial. Not *all* the properties of number and not *all* the properties of objects can be paired off in a systematic correspondence.   But *some* properties   of objects can be related by semantical rules to *some* properties of the numeral series. In particular, in dealing with the aspects of objects we can invoke empirical operations for determining equality (the basis for classifying things), for rank ordering, and for determining when differences and when rates between the aspects of objects are equal" (Stevens, 1951, p. 23).

Though the terms are often used interchangeably, Coombs, Dawes, & Tversky (1970, pp. 31f) distinguish between measurement and **SCALING**. Whereas the former is concerned with the construction of an AXIOMATIC model, the latter is concerned with the actual   process   of assigning numbers to objects or properties. The distinction can be seen most clearly in the difference between AXIOMATIC and NUMERICAL CONJOINT MEASUREMENT.

related   *terms*:   DIMENSION,   SCALES   of   MEASUREMENT,   CONJOINT MEASUREMENT, FUNCTIONAL MEASUREMENT.

METRIC

definition 1: A SCALE of MEASUREMENT with a fixed unit, that is, at least an INTERVAL (or possibly even an ORDERED-METRIC) scale.

definition 2: A fixed unit of measurement.

related terms: SCALES of MEASUREMENT, CARDINAL UTILITY.

MINIMAX CRITERION.

See MINIMAX REGRET CRITERION.

MINIMAX LOSS CRITERION.

See MINIMAX REGRET CRITERION.

MINIMAX LOSS STRATEGY.

See MINIMAX REGRET CRITERION.

MINIMAX REGRET CRITERION

definition: The strategy of choosing that alternative that minimizes the maximum REGRET, where regret is the difference between the UTILITY associated with a given alternative in a given state and the maximum utility associated with any alternative in that state (Savage, 1951). Once, one of the strategies recommended for DECISION MAKING under UNCERTAINTY, as opposed to RISK, particularly for decision making in competitive GAMES, and the main competitor to MAXIMIZATION of EXPECTED UTILITY as a principle of RATIONAL CHOICE. Now, of value primarily as a DESCRIPTIVE, rather than a NORMATIVE, MODEL. (See RISK DIMENSIONS, ELLSBERG PARADOX.) (See Luce & Raiffa, 1957, pp. 278ff; Miller & Starr, 1967, pp. 111ff.)

comment: The minimax regret criterion was suggested by Savage (1951) as an improvement over the **MAXIMIN UTILITY** (or **MAXIMIN GAIN**) criterion, associated with the names of Wald (1950) and von Neumann & Morgenstern (1947). The maximin utility criterion says that, under uncertainty, one should choose that act which maximizes the minimum utility, or payoff (Luce & Raiffa, 1957, pp. 278f). Consider the following PAYOFF **MATRIX**, in which A1 and A2 represent two alternative courses of action, S1 and S2 represent two possible states of nature, and the numbers in the matrix represent utilities of outcomes of payoffs:

	$s1$	$s2$	
$A1$	0	100	
$A2$	1	1	<--- maximin utility choice

The minimum utility for $A1$ is 0, and the minimum utility for $A2$ is 1. By selecting $A2$, one thus maximizes the minimum utility. (Since "it is customary in the literature to consider negative utility, disutility, or loss, as an index appraising consequences...the principle described above is usually called the **MINIMAX PRINCIPLE.**" Luce & Raiffa, 1957, p. 279.)

Critics point out that "this criterion would still select $A2$ even if the 1 were reduced to 0.00001 and the 100 increased to 10_6. These critics agree that act $A2$ is reasonable *if* player 2 is a conscious adversary of 1, for then 2 should choose $s1$, and $A2$ is best against $s1$; but, they emphasize, nature does not behave in that way..." (Luce & Raiffa, 1957, p. 280). It has been argued that the minimax strategy is too conservative even in competitive games. "...It gives up most possibilities of exploiting an opponent's mistakes. It is safe to say that a minimax businessman or poker player would soon go broke" (Edwards, Lindman, & Phillips, 1965, p. 279).

Savage (1951) suggested the minimax regret, or **MINIMAX LOSS,** criterion as an improvement over the maximin utility criterion. According to Edwards (1954, p. 409), "Savage believes (1951, also personal communication) that neither von Neumann and Morgenstern nor Wald actually intended to propose the principle of minimaxing loss; they confined their discussions to cases in which the concepts of minimax loss and minimax regret amount to the same thing." Minimax regret is based on a **REGRET MATRIX,** which is derived from a payoff matrix by computing regret for each state as the difference between the maximum utility for that state and the utility received (Luce & Raiffa, 1957, p. 280). The regret matrix corresponding to the payoff matrix above is shown below:

	$s1$	$s2$	
$A1$	1	0	<--- minimax regret choice
$A2$	0	99	

The maximum regret for $A1$ is 1, and the maximum regret for $A2$ is 99. The strategy, then, is to choose $A1$ and thus minimize the maximum regret.

While this strategy leads to the choice that seems intuitively reasonable in this case, it suffers from a weakness that has been characterized as "very serious" (Chernoff, 1954), dependence on IRRELEVANT ALTERNATIVES. Consider the following payoff matrix and its associated regret matrix, which are identical to the previous figures except for the addition of A3:

	$s1$	$s2$
$A1$	0	100
$A2$	1	1
$A3$	100	0

```
        s1    s2
A1    100     0
A2     99    99    <--- minimax regret choice
A3      0   100
```

The addition of an irrelevant alternative, A3, has changed the indicated choice from A1 to A2.

Both the maximin utility criterion and the minimax regret criterion are "ultraconservative (or PESSIMISTIC) in that, relative to each act, they concentrate upon the state having the worst consequence" (Luce & Raiffa, 1957, p. 282). The HURWICZ CRITERION (Hurwicz, 1951) permits one to select a preferred point on an OPTIMISM-pessimism continuum. It does this by associating with each alternative the index:

$$\alpha m_i + (1 - \alpha)M_i$$

where: m_i = the minimum utility for alternative i
M_i = the maximum utility for alternative i

and selecting the alternative with the highest index. If $\alpha = 1$, the criterion is the maximin utility criterion; if $\alpha = 0$, it is the MAXIMAX UTILITY CRITERION. "...By resolving a simple decision problem an α-level [that is appropriate for oneself] can be chosen empirically, which, in turn, can be employed in more complicated decisions" (Luce & Raiffa, 1957, p. 283).

"None of these principles commands general acceptance; each can be made to show peculiar consequences under some conditions" (Edwards, 1954, p. 409).

related terms: INSUFFICIENT REASON, ELLSBERG PARADOX, EXPECTED UTILITY, RISK DIMENSIONS.

MONEY PUMP.

See TRANSITIVITY.

MONOTONIC.

See FUNCTION FORM.

MONTE CARLO METHOD

definition: "A method of approximately solving mathematical and physical problems by the simulation of random quantities" (Sobol, 1974, p. 1). Because the Monte Carlo method can be used to simulate both (a) processes influenced by random factors and (b) PROBABILISTIC models devised for solving problems involving no chance, it can be considered a "universal method for solving mathematical problems" (Sobol, 1974, p. 3). Monte Carlo methods require less mathematical sophistication than computational methods and can often be used where computational methods would be too unwieldy.

example: A simple example is that of determining a binomial distribution by tossing, say 10 coins repeatedly, recording the proportion of heads on each toss, and plotting up the resulting distribution. The alternative would be to calculate the distribution.

comment: "The generally accepted birth date of the Monte Carlo method is 1949, when an article entitled 'The Monte Carlo Method' [Metropolis & Ulam, 1949] appeared. The American mathematicians J. Neyman and S. Ulam are considered its originators" (Sobol, 1974, p. 1).

synonym: **STATISTICAL TRIALS.**

related terms: DESCRIPTIVE MODELS.

MRS.

See TRADEOFF.

MRT.

See TRADEOFF.

MULTIATTRIBUTE DECISION MAKING

definition: Choosing from among a set of alternatives that are described in terms of multiple attributes, or DIMENSIONS.

comment: To be contrasted with **MULTIOBJECTIVE DECISION MAKING.** Multiobjective objective decision making methods "recognize that attributes of alternatives are often just means to higher ends--the decision maker's OBJECTIVES" (MacCrimmon, 1973, p. 19). Whereas mutliattribute decision making methods obtain PREFERENCES, usually in the form of FUNCTION FORMS and WEIGHTS, directly for levels on the attributes, multiobjective decision making methods derive these from the preferences among objectives and the functions relating attributes to objectives (MacCrimmon, 1973, p. 19). See PREFERENCE TREE. Keeney & Raiffa (1976, p. 32) provide an example of the difference between objectives and attributes: The overall objective "improve the well-being of the residents" might have as a lower-level objective "reduce the emission of pollutants from sources within the city", which, in turn, might be associated with an attribute such as "tons of sulfer dioxide emitted per year". The attribute indicates "the degree to which alternative policies meet the objective" (p. 19). In short, an attribute is a concrete descriptive variable, while an objective is a more abstract variable *with* a specification of the relative desirability of the levels of that variable. (See GOAL, FUNCTION FORM.)

In the MATHEMATICAL PROGRAMMING literature, an objective corresponds to what has here been defined as an attribute. Cohon (1978, p. 17), for example, distinguishes between an "ideal" and an objective on the basis of "operational usefulness". "An objective may lead to a mathematical statement in terms of the decision variables of a problem, i.e., an OBJECTIVE FUNCTION, while an ideal will never lead to such quantification" (p. 17).

related terms: GOALS, RELEVANCE TREE, COMPENSATORY MODELS, NONCOMPENSATORY MODELS.

MULTIATTRIBUTE UTILITY THEORY

definition: A theory for making multiple value dimensions COMMENSURABLE. in terms of a common scale of VALUE (Definition 2). Multiattribute utility theory frequently represents UTILITY

(Definition 1 or 2) in terms of a FUNCTION FORM and a WEIGHT for each dimension.

example: Examples include multiattribute utility theory for RISKLESS CHOICE (Gardiner & Edwards, 1975; see SMART) and for RISKY CHOICE (Keeney & Raiffa, 1976; see DECISION THEORY). The latter, for example, involves the following steps: (a) present the decision maker with multidimensional consequences (e.g., 4-door sedan, 20 m.p.g., $4000; camper, 30 m.p.g., $3800; etc.) and obtain decomposed judgments of von-NEUMANN-MORGENSTERN UTILITY varying one dimension at a time (testing first for UTILITY INDEPENDENCE); (b) compare full-range changes on two dimensions at a time, still using the von-Neumann-Morgenstern procedure, to obtain relative weights, or SCALING CONSTANTS; and, finally, (c) combine these decomposed judgments NORMATIVELY, by an ADDITIVE MODEL if the scaling constants sum to one and by a MULTIPLICATIVE MODEL otherwise (Keeney & Raiffa, 1976).

related terms: MULTIATTRIBUTE DECISION MAKING, COMPENSATORY MODELS, TRADEOFF, WEIGHT, FUNCTION FORM.

MULTIDIMENSIONAL SCALING

definition: In its broad sense, multidimensional scaling is any of an variety of methods for producing a geometrical representation of a matrix of data in order to reveal whatever structure may underlie those data (Carroll & Arabie, 1980, p. 608; Shepard, 1972a, p. 1). In this sense, the term includes CLUSTER ANALYSIS, FACTOR ANALYSIS, CONJOINT MEASUREMENT, and a variety of other methods, in addition to classical metric multidimensional scaling and, more recently, NONMETRIC multidimensional scaling and hierarchical clustering.

In its narrow sense, multidimensional scaling is to be distinguished from methods that do not take *proximity data* (measures of similarity, confusion, association, or correlation) as their input (Shepard, 1972a, p. 1; Nunnally, 1967, pp. 403-404). It is thus to be distinguished from (a) analysis of *dominance data* (measures of preference or of "winning"), (b) cluster analysis or factor analysis of *profile data* (measured values of objects on dimensions), and (c) analysis of conjoint measurement data (magnitudes of an effect of the joint values of input variables).

In classical metric multidimensional scaling (Torgerson, 1952), proximity data are related to distances among points in space in a way that depends on a function of some particular, specified form. (See FUNCTION FORM.) This is accomplished by using the form of the function to compute distance estimates from the proximity data and deriving characteristic roots and vectors of a scalar-product matrix from these distance estimates.

In nonmetric multidimensional scaling (Shepard, 1962a, 1962b; Kruskal, 1964a), proximity data are related to distances among points by a function that is merely MONOTONIC. This is accomplished by iterative adjustment of points (perhaps from an arbitrary start) so as to minimize some measure of departure from monotonicity (Shepard, 1972b, pp. 24-39).

comment: Multidimensional scaling can contribute to MULTIATTRIBUTE DECISION MAKING in any of three ways: (a) by revealing (see REVEALED PREFERENCE) the psychological DIMENSIONS along which alternatives are believed to differ, (b) by revealing the objective dimensions to which each psychological dimension is related, and (c) by revealing the psychophysical functions that relate objective dimensions to subjective ones (Green & Wind, 1973, pp. 60f.) A number of investigators have used multidimensional scaling to predict multiattribute decision making (e.g., Bass, Pessemier, & Lehmann, 1972; Green & Wind, 1973; Klahr, 1969.)

related terms: MULTIVARIATE ANALYSIS, CLUSTER ANALYSIS, STRUCTURAL MODELING, FACTOR ANALYSIS, CONJOINT MEASUREMENT, FUNCTIONAL MEASUREMENT, METRIC, NONMETRIC, GRAPHIC AIDS.

MULTILINEAR MODEL

definition: A LINEAR MODEL that AGGREGATES information from different VARIABLES by (a) adding the input variables to one another (ADDING MODEL), and/or (b) multiplying the input variables by one another (MULTIPLYING MODEL.) Thus,

$$Y = b_1 X_1 + b_2 X_2 + b_3 X_1 X_2$$

e.g., Keeney & Raiffa, 1976, p. 233.) It is important to note that the transformation of variables (for example, by VALUE or UTILITY FUNCTIONS) is a separate matter from their aggregation. Linear aggregation rules can take as inputs the outputs of either linear or nonlinear transformations. A multilinear model is the most general case of a linear model. The first two terms in the equation above correspond to an ADDING MODEL, and the last, to a MULTIPLYING MODEL (Keeney & Raiffa, 1976, p. 233). The multiplicative component is often referred to as the **BILINEAR TERM** when there are two input variables as the **MULTILINEAR TERM** when there are more than two, and, in either case, as a **LINEAR INTERACTION** term.

comment: The multilinear model, like the adding and multiplying models of which it is composed, exhibits ADDITIVE INDEPENDENCE.

related terms: LINEAR MODEL, ADDING MODEL, AVERAGING MODEL, MULTIPLYING MODEL, INDEPENDENCE.

MULTILINEAR TERM.

See MULTILINEAR MODEL.

MULTIOBJECTIVE DECISION MAKING.

See MULTIATTRIBUTE DECISION MAKING.

MULTIPLE-CUE PROBABILITY LEARNING

definition: An inductive INFERENCE task in which the subject is required to learn to infer the state of a criterion VARIABLE on the basis of the states of a number of predictor variables, or CUES, (Brehmer, 1976b, p. 1.)

comment: Multiple-cue research is a standard research paradigm in SJT, where it is argued that this paradigm is representative of the most frequently encountered cognitive tasks. Most studies rely upon the LENS MODEL for conceptual and analytical guidance. Independent variables have included: number of cues (Hoffman & Blanchard, 1961; Hayes, 1964; Oskamp, 1965); degree of correlation between cues and criterion (ECOLOGICAL VALIDITY) (Peterson, Hammond, & Summers, 1965a, 1965b; Summers, 1969); FUNCTION FORMS relating cues and criterion (Lee & Tucker, 1962; Uhl, 1963; Brehmer, 1969a; Hammond & Summers, 1965;

Summers, 1967; and Summers, Summers, & Karkau, 1969); degree and direction of correlation among cues (REDUNDANCY and CONFLICT) (Slovic, 1966; L. W. Dudycha & Naylor, 1966); and type of feedback (OUTCOME FEEDBACK vs. COGNITIVE FEEDBACK) (Hammond, 1971; Hammond & Boyle, 1970; Newton, 1965; Todd & .Hammond, 1965.)

synonym: **MCPL**, INTERVAL CONCEPT LEARNING.

related terms: SOCIAL JUDGMENT THEORY, DOUBLE-SYSTEM CASE, LENS MODEL, REPRESENTATIVE DESIGN.

MULTIPLE CUTOFFS.

See CONJUNCTIVE and DISJUNCTIVE MODELS.

MULTIPLE-CUTTING-POINT MODEL.

See CONJUNCTIVE and DISJUNCTIVE MODELS.

MULTIPLE REGRESSION.

See REGRESSION ANALYSIS.

MULTIPLE REGRESSION FORECASTING.

See FORECASTING.

MULTIPLICATIVE MODEL.

See MULTIPLYING MODEL.

MULTIPLYING MODEL

definition: A LINEAR MODEL that AGGREGATES information from different VARIABLES by multiplying those variables (Anderson, 1981, pp. 47ff; Keeney & Raiffa, 1976, p. 238). Thus,

$$Y = bX_1X_2.$$

It is important   note that the transformation of variables (for example, by VALUE or UTILITY FUNCTIONS) is a separate matter from their aggregation. Linear aggregation rules, such as multiplying, can

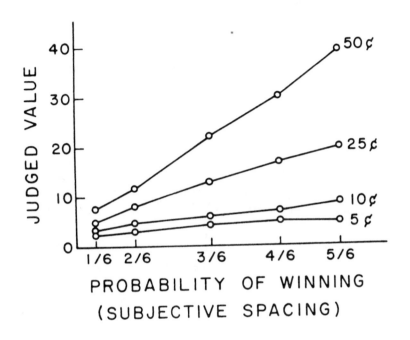

A Linear Fan

From Anderson & Shanteau, 1970. Copyright   1970 by   the   American Psychological Association. Reprinted by permission.

take   as   inputs   the   outputs   of either   linear   or nonlinear transformations.

examples: One example of a multiplying model would be the combining of PROBABILITY and VALUE in determining EXPECTED VALUE (Shanteau,

1975). Another is BAYES' THEOREM. Still another is the multiplication of height by width, by adults, in estimating area (Anderson & Cuneo, 1978). Also, job performance has been hypothesized to be the product of motivation and ability, and many situations are hypothesized to follow a general expectancy-times-valence formulation.

comment: In analysis of variance, a multiplying model would show up as an interaction, though other patterns of interaction are possible (see CONFIGURAL MODEL). A multiplying model is indicated graphically by a LINEAR FAN pattern (see figure on preceding page) among the functions relating X_1 to Y at different levels of X_2.

synonyms: **MULTIPLICATIVE MODEL.**

related terms: LINEAR FAN, INDEPENDENCE, CONFIGURAL MODEL, INTERACTION, MULTILINEAR MODEL.

MULTIVARIATE ANALYSIS

definition: The use of mathematical techniques for (a) discovering regularities in the behavior of multiple VARIABLES, or (b) testing alternative models of association between multiple variables (Green, 1976, p. 1.)

examples and comment: Multivariate methods can be broadly divided into (a) those that are concerned with the *internal structure* of a set of variables (or of a set of entities described in terms of multiple variables) and (b) those that are concerned with the *external structure* that relates one set of variables (predictor variables) to another set of variables (criterion variable or variables)(see Green, 1976, p. 8.) The former, which include FACTOR ANALYSIS, MULTIDIMENSIONAL SCALING, and CLUSTER ANALYSIS, are less commonly used in JUDGMENT and DECISION ANALYSIS.

Multivariate methods that are concerned with the structure between predictors and criteria are divided into methods for dealing with a single criterion (MULTIPLE REGRESSION, analysis of variance (for example, FUNCTIONAL MEASUREMENT), analysis of covariance, two-group discriminant analysis, and CONJOINT MEASUREMENT) and methods for dealing with multiple criteria (canonical correlation, multivariate analysis of variance and analysis of covariance, and multiple discriminant analysis.) Those that deal with a single criterion are most directly related to JUDGMENT and DECISION analysis, which is usually concerned with predicting the single criterion of SUBJECTIVE PROBABILITY or that of PREFERENCE or UTILITY. Multiple regression techniques are employed by SJT; analysis of variance techniques, by IIT; THEORY; and CONJOINT MEASUREMENT techniques, by DT and by such researchers as Krantz, Tversky, Coombs, Green, and McClelland.

related terms: REGRESSION ANALYSIS, CONJOINT MEASUREMENT, MULTIDIMENSIONAL SCALING, CLUSTER ANALYSIS, DT, IIT, SJT.

N-SYSTEM CASE.

   See COGNITIVE SYSTEM.

NEGATIVE FEEDBACK CONTROL.

   See FEEDBACK.

NEGATIVELY ACCELERATED.

   See FUNCTION FORM.

NEPA.

   See ENVIRONMENTAL IMPACT ASSESSMENT.

NET PRESENT VALUE.

   See COST-BENEFIT ANALYSIS.

NET PRESENT WORTH.

   See COST-BENEFIT ANALYSIS.

NOMINAL.

See SCALES of MEASUREMENT.

NOMOTHETIC

definition: A term coined by the philosopher Windelband (1904) to refer to the study of the general case. An approach to data analysis in which the analysis is performed on data that have been AGGREGATED across people (e.g., on group means). In a judgment analysis context, this approach assumes that "all judges are essentially replicates of one another," differing only with respect to random error; the aggregation serves to reduce random error (Hammond, McClelland, & Mumpower, 1980, pp. 115 ff.).

comment: The advantages of the nomothetic method are simplicity and statistical power. The disadvantage is the risk of erroneous inference about individuals' characteristics from aggregated data when individuals are *not* essentially replicates of one another; that is, when individuals differ systematically as well as randomly. The results of nomothetic analysis in this case may be seriously misleading: "Grouped data may fit a given model even though the judgments of every individual do not, and grouped data may not fit a model even though the data from all individuals do fit that model" (Hammond *et al.*, 1980, pp. 123-4). Langbein and Lichtman (1978), following Robinson (1950), term such erroneous inference the **"ECOLOGICAL FALLACY"** in a related discussion of **ECOLOGICAL INFERENCE,** that is, inference about individuals' characteristics from aggregate data.

related terms: IDIOGRAPHIC, DESCRIPTIVE.

NON-DOMINATED SET.

See PARETO FRONTIER, EFFICIENT FRONTIER.

NONCOMPENSATORY MODEL

definition: A model for AGGREGATING information from different DIMENSIONS that does not permit a low VALUE on one dimension to be compensated for by a high value on another. LEXICOGRAPHIC, CONJUNCTIVE, DISJUNCTIVE, SATISFICING, and MINIMAX MODELS are examples of noncompensatory models.

related terms: COMPENSATORY MODEL, CONJUNCTIVE and DISJUNCTIVE MODEL, LEXICOGRAPHIC MODEL, SATISFICING, MINIMAX REGRET, CONCEPT LEARNING.

NONLINEAR.

See LINEAR RELATIONSHIP, LINEAR MODEL.

NONLINEAR PROGRAMMING.

See MATHEMATICAL PROGRAMMING.

NONMARKETED GOOD

definition: A commodity (good, service, or characteristic thereof, tangible or intangible) that is not directly exchanged in economic markets and that therefore lacks a monetary MARKET PRICE which (under ideal conditions) would indicate its VALUE (Definition 2a) and production cost relative to the costs of other commodities (see TRADEOFF). (Freeman, 1979; Layard, 1972; Sinden & Worrell, 1979, Ch. 1; Stokey & Zeckhauser, 1978, Ch. 14.)

synonym: **UNPRICED GOOD.**

examples: Environmental quality (e.g., clean air, clean water, scenic beauty); national defense; police and fire services; national forest recreation.

comment: Nonmarketed goods are almost entirely PUBLIC GOODS (which see).

There are three basic approaches to estimating the VALUES (Definition 2) of nonmarketed goods (Freeman, 1979, Ch. 1). The *first* is direct surveys in which individuals are asked, using BIDDING GAMES, to state their WILLINGNESS to PAY or WILLINGNESS to ACCEPT PAYMENT for those goods. The *second* (applicable only to public goods) is to hold a referendum vote on proposals for alternative levels of governmental provision of the good. The *third* is to study transactions in marketed commodities which are related to the nonmarketed goods in production or consumption.

The third approach includes at least three variants which are applicable in different circumstances (Freeman, 1979, Chs. 4, 6-9). Take air pollution (negative air quality) as the nonmarketed good in question. One variant could involve studying agricultural productivity and prices to assess pollution effects on vegetable crops and markets, considering the nonmarketed good as a factor in production of marketed goods. A second variant would involve studying variation in housing price (indicating value to consumers) as a function of variation in metropolitan pollution level, considering the nonmarketed good as entering directly into consumers' UTILITY [Definition 1] functions) and therefore as affecting the value of marketed goods that incorporate it as a component. (When buying a "house" one really buys a bundle of characteristics, or DIMENSIONS, which includes aspects of the building itself, the lot, the social environment, the physical environment, etc.) A third variant could involve studying variation in expenditures on medical care and supplies, house painting, air filtration systems, etc., made to offset adverse effects of existing or expected pollution; this would consider the nonmarketed good as something consumers value indirectly, through its causation of adverse, directly-valued, consequences. The second and third variants both exemplify the study of "averting behavior", the actions people take to avoid or mitigate adverse effects of unfavorable externalities (see EXTERNALITY); (Zeckhauser & Fisher, 1976, cited by Freeman, 1979, p. 132).

related terms: PUBLIC GOOD, MARKET PRICE, SHADOW PRICE, COST-BENEFIT ANALYSIS, COST-EFFECTIVENESS ANALYSIS, VALUE, TRADEOFF.

NONMETRIC

definition: Referring to MEASUREMENT without a fixed unit, that is, on an ORDINAL or NOMINAL scale. (See SCALES of MEASUREMENT.)

related terms: SCALES of MEASUREMENT.

NONMONOTONIC.

See FUNCTION FORM.

NON-REGRESSIVENESS BIAS

definition: The tendency to make insufficient or no allowance for REGRESSION towards the MEAN when predicting on the basis of a predictor that is not perfectly correlated with the criterion (has less than perfect DIAGNOSTICITY).

example: "Suppose one is told that a college freshman has been described by a counselor as intelligent, self-confident, well-read, hard-working, and inquisitive. Consider two types of questions that might be asked about this description:

> (a) *Evaluation*: How does this description impress you with respect to academic ability? What percentage of descriptions of freshmen do you believe would impress you more? (b) *Prediction*: What is your estimate of the grade point average that this student will obtain? What is the percentage of freshman who obtain a higher grade point average?

"There is an important difference between the two questions. In the first, you evaluate the input; in the second, you predict an OUTCOME. Since there is surely greater UNCERTAINTY about the second question than about the first, your prediction should be more regressive than your evaluation. That is, the percentage you give as a prediction should be closer to 50% than the percentage you give as an evaluation....

"The REPRESENTATIVENESS hypothesis, however, entails that prediction and evaluation should coincide. In evaluating a given description, people select a score which, presumably, is most representative of the description. If people predict by representativeness, they will also select the most representative score as their prediction" (Kahneman & Tversky, 1973, pp. 243-244).

Einhorn & Hogarth (1981, p. 4) add an important qualification, that "extreme predictions are not suboptimal in non-stationary processes", that, "given a changing process, regressive predictions are suboptimal." They give as an example Chrysler's recent large losses, pointing out that, if one takes these as indicative of a deteriorating quality of management and worsening market conditions, one should predict even *more* extreme losses.

related terms: REGRESSION towards the MEAN, DIAGNOSTICITY, BASE-RATE FALLACY, REPRESENTATIVENESS.

NORMATIVE MODEL

definition: A set of rules specifying what people should do in order to be self-consistent, or RATIONAL. A normative model for DECISION MAKING thus specifies what decision a person should make, given certain BELIEFS and VALUES and the desire to be self-consistent. (Edwards, Lindman, & Phillips, 1965, pp. 263f.)

related terms: PRESCRIPTIVE MODEL, DESCRIPTIVE MODEL, RATIONALITY, AXIOM, DECISION AID.

NPV.

See NET PRESENT VALUE.

NPW.

See NET PRESENT WORTH.

NUMERAIRE.

See VALUE.

NUMERICAL CONJOINT MEASUREMENT.

See CONJOINT MEASUREMENT.

OBJECTIVE.

See GOAL, MULTIATTRIBUTE DECISION MAKING.

OBJECTIVE FUNCTION

definition: In MATHEMATICAL PROGRAMMING, the measure of effectiveness, or criterion of optimality, of a system (see OPTIMIZATION). "...The objective function acts as an indicator for the achievement of the optimum solution," since "In general, the *optimum* solution to the model is obtained when the corresponding values of the DECISION VARIABLES yield the *best* value of the objective function while satisfying all constraints" (Taha, 1976, p. 6).

comment: The objective function is defined as a mathematical function of either the decision variables or of output (outcome) variables whose levels are determined (driven) by the decision variables. It is usually defined as a function of decision variables in LINEAR PROGRAMMING, but as a function of output variables in GOAL PROGRAMMING (Taha, 1976; Cohon, 1978).

related terms: MATHEMATICAL PROGRAMMING, OPTIMIZATION, MAXIMIZATION.

OBJECTIVE PROBABILITY

definition: A number that represents the likelihood of an event in terms of the number of outcomes of interest relative to the total number of outcomes (Raiffa, 1968, p. 273).

Objective probabilities, like all probabilities, (a) range from 0, for impossibility, to 1, for certainty, (b) can be added to yield the p's for sets of events that are mutually exclusive, and (c) add to 1 for sets of events that are mutually exclusive and exhaustive. Objective probabilities are based on counting, in contrast to subjective probabilities, which are based on JUDGMENT.

comment: Actually, the objectivist view of probability is based on two approaches. One, the **CLASSICAL, ANALYTICAL,** or **CANONICAL** approach (Cardano, 1501-1576, reprinted 1953; Feller, 1968), defines probability in terms of *conceptual experiments*. Thus, probability is a number that represents the likelihood of an event in terms of the number of *conceivable* outcomes on which the event would occur relative to the total number of *conceivable* outcomes, "conceivable outcomes" being understood to be equally likely. Thus, the probability of rolling a one on a die is 1/6, but the die must be fair.

The other, **EMPIRICAL FREQUENCY,** approach (Poisson, 1837), defines probability in terms of *empirical experiments*. Thus, probability is a number that represents the likelihood of an event in terms of the limit of the number of *actual* outcomes on which the event occurs relative to the total number of *actual* outcomes, as the experiment is repeated indefinitely. Thus, the probability of rolling a one on a die is the limit of the proportion of times a one actually comes up on repeated rolls, and a fair die is not required.

For an excellent review of the history of approaches to probability, see Raiffa (1968, pp. 273-278).

synonyms: **PHYSICAL PROBABILITY, CLASSICAL PROBABILITY, FREQUENTISTIC PROBABILITY,** ACTUARIAL PREDICTION.

related terms: SUBJECTIVE PROBABILITY, RISK, CHANCE FORK.

ODDS

definition: The ratio between two probabilities, usually the probabilities of alternative hypotheses conditional upon some datum. Given two alternative hypotheses, H_1 and H_2, and a datum, D, BAYES' THEOREM states that:

$$p(H_1 | D) = \frac{p(D | H_1) p(H_1)}{p(D)}$$

and

$$p(H_2 | D) = \frac{p(D | H_2) p(H_2)}{p(D)}$$

The necessity of computing $p(D)$ can be eliminated by dividing one of these equations by the other to yield:

$$\frac{p(H_1 | D)}{p(H_2 | D)} = \frac{p(D | H_1) p(H_1)}{p(D | H_2) p(H_2)}$$

For this form, new symbols are introduced:

$$\Omega_1 = LR \times \Omega_0,$$

where Ω_1 is the POSTERIOR ODDS, LR the LIKELIHOOD RATIO, and Ω_0 the PRIOR ODDS (Edwards, Lindman & Savage, 1963, p. 218; Slovic & Lichtenstein, 1973, p. 31.)

comment: According to Edwards (1968a, p. 26), odds or log odds is more intuitive than probability for naive subjects (hence, its use in the gambling industry.) Use of odds produces less CONSERVATISM than use of probabilities, presumably because the scale is not bounded (Phillips & Edwards, 1966; Slovic & Lichtenstein, 1973.) Furthermore, log odds is unique among the common measures of uncertainty in that "the amount of change in opinion produced by a piece of evidence is independent of where the opinion was to start with" (Edwards, 1968a, p. 26.) This is so because log odds results in an additive model:

$$\log \Omega_1 = \log LR + \log \Omega_0.$$

related terms: PROBABILITY, PRIOR PROBABILITY, POSTERIOR PROBABILITY.

OPERATIONS RESEARCH

definition: An analytic approach to DECISION MAKING developed in England during World War II for OPTIMIZING the utilization of scarce military resources and later adopted and extended by the United States military. Operations research includes a variety of techniques, among them DECISION ANALYSIS, LINEAR PROGRAMMING, NONLINEAR PROGRAMMING, INTEGER PROGRAMMING, DYNAMIC PROGRAMMING, FORECASTING techniques, queueing theory, critical-path methods for scheduling, network methods for routing, and inventory models (Raiffa, 1968, pp. 295f; Siemens, et al., 1973; Taha, 1971; Dannenbring & Starr, 1981).

synonym: OR.

related terms: MATHEMATICAL PROGRAMMING, FORECASTING, STRUCTURAL MODELING, CROSS-IMPACT ANALYSIS, DECISION THEORY.

OPPORTUNITY COST.

See DISCOUNTING, COST-BENEFIT ANALYSIS.

OPTIMISM.

See HURWICZ CRITERION.

OPTIMIZATION

See MAXIMIZATION.

OR.

See OPERATIONS RESEARCH.

ORDERED-METRIC.

See SCALES of MEASUREMENT.

ORDINAL.

See SCALES of MEASUREMENT.

ORDINAL UTILITY

definition: UTILITY measured only on an ORDINAL scale, not on a higher-order (ORDERED-METRIC, INTERVAL, RATIO, or ABSOLUTE) scale (See Edwards, 1954, p. 384.)

comment: Ordinal utility permits analysis of DOMINANCE, but not of TRADEOFFS or of RISK.

synonym: **PREFERENCE.**

related terms: UTILITY, CARDINAL UTILITY, PREFERENCE STRUCTURE, DOMINANCE, SCALES of MEASUREMENT.

ORGANIZATION.

See AGGREGATION.

ORGANIZING.

See AGGREGATION.

ORGANIZING PRINCIPLE.

See AGGREGATION RULE.

OUTCOME.

See VALUE.

OUTCOME FEEDBACK.

See FEEDBACK.

OVERCONFIDENCE EFFECT

definition: An unwarranted BELIEF in the correctness of one's answers (Lichtenstein, Fischhoff, & Phillips, 1977). Excessive narrowness of SUBJECTIVE PROBABILITY distributions. In one study (Alpert & Raiffa, 1969), for example, among answers assigned probabilities of .90 of being correct, only 75% turned out, in fact, to be correct; and, among answers assigned probabilities of 1.00 of being correct, only 80% turned out to be correct.

comment: See ANCHORING and ADJUSTMENT for an explanation and corrective JUDGMENT elicitation method.

related terms: CALIBRATION, SUBJECTIVE PROBABILITY, BIAS, ILLUSORY CORRELATION, ANCHORING and ADJUSTMENT.

PARALLEL CONCEPTS

definition: The principle that "organismic and environmental systems should be described in symmetrical terms" (Hammond, Stewart, Brehmer, & Steinmann, 1975, p. 274).

example: "As Brunswik describes the LENS MODEL, it becomes clear that he employs a principle of parallel concepts, for each concept on one side is paralleled by a similar concept on the other. Thus, CUES on the task, or ecological, side vary in ECOLOGICAL VALIDITY, and on the organismic side there is variation in CUE UTILIZATION by the subject.... SOCIAL JUDGMENT theorists are also concerned with the extent to which the principles of ORGANIZATION that control the task system are reflected in the principles of organization that control the cognitive system of the subject" (Hammond, *et al.*, 1975, pp. 274-275).

comment: For DT, BDT, and PDT, as well as SJT, "the models they construct of judges' cognitive systems are similar to the models they assume best describe environmental systems" (Hammond, McClelland, & Mumpower, 1980, p. 192).

related terms: LENS MODEL.

PARALLELISM.

  See ADDING MODEL.

PARAMORPHIC MODEL

definition: A representation that has the same output (for a given set of inputs) as the process being represented, though it may not arrive at it by the same process (Hoffman, 1960.)

comment: Hoffman (1960, 1968) observed that (a) two or more models of judgment may be algebraically equivalent yet suggestive of radically different underlying processes, and (b) two or more models may be algebraically different yet equally predictive, given fallible data. Hoffman introduced the term "paramorphic representation" to remind psychologists that "the mathematical description of JUDGMENT is inevitably incomplete..., and it is not known how completely or how accurately the underlying process has been represented" (1960, p. 125.) (In mineralogy, the word "paramorph" is used "to describe a substance having crystalline structural properties which differ from those of another substance with the identical chemical composition" (Hoffman, 1960, pp. 124-125).) Algebraic models (including ADDING, AVERAGING, MULTIPLYING, and BAYESIAN) are all paramorphic. Dawes (1979) has recently argued for the usefulness of paramorphic models, particularly LINEAR MODELS, for ACTUARIAL PREDICTION or for BOOTSTRAPPING. Paramorphic models are to be contrasted with PROCESS-TRACING MODELS. It should be noted that the ability of a paramorphic model to produce the same output as the process being represented may be restricted to the input set for which it was established.

related terms: BOOTSTRAPPING, PROCESS TRACING MODEL.

PARETO FRONTIER

definition: The set of alternatives no one of which is DOMINATED by any other alternative (see, e.g., Coombs & Avrunin, 1977, p. 220). In the figure on the next page (which is drawn so that the most desirable region is in the southeast portion), point B lies on the Pareto frontier but the points on the line between A and C do not. See EFFICIENT FRONTIER.

comment: Note that, while no alternative on the Pareto frontier is dominated by any alternative on or off the frontier, it is not necessarily the case that every alternative on the frontier dominates every alternative not on the frontier.

Pareto (1906) was the first to emphasize that ORDINAL UTILITY can serve most of the purposes of CARDINAL UTILITY.   The association of his name with this frontier "serves to emphasize the property's purely ORDINAL character" (Coombs & Avrunin, 1977, p. 220). The **PARETO PRINCIPLE** states that increasing one person's wealth while leaving another's unchanged results in a socially more desirable state.

CHOICE among alternatives on the Pareto frontier requires making TRADEOFFS.

synonyms: **PARETO OPTIMAL SET, NON-DOMINATED SET.** Sometimes (e.g.,

Keeney & Raiffa, 1976, p.   71) used   synonymously   with EFFICIENT
FRONTIER.

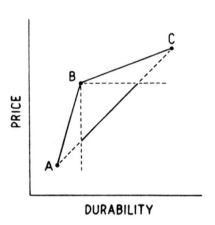

DURABILITY

Pareto and Efficient Frontiers

From Coombs & Avrunin, 1970, p. 220. Copyright 1977 by the American
Psychological Association. Reprinted by permission.

related terms: DOMINANCE, EFFICIENT FRONTIER, EQUITY.

PARETO OPTIMAL SET.

   See PARETO FRONTIER.

PARETO PRINCIPLE.

   See PARETO FRONTIER.

PAYOFF MATRIX.

See MINIMAX REGRET CRITERION

PDT.

See PSYCHOLOGICAL DECISION THEORY.

PERCEPTUAL ACHIEVEMENT.

See LENS MODEL.

PERIPHERAL.

See LENS MODEL.

PERSONAL PROBABILITY.

See SUBJECTIVE PROBABILITY.

PESSIMISM.

See HURWICZ CRITERION.

PHYSICAL PROBABILITY.

See OBJECTIVE PROBABILITY.

PIP

definition: Probabilistic Information Processing. "A probabilistic information processing system (PIP) would accept relevant information from men and sensors in explicitly PROBABILISTIC form, would process it by using appropriate procedures based on BAYES'S THEOREM, and would produce and display as output numerical probabilities for each hypothesis or evaluation of interest to the system" (Edwards &

Phillips, 1964, p. 361). It is expected that such a system will be able to reach conclusions at a predetermined LEVEL OF CONFIDENCE on the basis of substantially fewer data than unaided humans (Edwards & Phillips, 1964, p. 361, pp. 376f.) Evaluations in a number of realistically complex environments have supported this expectation (Edwards, Phillips, Hays, & Goodman, 1968; Phillips, 1966; Kaplan & Newman, 1966; Howell, 1967.)

comment: "Experiments and calculations suggest for three reasons that a PIP may be able to diagnose correctly the state of its environment on the basis of considerably less information than a deterministic system would require. First, a probabilistic system based on Bayes's theorem is optimal, in a formal mathematical sense, for extracting as much certainty as possible from the available information. Second, a probabilistic system can afford to accept and use with profit information so seriously fallible or degraded that it would be excluded or ignored in deterministic systems. Third, a probabilistic system permits a novel allocation of the elements of probabilistic inference between men and machines, an allocation which, research suggests, may be much better than that possible in deterministic systems" (Edwards & Phillips, 1964, p. 361).

related terms: BAYESIAN, BAYES' THEOREM, CONSERVATISM, INFERENCE.

PLAUSIBLE REASONING.

See INFERENCE.

POLICY

definition: A guide for action or general rule for making JUDGMENTS and DECISIONS in specific cases (Hammond & Brehmer, 1973, p. 339). A policy specifies (a) the information that is relevant to the judgment or decision and (b) the relationship between that information and the resulting judgment or course of action.

comment: Policies can be described by means of either PARAMORPHIC or PROCESS TRACING MODELS. Researchers in SJT describe policies in terms of a LINEAR MODEL. Note that "policy" is not to be confused with "POLICY", which is an interactive computer program used as a DECISION

AID. (See "POLICY" AID.)

related terms: JUDGMENT, DECISION, LINEAR MODEL, POLICY CAPTURING.

"POLICY" AID

definition: An interactive computer program developed by Hammond and his associates (Hammond, 1971; Hammond, Stewart, Brehmer, & Steinmann, 1975) for describing (see POLICY CAPTURING) and applying the JUDGMENT POLICIES of DECISION makers.   In a typical application, a decision maker would be shown a series of profiles of actual or hypothetical decision alternatives and would use a numerical rating scale to evaluate each. The individual's judgments would then be analyzed by means of a stepwise MULTIPLE-REGRESSION ANALYSIS, and graphical displays (see Hammond, 1971) of WEIGHTS and FUNCTION FORMS would be printed out at the computer terminal. The decision maker would then have an opportunity to modify this policy description on the basis of these displays or on the basis of the evaluations generated by alternative policies for each of the case profiles. If more than one decision maker is involved, the policies of pairs of individuals can be compared or a CLUSTER ANALYSIS can be performed to determine sources of CONFLICT.   POLICY employs (a) COGNITIVE FEEDBACK to aid individual learning and interpersonal learning and (b) BOOTSTRAPPING to improve ACHIEVEMENT and reduce interpersonal conflict. Cognitive feedback allows the policy captured A POSTERIORI by the POLICY program to be compared with a policy specified A PRIORI by the same judge. POLICY can be used to capture both policies for FACT judgment and policies for VALUE judgment.

comment: POLICY is available on an international timesharing network (the General Electric MARK III System); participants can interact with each other using the POLICY program and terminals located anywhere in the world having access to the timesharing system.   The program includes a capability for direct access to an interactive statistical package, including a routine for applying the judgment policies of participants to information stored in a data base to obtain predicted evaluations sorted in order of desirability.

related terms: WEIGHT, FUNCTION FORM, FEEDBACK, POLICY EQUATION, POLICY CAPTURING, BOOTSTRAPPING, A POSTERIORI DECOMPOSITION, A PRIORI DECOMPOSITION.

POLICY CAPTURING

definition: The use of statistical analysis of WHOLISTIC JUDGMENTS to obtain a PARAMORPHIC MODEL of the judgment process that generated those judgments (Goldberg, 1968; Hammond, Hursch, and Todd, 1964; Hammond *et al.*, 1975; Hoffman, 1960; Slovic and Lichtenstein, 1973); that is, to obtain a POLICY that reproduces an individual's (or group's, or organization's) judgments or DECISIONS.

comment: The judgments analyzed in policy capturing may reflect either real-world behavior (e.g., a college admissions committee's evaluations of applicants for graduate school) or responses to hypothetical questions.

Three statistical techniques are most commonly used in policy capturing: MULTIPLE REGRESSION ANALYSIS (Hammond, Hursch, and Todd, 1964; Hammond *et al.*, 1975), analysis of variance (Hoffman, Slovic, & Rorer, 1968; Anderson, 1974a,b,c) and CONJOINT MEASUREMENT (Green and Wind, 1973; Krantz and Tversky, 1971), all discussed by Hammond, McClelland, and Mumpower (1980) and by Slovic and Lichtenstein (1973).

The judgment models obtained through policy capturing can be used in numerous ways, as discussed by Hammond *et al.* (1975), Slovic & Lichtenstein (1973), and Slovic, Fischhoff, & Lichtenstein (1977), among others. Principal uses include prediction of further judgments by the same judges; representation of judges in situations where it is not feasible for them to make direct judgments; substitution for judges in order to improve judgments by increasing judgmental reliability (BOOTSTRAPPING; see especially Goldberg, 1970); improvement of judges' self-insight through COGNITIVE FEEDBACK (often in comparison with the judges' subjective descriptions of their policies); improvement of interpersonal (intergroup) communication; and management of inter- personal CONFLICT.

The earliest known work on policy capturing was by Edward L. Thorndike (1918) in which he compared intuitive judgment to multiple correlation. Later, Henry A. Wallace, who was to become U. S. Secretary of Agriculture and then Vice President, used multiple correlation to capture the policies used by corn judges in evaluating crop quality (Wallace, 1923).

related terms: POLICY, PARAMORPHIC, BOOTSTRAPPING, REGRESSION ANALYSIS, FUNCTIONAL MEASUREMENT, CONJOINT MEASUREMENT.

POLICY CONFLICT.

See POLICY SIMILARITY, CONFLICT

POLICY SIMILARITY

definition: The correlation between the predictable variance in the JUDGMENTS of two judges (Brehmer, 1976a, p. 987.) Considering only LINEAR similarity:

$R(S_1)$ = the multiple correlation between the CUES
and the judgments made by S_1,

$R(S_2)$ = the multiple correlation between the cues
and the judgments made by S_2,

$R(A)$ = AGREEMENT, the correlation between the
judgments made by S_1 and those made by
S_2.

G = (linear) Policy Similarity,

$$G = \frac{R(A)}{R(S_1)R(S_2)}$$

(Brehmer, 1976a, p. 987.) See LENS MODEL EQUATION for generalization to NONLINEAR similarity.

comment: Policy similarity and POLICY CONFLICT are but different regions on the same DIMENSION, G.

Solving the above equation for $R(A)$, a measure of Agreement, yields:

$$R(A) = G[R(S_1)R(S_2)],$$

which shows that disagreement can result either from policy conflict ($G < 1.00$) or from individual inconsistency in the application of POLICY ($R(S_i) < 1.00$). Brehmer (1969b) has found that a joint task that reduces policy conflict at the same time increases individual inconsistency, with the result that there is little reduction in disagreement. For this reason, SJT employs the POLICY interactive computer program (see "POLICY" AID) (a) to provide COGNITIVE FEEDBACK, and thus to reduce policy conflict, while at the same time (b) maintaining COGNITIVE CONTROL, and thus reducing individual inconsistency (See Hammond & Boyle, 1970; Hammond & Brehmer, 1970.)

related terms: LENS MODEL EQUATION, CONFLICT, SOCIAL JUDGMENT THEORY.

PORTFOLIO THEORY

definition: A DESCRIPTIVE MODEL of DECISION MAKING under conditions of RISK, developed by Clyde H. Coombs and based on the application of UNFOLDING THEORY to RISK (Coombs, 1969, 1975; Coombs & Pruitt, 1960; Coombs & Meyer, 1969; Coombs & Huang, 1970). The principal assumptions of the theory are (a) that CHOICE in risky situations is based on both the mean of the PROBABILITY distribution over OUTCOMES and some measure of risk and (b) that an individual's PREFERENCE for risk decreases MONOTONICALLY on both sides of an ideal point (that is, is SINGLE-PEAKED). Other theories assume that one always should, or always does, seek to *minimize* risk.

example: A person might prefer the probabilities .3, .4, .3 for the events -$5, $0, +$5 to either the probabilities .4, .2, .4 or the probabilities .05, .9, .05, respectively, for the same events (Coombs, 1975, p. 74).

comment: The second assumption of unfolding theory intentionally violates the BETWEENNESS PROPERTY of UTILITY theory, which states that "Any object which is a combination of other objects with stated probabilities is never preferred to every one of these other objects, nor is every one of them ever preferred to the combination" (Friedman & Savage, 1948, p. 288). There is evidence (e.g., Lehner, 1980) that this assumption of portfolio theory is in error.

related terms: VARIANCE PREFERENCES, UNFOLDING THEORY, RISK DIMENSIONS, RISK.

POSITIVE FEEDBACK CONTROL.

See FEEDBACK.

POSITIVELY ACCELERATED.

See FUNCTION FORM.

POSSIBILITY FRONTIER.

See EFFICIENT FRONTIER.

POSTERIOR PROBABILITY.

See BAYES' THEOREM.

PREDICTABILITY, ENVIRONMENTAL.

See LENS MODEL EQUATION.

PREDICTABILITY, JUDGMENTAL.

See LENS MODEL EQUATION.

PREFERENCE.

See ORDINAL UTILITY.

PREFERENCE STRUCTURE.

See INDIFFERENCE CURVE.

PREFERENCE TREE

definition: A model of CHOICE proposed by Tversky & Sattath (1979) in which each alternative is represented as a collection of aspects, the entire set of aspects is assumed to have a TREE structure, and DECISION MAKING is assumed to be a process of PROBABILISTICALLY selecting branches and sub-branches from the tree.

comment: The principal difference between the earlier ELIMINATION-by-ASPECTS model and the preference tree model lies in the TREE structure of the latter, which greatly reduces the complexity of the search process.

related terms: ELIMINATION-by-ASPECTS, TREE, LEXICOGRAPHIC, NONCOMPENSATORY.

PREFERENTIAL INDEPENDENCE

definition: "The set of ATTRIBUTES *Y* is *preferentially independent of the complementary set Z* if and only if the conditional preference structure in the *Y* space given z' does not depend on z'" (Keeney & Raiffa, 1976, p. 109), where *Y* and *Z* refer to sets of attributes and z' refers to a particular set of LEVELS on attribute *Z*. This means that the ORDINAL relation between levels of *Y* and judged VALUE (Definition 2)--the relative desirability of different *Y* levels--is not systematically different at different levels of *Z*. In still other terms, the FUNCTION FORM relating *Y* and *V*(*Y*) exhibits **SIMPLE INDEPENDENCE** (Fischer, 1976; Krantz & Tversky, 1971).

The set *Y* will be an *n*-tuple of attributes where *n* can in principle range from 1 to infinity. In the special case where *n* = 2, the VALUE TRADEOFF, or MARGINAL RATE of SUBSTITUTION, between attributes Y_1 and Y_2 at any point (y_1, y_2), given level z' of *Z*, is independent of z' for all y_1, y_2, and z'. That is, the set of INDIFFERENCE CURVES in (Y_1, Y_2) space does not depend on z' (Keeney & Raiffa, 1976, p. 101). When *n* is greater than or equal to 3, however, the value tradeoffs among the members of any 2...*n*-tuple subset of *Y* may or may not be preferentially independent either of that subset's complement (the remaining attributes) within *Y* or of *Z* (Keeney & Raiffa, 1976, pp. 100-114).

examples: When *n* = 1, the questions used to assess preferential independence would be ones such as:

> a. Assuming a 0% population increase, would you prefer an income of $20,000 or one of $40,000?

> b. Assuming a 10% population increase, would you prefer an income of $20,000 or one of $40,000?

If the same income level is preferred in both cases, income is preferentially independent of population, at least over these ranges.

When $n = 2$, questions used to assess preferential independence would be ones such as:

    a. Assuming a 0% population increase, would you prefer an income of $20,000 and a four-week annual vacation or an income of $40,000 and a one-week annual vacation?

    b. Assuming a 10% population increase, would you prefer an income of $20,000 and a four-week annual vacation or an income of $40,000 and a one-week annual vacation?

If the same income-vacation combination is preferred in both cases, the attribute set comprised of income and vacation length is preferentially independent of population, at least over these ranges.

comment: Preferential independence is not necessarily symmetrical. If set Y is preferentially independent of set Z, Z may or may not be preferentially independent of Y.

In riskless cases, when $n = 1$ in Y, preferential independence is sufficient for eliminating DOMINATED alternatives, but not for dealing with tradeoffs. When n is equal to or greater than 2 in Y, preferential independence is sufficient for dealing with tradeoffs within Y if the attributes of Y are **MUTUALLY PREFERENTIALLY INDEPENDENT**--a condition holding when "every subset of those attributes is preferentially independent of its complementary set" (Keeney & Raiffa, 1976, p. 111)--or, synonymously, **JOINTLY INDEPENDENT** (Fischer, 1976; Krantz & Tversky, 1971). Whatever the sizes of sets Y and Z, preferential independence is sufficient for dealing with tradeoffs between Y and Z if the sets are mutually preferentially independent, regardless of whether the attributes within Y or within Z are so or not (Keeney & Raiffa, 1976, pp. 110-111).

UTILITY INDEPENDENCE (which see) is necessary for dealing with RISKY cases.

related terms: INDEPENDENCE, UTILITY INDEPENDENCE, VALUE, FUNCTION
FORM, DOMINANCE, INDIFFERENCE CURVE, RISK, RISKLESS.

PREFERRED PROPORTIONS TRADEOFF METHOD.

See TRADEOFF.

PRESCRIPTIVE MODEL

definition: A set of rules recommending what people can do to improve
their self-consistency or RATIONALITY. Sometimes distinguished from a
NORMATIVE MODEL in that it takes account of the limited abilities of
human beings (Keeney & Raiffa, 1976, p. vii.), sometimes not (Dawes &
Corrigan, 1974, p. 96.)

related terms: NORMATIVE MODEL, DESCRIPTIVE MODEL, RATIONALITY.

PRICING OUT.

See WILLINGNESS to PAY.

PRIOR PROBABILITY.

See BAYES' THEOREM.

PRISONER'S DILEMMA

definition: A SOCIAL DILEMMA, attributed to A. W. Tucker (See Luce
& Raiffa, 1957, p. 94), in which two persons are involved and in
which (a) "all harm for defection is visited completely on the other
player", (b) "each player knows with certainty how the other has
behaved", and (c) "each player has total reinforcement control over
the other" (Dawes, 1980, pp. 182f.)

comment: "The name 'prisoner's dilemma' derives from an anecdote
concerning two prisoners who have jointly committed a felony and who
have been apprehended by a District Attorney who cannot prove their
guilt. The District Attorney holds them incommunicado and offers each

the chance to confess. If one confesses and the other doesn't, the one who confesses will go free while the other will receive a maximum sentence. If both confess they will both receive a moderate sentence, while if neither confesses both will receive a minimum sentence. In this situation, confession is a DOMINANT strategy. If the other confesses, confession leads to a moderate sentence rather than to a maximum one; if the other doesn't, it leads to freedom rather than to a minimum sentence. But confession leads to a deficient equilibrium, because dual confession results in moderate sentences, whereas a minimum sentence could be achieved by neither confessing. Hence, the dilemma" (Dawes, 1980, p. 182.)

related terms: SOCIAL DILEMMA.

PROBABILISTIC FUNCTIONALISM.

See LENS MODEL.

PROBABILISTIC INFORMATION PROCESSING.

See PIP.

PROBABILITY.

See OBJECTIVE PROBABILITY, SUBJECTIVE PROBABILITY.

PROBABILITY ESTIMATION.

See ANCHORING and ADJUSTMENT.

PROBABILITY TREE.

See DECISION TREE.

PROBABLE INFERENCE.

See INFERENCE.

PROBLEM STRUCTURING

definition: Determining the alternative courses of action, the possible states of nature, the sequencing of acts and events, the information needed about the possible states of nature, and the VALUE DIMENSIONS on which the possible outcomes differ. (See, for example, Keeney & Raiffa, 1976, p. 5, though they do not mention values.)

comment: It is widely agreed that problem structuring is usually the most important (and least understood) part of a JUDGMENT and DECISION ANALYSIS. However, as Hammond, McClelland, & Mumpower (1980, p. 159) point out, "all approaches seem to have left the problems of eliciting, defining, and transforming ATTRIBUTES as 'tricks of the trade'".

related terms: DECISION FRAME, FACT-VALUE DISTINCTION, GOAL SET, DECISION TREE.

PROCESS-TRACING MODEL

definition: A model of the sequence of operations or thoughts involved in carrying out a cognitive task (Einhorn, Kleinmuntz, & Kleinmuntz, 1979, Hogarth, 1974; Simon, 1979a). Such models are commonly developed from the verbal protocols (Newell & Simon, 1972; Payne, Braunstein, & Carroll, 1978) or eye movements (Russo & Rosen, 1975) of judges and expressed as flow diagrams or computer programs.

examples: Subjects in a MULTIPLE-CUE PROBABILITY LEARNING experiment learn to use appropriate WEIGHTS, but their introspective accounts suggest that they are learning a sequence of simple operations rather than adjusting weights (Azuma & Cronbach, 1966).

Similarly, in DECISION MAKING under RISK, the way in which

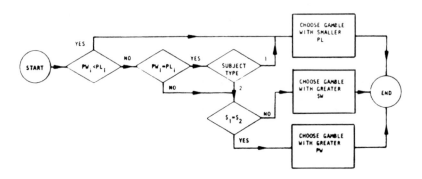

A Process-Tracing Model of Decision Making Under Risk

From Payne & Braunstein, 1971.   Copyright 1971   by   the   American
Psychological Association.   Reprinted by permission.

subjects might take into account various DIMENSIONS   of   RISK   can   be
described   in   terms of a process-tracing model.   An example of such a
model is that suggested by Payne & Braunstein (1971), based on work by
Slovic & Lichtenstein (1968), in which:

   (a) when   the   probability of winning is less than the
       probability of losing, the gamble with   the   lower
       probability of losing is chosen;

   (b) when   the   probability   of winning is greater than
       the probability of losing,   the   gamble   with   the
       greater amount to be won is chosen;

   (c) when   the   probability   of winning is equal to the
       probability   of   losing,   individual   differences
       determine whether the CHOICE is of the alternative
       with   the   lower   probability   of   losing   or   the
       alternative with the greater amount to be won.

Such   a   model can be represented in terms of a flow diagram, as shown
above.

comment: Information-processing models are to be contrasted with PARAMORPHIC, or "black box", models, which describe input-output relations statistically but do not concern themselves with the processes that intervene between input and output. Process-tracing and paramorphic models are coming to be viewed as complementary (Einhorn, Kleinmuntz, & Kleinmuntz, 1979).

synonym: INFORMATION-PROCESSING MODEL.

related terms: PARAMORPHIC MODEL.

PRODUCTION POSSIBILITY FRONTIER.

See EFFICIENT FRONTIER.

PROPER LINEAR MODEL

definition: A term coined by Dawes (1979) to refer to a LINEAR MODEL in which the WEIGHTS given to the predictor VARIABLES are chosen in such a way as to OPTIMIZE the relationship between the prediction and the criterion.

examples:
Examples are models produced by least-squares REGRESSION ANALYSIS, discriminant function analysis, and RIDGE REGRESSION.

related terms: IMPROPER LINEAR MODEL

PROPER SCORING RULE

definition: A SCORING RULE is a rule for providing JUDGES with FEEDBACK in CALIBRATION training; a proper scoring rule is a scoring rule for which the reporting strategy that yields the highest score is simply reporting one's true BELIEFS (Lichtenstein & Fischhoff, 1980; Lichtenstein, Fischhoff, & Phillips, 1977).

related terms: CALIBRATION, FEEDBACK.

PROSPECT
‾‾‾‾‾‾‾‾

definition: A prospect (x1, p1; ...; xn, pn) is "a contract that yields OUTCOME xi with PROBABILITY pi... The (RISKLESS) prospect that yields x with certainty is denoted by (x)" (Kahneman & Tversky, 1979b, p. 263.)

related terms: LOTTERY, PROSPECT THEORY.

PROSPECT THEORY
‾‾‾‾‾‾‾‾ ‾‾‾‾‾‾

definition: An "alternative", proposed by Kahneman & Tversky (1979b), to "EXPECTED UTILITY theory as a DESCRIPTIVE MODEL of DECISION MAKING under RISK" (Kahneman & Tversky, 1979b, p. 263). The model accounts for:

      a. the tendency to underweight OUTCOMES that are merely probable in comparison with outcomes that are obtained with certainty... called the CERTAINTY EFFECT, [which] contributes to RISK AVERSION in CHOICES involving sure gains and RISK SEEKING in choices involving sure losses" (Kahneman & Tversky, 1979b, p.263); and

      b. the tendency to "disregard components that are shared by all PROSPECTS under consideration ...called the ISOLATION EFFECT, which leads to inconsistent PREFERENCES when the same choice is presented in different forms", (Kahneman & Tversky, 1979b, p. 263) or DECISION FRAMES.

In prospect theory, probabilities are replaced by DECISION WEIGHTS, which are generally lower than the corresponding probabilities, except in the range of low probabilities, and VALUE is assigned to GAINS and LOSSES, rather than to final assets.

related terms: PROSPECT, EXPECTED UTILITY, CERTAINTY EFFECT, ISOLATION EFFECT, GAINS and LOSSES.

PROSPECTIVE EVALUATION.

See COST-BENEFIT ANALYSIS.

PROXIMAL.

See LENS MODEL.

PROXY ATTRIBUTE

definition: An objectively measurable VARIABLE used as an indirect MEASURE, or INDICATOR, of the extent to which a related OBJECTIVE is met (Keeney & Raiffa, 1976, p. 55ff). (See MULTIATTRIBUTE DECISION MAKING, RELEVANCE TREE.) A proxy attribute may be related to the corresponding objective as a cause, a consequence, or an otherwise partial and fallible indicator off its attainment. (See NON-REGRESSIVENESS BIAS.) "It could be argued that essentially all attributes are proxy attributes because nothing can be absolutely measured. There are just varying degrees to which an objective is directly measured" (Keeney & Raiffa, 1976, p. 55).

examples: Proxy attributes that are (assumed) causes of attainment of the corresponding objectives include (a) ambulance response time, used as a proxy for the objective "minimize probability of death on arrival" on the assumption that minimizing response time improves the patient's survival chances, and (b) monetary worth, used as a proxy for the objective "maximize UTILITY (Definition 1), or WELFARE", in the assumption that wealth contributes to material and psychological welfare. (See COST-BENEFIT ANALYSIS.) Proxy attributes that are (assumed) consequences of attainment of the corresponding objectives include (a) number of citizen complaints, used to indicate adequacy of municipal services that the complaints would concern, and (b) students' performance on standardized tests, used to indicate the adequacy of the extent to which those students have learned the corresponding topics.

comment: Rigorous use of a proxy attribute for estimating the utility of an alternative on an outcome objective involves a three-step process, incorporating FACT-VALUE SEPARATION:

        a. Estimate a (conditional) PROBABILITY distribu-

tion over the various possible levels of the
attribute, given implementation of the
alternative (FACT JUDGMENT);

b. Assess a (conditional) UTILITY function over
those attribute levels (VALUE JUDGMENT); and

c. Calculate (subjective) EXPECTED UTILITY on the
basis of (a) and (b) (analytic AGGREGATION of
fact judgments and value judgments).

The fact-value separation is not complete, however, since the
decision maker's utility judgments in step (b) must be predicated on
his/her implicit estimation of (a) a conditional *probability*
distribution over levels of attainment of the objective itself for
each proxy attribute level, and (b) a conditional *utility* function
over levels of attainment of the objective. The greater the
conceptual or temporal distance between the attribute and the
objective, the more the decision maker must rely on such implicit
estimates and the less complete the fact-value separation. See
discussion under FACT-VALUE SEPARATION.

Use of proxy attributes is one of three options identified by
Keeney & Raiffa for estimating the utility of an alternative on a
SUBJECTIVE ATTRIBUTE. The others are use of a SUBJECTIVE INDEX, which
likewise requires a three-step separation and analytic integration of
fact and value, and use of DIRECT PREFERENCE MEASUREMENT, which
collapses the three steps into a single step performed subjectively by
the decision maker. (See Keeney & Raiffa, 1976, pp. 61-62.)

related terms: DECOMPOSITION, PRESCRIPTIVE MODEL, MULTIATTRIBUTE
DECISION MAKING, DECISION THEORY.

PSYCHOLOGICAL DECISION THEORY

definition: A DESCRIPTIVE and NORMATIVE approach to JUDGMENT and
DECISION MAKING developed by Daniel Kahneman and Amos Tversky (1972,
1973, 1978, 1979a,b; Tversky & Kahneman, 1971, 1973, 1974, 1980); Paul
Slovic and Sarah Lichtenstein (Slovic & Lichtenstein, 1974) and Baruch
Fischhoff (Fischhoff, 1975; Fischhoff, Lichtenstein, & Slovic 1971).
The psychological concepts employed by Psychological Decision Theory

(PDT) include the HEURISTICS of REPRESENTATIVENESS, AVAILABILITY, and ANCHORING and ADJUSTMENT and the notion of HINDSIGHT BIAS for judgment and RISK DIMENSIONS, PREFERENCE TREES, and PROSPECT THEORY for decision making. Suggested DECISION AIDS consist of DEBIASING procedures (Kahneman & Tversky, 1979a).

synonym: PDT.

related terms: JUDGMENT vs. DECISION THEORIES, HEURISTICS, HINDSIGHT BIAS, RISK DIMENSIONS, PREFERENCE TREES, PROSPECT THEORY, BOUNDED RATIONALITY.

PUBLIC GOOD

definition: A good (commodity) that is held in common, characterized by three principal attributes (Stokey & Zeckhauser, 1978, pp. 305-308):

1. *Underprovision*. The good is underprovided in the private sector because its full cost is greater than the benefit any individual gains from it and often greater than any individual can afford, although total societal benefit exceeds total societal cost if public provision is justified.

2. *Nonrivalry*. Any one person's use does not significantly reduce another's benefit from use, though the good may be congestible (thus reducing each user's benefit) when there are many simultaneous users.

3. *Nonexcludability (nonappropriability)*. It is impossible or impracticable to exclude noncontributors (those who do not pay for benefits of use; "free riders").

"Publicness is a matter of degree" (p. 308).

examples: Military defense; police and fire protection; conventional radio broadcasts; public parks; environmental (air and water) quality.

comment: Public goods comprise the bulk of NONMARKETED GOODS

(UNPRICED GOODS). Public goods are nonmarketed (unpriced) because a good can be marketed for a price only if potential sellers can withhold it from the market if the price is not met; the nonexcludability precludes such withholding.

Public goods provide favorable externalities (see EXTERNALITY) to free riders. Public goods may provide favorable externalities to contributors as well, since if a contributor's benefits exceed his costs, the source of that excess benefit is the full set of contributors without whom the good normally would not have been provided. Provision of such a good in the private sector is an extreme case of favorable externality because the nonexcludability of noncontributors ensures that most benefits accrue to parties other than the provider. This preponderance of externalities explains (in a market whose actors are motivated primarily by self-interest rather than altruism) why public goods are underprovided in the private sector.

related terms: WILLINGNESS TO PAY, WILLINGNESS TO ACCEPT PAYMENT, BIDDING GAME, SHADOW PRICE, MARKET PRICE, COST-BENEFIT ANALYSIS, COST-EFFECTIVENESS ANALYSIS, VALUE, TRADEOFF.

PURELY SUBJECTIVE DIMENSION.

See SUBJECTIVE ATTRIBUTE.

QUALITATIVE AXIOM.

See AXIOM.

QUASI-RATIONALITY

definition: A term introduced by Brunswik (1952, pp. 23-24; 1956, pp. 89-93) to refer to processes that, while not RATIONAL, are "RATIOMORPHIC", or "REASONING-like". While the ends of rational and quasi-rational processes are the same (see also SYSTEMIC RATIONALITY). the processes, themselves, are different. Brunswik writes (1952, p. 24), "All evidence may best be summarized by designating perception as a 'quasi-rational' rather than a rational system. Perception is what Werner has labelled 'an analogous function (or process)' to reasoning,

more primitive in its organization but vested with the same purpose".
Brunswik (1952, pp. 23-24) contrasts the PROBABILISTIC FUNCTIONING
that is characteristic of perception with the deterministic
functioning that is characteristic of reasoning, emphasizing that
perception is seldom perfect but also seldom greatly in error, while
reasoning is often perfect but also often greatly in error. The
processes of quasi-rationality are "UNCERTAINTY-geared" and involve
VICARIOUS FUNCTIONING.

comment: Hammond (1966) has extended the concept of quasirationality
from a dichotomy to a continuum. Hammond & Brehmer (1973, p. 340)
write that intuitive and analytic forms of thinking "are not different
in kind; rather, they are the endpoints of a continuum. ...Most
instances of thinking will have *both* intuitive and analytical
components. We will refer to this composite as *quasi-rational
thought*." They (1973, p. 340) define the ends of the COGNITIVE
CONTINUUM as follows: "The ANALYTICAL end of the continuum is
characterized by a form of thinking that is *explicit*, *sequential*, and
recoverable. That is, it consists of a series of steps that transform
information according to certain rules. These rules, whatever they
are, can be reported by the thinker.... INTUITIVE thinking, on the
other hand, is *implicit*, *nonsequential*, and *nonrecoverable*. Usually,
the thinker can report no more than the outcome of his thinking."
Hammond (1980) has compared quasi-rationality with Simon's BOUNDED
RATIONALITY.

related terms: BOUNDED RATIONALITY, SYSTEMIC RATIONALITY,
RATIONALITY, VICARIOUS FUNCTIONING, LENS MODEL.

RANGE-ADJUSTED WEIGHT.

See WEIGHT.

RANGE EFFECT.

See WEIGHT.

RATIO.
___

See SCALES of MEASUREMENT.

RATIOMORPHIC.
___

See QUASI-RATIONALITY.

RATIONALIST APPROACH to PROBABILITY.
___

See SUBJECTIVE PROBABILITY.

RATIONALITY
___

suggested definition: Justifiability of VALUES, BELIEFS, and/or behavior in terms of the principles of inductive and deductive REASONING.

comment: According to Webster's (1976, p. 1885), "rational usu. implies a latent or active power to make logical INFERENCES and draw conclusions that enable one to understand the world about him and relate such knowledge to the attainment of ends.... in application to policies, projects, or acts, rational implies satisfactory to the reason or chiefly activated by reason". According to the philosopher Lonergan (1970), "...Rational consciousness...is the emergence and the effective operation of a single law of utmost generality, the law of sufficient reason..." (p. 322). Rational consciousness "seeks groundedness for objects of thought" (p. 323). "...I become rationally *self*-conscious [emphasis added] inasmuch as I am concerned with reasons for my own acts..." (p. 611). "Man is not only a knower but also a doer; the same intelligent and rational consciousness grounds the doing as well as the knowing; and from that identity of consciousness there springs inevitably an exigence for self-consistency in knowing and doing" (p. 599). By embracing the principles of inductive reasoning, as well as those of deductive reasoning, both Webster's and Lonergan's definitions would reject, for example, as not rational the beliefs of a paranoid that, while internally consistent, fail to satisfy the inductive requirement of falsifiability.

Those workers in JUDGMENT and DECISION MAKING who have addressed the question of rationality, while not denying the importance of inductive reasoning, have tended to emphasize principles of deductive reasoning. The dominant view is that rational beliefs are logically consistent (see BAYES' THEOREM), rational PREFERENCES are TRANSITIVE, and rational behavior is behavior that MAXIMIZES EXPECTED UTILITY (or, alternatively, SUBJECTIVE EXPECTED UTILITY), though views of rationality based on MINIMAX principles have also been put forth. (See, e.g., Simon, 1957, p. 245; Edwards, 1954; Coombs, Dawes, & Tversky, 1970, p. 122; Luce & Raiffa, 1957, p. 5; Rapoport & Chammah, 1965, p. 14.) Rationality in the context of competitive GAMES has also been defined in terms of choosing those courses of action "which are most conducive to maximizing one's own payoff" (Rapoport & Chammah, 1965, p. 14).

However, Hammond, McClelland, & Mumpower (1980, pp. 58-59) observe that "In Group I [DT, BDT, and PDT], evaluation of the subjects' decision behavior is carried out with reference to the decision behavior of a mathematical model of rationality; the model is used to evaluate logical correctness.... ...No empirically correct answer need be available in order to evaluate the subjects' behavior....

"BAYESIAN research and PDT research move one step closer to empirical, as against logical, evaluation of the subjects' performance by calculating the correct answer to a decision problem through the use of a statistical model....

"In contrast, on the other side of the conceptual watershed, when SJT and AT evaluate subjects' performance in judgment tasks they do so in terms of the subjects' ACHIEVEMENT of an *empirical* criterion."

March (1978) distinguishes between "CALCULATED RATIONALITY", where "action is presumed to follow...from explicit calculation of its consequences in terms of OBJECTIVES" (p. 591) and "SYSTEMIC RATIONALITY" (which, together with calculated rationality, appears to exhaust the possible meanings of "ADAPTIVE behavior"), where "action is presumed to follow...from rules of behavior that have evolved through processes that are sensible but which obscure from present knowledge full information on the rational justification for any specific rule" (p. 591). Simon (1955, 1979b) points to processes of BOUNDED RATIONALITY. And Brunswik (1952, 1956) and Hammond (Hammond & Brehmer, 1973; Hammond, Stewart, Brehmer, & Steinmann, 1975) point to

QUASIRATIONAL processes, such as those involved in judgment, that are some mix of INTUITIVE and ANALYTIC processes and more "RATIOMORPHIC" than rational.

related terms: BOUNDED RATIONALITY, QUASI-RATIONALITY, VIGILANCE, AXIOM, TRANSITIVITY, MAXIMIZATION, EXPECTED UTILITY, SUBJECTIVE EXPECTED UTILITY, MIMINAX, DECISION AID.

REASONING.

See INFERENCE, RATIONALITY.

REDUNDANCY

definition: The presence of more information than is necessary to perform a given task. The presence of "surplus information" (Evans, 1967.)

comment: There seem to be two kinds of redundancy, which have opposite effects on patterns as well as opposite implications for performance (Alluisi, 1960.) Evans (1967, p. 104) calls attention to the following two lists:

WA 5-3172	872-3185
WA 5-7393	296-2618
WA 5-8286	513-2366

"In which list are the examples more redundant? The answer depends on the purpose involved. If one is going to memorize the lists, the first list is more redundant because a part of each item is surplus; it need not be memorized for each item. But if one is going to discriminate between pairs of items, the second list exhibits greater redundancy because pairs of items in the second list have more elements differing between them" (Evans, 1967, p. 104).

The first list illustrates what Evans (1967, p. 105) calls "SCHEMATIC REDUNDANCY." "This term is derived from suggestions by Woodworth (1938), Attneave (1957), and Oldfield (1954) that humans make use of the common (or redundant) aspects of a family of patterns by abstracting and encoding those aspects which partially describe every member of the family. An individual pattern may then be remembered by storing only those aspects which are not correctly given by the schema" (Evans, 1967, pp. 104-105). The second list illustrates what Evans (1967, p. 105) calls "DISCRIMINATION REDUNDANCY" because the information is "surplus with respect to a discrimination task".

"In terms of a schema-plus-correction hypothesis, we may conceive of a pattern as partitioned into two subsets of ATTRIBUTES, those which belong to the schema and those which are distinctive and belong to the correction portion of the description. Schematic redundancy is increased by increasing the schema set; discrimination redundancy, by increasing the correction set" (Evans, 1967, p. 105).

Shannon and Weaver (1949) defined the redundancy of a source as "one minus the relative entropy." In symbols, this definition may be expressed as:

$$R_S = 1 - H_a/H_{max}.$$

where Ha represents the actual UNCERTAINTY of the source while Hmax represents the maximum possible uncertainty. Increasing Hmax tends to make patterns more complex and more different, while decreasing Ha makes patterns simpler and more similar. Yet "both operations have the same effect on the redundancy measure. Technical redundancy cannot serve satisfactorily as a psychological variable in the context of pattern perception unless distinction is made between the two methods of producing redundancy" (Evans, 1967, p. 105).

The kind of redundancy that seems to have been studied in JUDGMENT and DECISION tasks is schematic redundancy. For example, in an IMPRESSION FORMATION task, the descriptive adjectives "handsome" and "attractive" would be redundant in the sense of schematic redundancy. Redundant and INCONSISTENT information has been found to have less impact in impression formation tasks than INDEPENDENT information (Anderson & Jacobson, 1965; Wyer, 1968, 1970). However, in MULTIPLE-CUE PROBABILITY LEARNING tasks, subjects' BETA WEIGHTS match the CUE-criterion correlations, rather than the cue-criterion beta weights, indicating a failure to take account of redundancy (Armelius & Lenntoft, 1970; Naylor & Schenck, 1968).

When cues are *positively* correlated, a variety of strategies (CONJUNCTIVE, DISJUNCTIVE, LINEAR; Einhorn, Kleinmuntz, & Kleinmuntz, 1979) and a variety of weighting schemes (Dawes & Corrigan, 1974) will classify alternatives similarly. As Einhorn, et al. (1979, p. 480) point out, "this has two implications: (a) from the organism's perspective, the benefits of using one strategy or another may be so small as to make the simpler, NONCOMPENSATORY strategies preferable.... (b) from an experimental point of view, unless cues are negatively correlated, the ability to discriminate among competing strategies will be greatly diminished."

In MULTIPLE-OBJECTIVE DECISION MAKING, failure to take account of schematic redundancy in GOAL SETS leads to DOUBLE COUNTING.

synonyms: VICARIOUS **MEDIATION**.

related terms: DOUBLE COUNTING, VICARIOUS MEDIATION, CONFLICT, INDEPENDENCE.

REFERENCE EFFECT

definition: "Changes in PREFERENCES due to a shift in the reference point [or "adaptation level," or DECISION FRAME] are called reference effects" (Tversky, 1977, p. 212).

example: "...The consequences of DECISIONS are commonly perceived and evaluated as positive or negative changes from some neutral reference point" (Tversky, 1977, p. 212). Changing the reference point can change the preference ordering among a given set of alternatives. When people are asked to evaluate total number of fatalities, for example, "zero fatalities is the natural reference point, and most people prefer an even chance of losing 500 lives or nothing to an even chance of losing 100 or 400 lives When the problem is stated in terms of changes in the number of fatalities, the current level serves as the reference point. Suppose the current (yearly) death toll is 500 lives; the problem then becomes a CHOICE between an even chance to save 500 lives or nothing and an even chance to save 100 or 400 lives. Here, almost all respondents prefer the latter option, contrary to their earlier choice" (Tversky, 1977, p. 215.)

comment: The manner in which the problem is formulated can affect one's reference point, and this, in turn, can affect the shape of the UTILITY CURVE.

related terms: DECISION FRAME, PROBLEM STRUCTURING, PROSPECT THEORY, ANCHORING and ADJUSTMENT.

REFLECTION EFFECT

definition: The fact that the CERTAINTY EFFECT leads to "RISK AVERSION in the positive domain" and "RISK-SEEKING in the negative domain," thus distinguishing it from ATTITUDE TOWARD RISK as an effect that increases the aversiveness of losses as well as the desirability of gains (Kahnemann & Tversky, 1979b, pp. 268f.)

example: Preference for a sure gain (e.g., 3000 for sure) to a larger gain that is merely PROBABLE (e.g., a .80 chance on 4000) illustrates risk-aversion in the positive domain. Preference for a loss that is merely probable (e.g., a .80 chance on a loss of 4000) over a smaller loss that is certain (e.g., a loss of 3000 for sure) illustrates risk-seeking in the negative domain.

related terms: CERTAINTY EFFECT, RISK AVERSION, RISK SEEKING.

REGRESSION ANALYSIS

definition: Analysis of the predictability of a criterion on the basis of one or more predictors that takes into account the degree of correlation between each predictor and the criterion and thus the extent to which the predictor would be expected to REGRESS TOWARDS THE MEAN. Includes multiple regression, analysis of variance, analysis of covariance, and canonical correlation.

comment: The OPTIMALITY of regression analysis depends on the acceptance of a built-in PAYOFF function: the least-squares criterion of goodness of fit. The POSTERIOR PROBABILITIES of the BAYESIAN model, by way of contrast, can be combined with any payoff function (Slovic & Lichtenstein, 1973, pp. 39f.)

related terms: MULTIPLE REGRESSION, BETA WEIGHT, MULTIVARIATE ANALYSIS.

REGRESSION COEFFICIENT.

   See BETA WEIGHT.

REGRESSION TOWARDS the MEAN

definition: The tendency for the true VALUE to lie closer to the mean than the predicted value.

example: Consider two VARIABLES X and Y, which have the same distribution. If one selects individuals whose average score departs from the mean of X by k standard deviations, their average departure from the mean of Y will ordinarily be less than k standard deviations. If X is parent's adult height and Y is child's adult height, regression toward the mean is the tendency for tall parents to have children shorter than themselves and short parents to have children taller than themselves. Height thus regresses towards the mean.

comment: The amount of regression depends on the correlation between X and Y. If the correlation between X and Y is 1.00, there will be no regression. If the correlation is 0, regression will be all the way to the mean, that is, the EXPECTED VALUE of Y will be the mean of Y, no matter what the value of X.

related terms: REGRESSION ANALYSIS, NON-REGRESSIVENESS BIAS, DIAGNOSTICITY.

REGRESSION WEIGHT.

   See BETA WEIGHT.

REGRET.

   See MINIMAX REGRET CRITERION.

REGRET MATRIX.

   See MINIMAX REGRET CRITERION.

RELATIVE WEIGHT.

See WEIGHT.

RELEVANCE TREE

definition: A TREE of superordinate and subordinate OBJECTIVES that indicates the degree of relevance of each subordinate objective for the achievement of its superordinate objective. The lowest levels in such a tree would ordinarily represent ATTRIBUTES.

comment: The TREE structure tends to ensure that the set of objectives, or GOAL SET, involves no DOUBLE COUNTING and that it is complete. (The DIMENSIONS in a goal set should also be checked for INDEPENDENCE.)

The relevance of a subordinate objective for the objective immediately superordinate to it is indicated by an index that ranges from 0 to 1.00 and that sums to 1.00 for all the objectives immediately subordinate to the same objective. The relevance of a subordinate objective for objectives not immediately superordinate to it is obtained by calculation. For example, if an objective at Level III has a relevance index of .20 for its superordinate objective at Level II, and this objective, in turn, has a relevance index of .10 for its superordinate objective at Level I, then one can multiply these relevance indices to obtain .20 x .10 = .02 for the relevance of the objective at Level III to the objective at Level I.

synonym: GOAL TREE (in which case one speaks of goals and subgoals).

related terms: GOAL, TREE, DOUBLE-COUNTING, INDEPENDENCE, INFERENCE, WEIGHT, MULTIOBJECTIVE DECISION MAKING.

REPRESENTATION THEOREM.

See AXIOM.

REPRESENTATIVE DESIGN

definition: A form of experimental design in which the independent
VARIABLES are arranged to be representative of the ecological
conditions toward which the experimenter wishes to generalize
(Brunswik, 1956, especially pp. 7-10; see also Hammond, 1966). To be
contrasted with conventional SYSTEMATIC DESIGN, in which the
independent variables are manipulated without regard to ecological
generalization.

comment: The concept of representative design of experiments was
introduced by Brunswik in 1947 (see Brunswik, 1956; Hammond, 1966) to
counteract what he called a "double-standard" in psychological
research: whereas subjects are carefully sampled in order to satisfy
the logic of statistical INFERENCE, experimental situations are not.
Particularly cogent examples of this "double-standard" can still be
found in research in the social psychology of JUDGMENT, where
experiments are designed in which many and carefully sampled subjects
judge the attributes of only one person. The results are thus
contingent upon the particular characteristics of the person judged
and cannot be expected to hold when a new experimenter employs a
different person with different characteristics to be judged.
(Examples are provided in Hammond, 1980.) More specifically,
representative design calls for ecological representativeness with
regard to the manner in which the independent variables of the
experiment are varied. According to Brunswik, the "generalizability
of results concerning...the [independent] variables must remain
limited unless at least the RANGE, but better also the
distribution...of each variable, has been made representative of a
carefully defined set of conditions" (1956, p. 53). Representative
design also calls for the covariation between the independent
variables of an experiment to be ecologically representative. The
conventional factorial design of experiments fails to meet this
requirement because in this design independent variables are
arbitrarily made to be orthogonal to one another, whereas this is
seldom the case in the real world. In Brunswik's terms, orthogonal
arrangements "systematically untie" variables that are "ecologically
tied", yet experimenters arbitrarily generalize their results from the
factorial experiment to the organism's nonfactorial ecology.

The concept of representative design is of particular importance
in judgment and DECISION research because in this field generalization
over task conditions (the main point of representative design) has

generally been of greater concern than generalization over subjects. Therefore, many researchers in this field have made efforts to arrange their task conditions (e.g., number of CUES, range and distribution of cue VALUES, covariation between cues) to be representative of real-world task conditions. For a brief history of representative design and an appraisal of its current status, see Hammond & Wascoe (1980). See also Meehl (1978) for a general criticism of conventional methodology in psychology in which the importance of Brunswik's critique is indicated.

related terms: SYSTEMATIC DESIGN.

REPRESENTATIVENESS

definition: A judgmental HEURISTIC, identified by Kahneman and Tversky (1972, 1973), according to which the SUBJECTIVE PROBABILITY of an event is judged by the degree to which the event is similar to (representative of) its parent population or reflects the features of the process by which it is generated. (See SCRIPT.) Thus, the sequence of heads and tails, HHTHTH, is seen to be more probable (presumably because it is more like a random sequence) than the sequence, HHHTTT, though they are equally probable. And the description, "meticulous, introverted, meek, and solemn," is seen as more probably describing an engineer than a lawyer. (See also Dale, 1968; Lichtenstein & Feeney, 1968.)

comment: This heuristic ignores such factors as base rate, (see BASE-RATE FALLACY) sample size (see LAW of SMALL NUMBERS), and REGRESSION TOWARDS the MEAN (see NON-REGRESSIVENESS BIAS).

Subjects who were presented with the description, "meticulous, introverted, meek, and solemn," and told that it described a man who had been drawn at random from 70 engineers and 30 lawyers, and subjects who were presented with the same description but told that it described a man who had been drawn at random from 30 engineers and 70 lawyers, gave essentially the same JUDGMENTS of the probability that the man was an engineer. Apparently, subjects evaluated the likelihood that a particular description belonged to an engineer rather than to a lawyer by the degree to which this description was representative of the respective stereotypes, with little or no regard for the PRIOR PROBABILITIES of the two outcomes. Representativeness thus leads to the base-rate fallacy.

The major difference between AVAILABILITY and representativeness is that the former evaluates subjective probability by "the difficulty of retrieval or construction of instances," thus focussing on "the particular instances, or the denotation of the event"; whereas the latter evaluates subjective probability by the degree of correspondence between the sample and the population, or between an occurrence and a model," thus focussing on "the generic features, or the connotation, of the event." "Thus, the representation heuristic is more likely to be employed when events are characterized in terms of their general properties; whereas the availability heuristic is more likely to be employed when events are more naturally thought of in terms of specific occurrences." (Kahneman & Tversky, 1972, pp. 451-452.)

related terms: HEURISTIC, SUBJECTIVE PROBABILITY, BASE-RATE FALLACY, SCRIPT, AVAILABILITY, ANCHORING-and-ADJUSTMENT, NON-REGRESSIVENESS BIAS, LAW of SMALL NUMBERS.

RESPONSE LINEARITY.

See COGNITIVE CONTROL.

RETRACEABILITY

definition 1: Sufficient completeness and clarity in one's own mental representation of a cognitive process one has engaged in to enable one to retrace the steps in the process.

definition 2: Sufficient completeness and clarity in the description of a process (e.g., a POLICY analysis) to enable another party to retrace the steps in the process.

general comment: Retraceability is one of the criteria employed to evaluate the quality of a DECISION-MAKING process. The inability to explicate the reasons for taking one branch or another at a CHOICE point diminishes the quality of a decision process (though not necessarily of the decision). Lack of retraceability leads to interpersonal CONFLICT (Brehmer & Hammond, 1977).

RETROSPECTIVE EVALUATION.

See COST-BENEFIT ANALYSIS.

REVEALED PREFERENCE

definition: The use of actual CHOICES as a basis for inferring degree of BELIEF, or SUBJECTIVE PROBABILITY, (Ramsey, 1931; Savage, 1954) and PREFERENCE, or UTILITY, (von Neumann & Morgenstern, 1947). The choices may be in either a MARKET situation or an experimental situation (MacCrimmon & Siu, 1974, p. 98).

comment: This approach was pioneered by Samuelson (1938, 1947, 1948). (See Edwards, 1954, pp. 385 f.) Of course, factors that might affect utility must be controlled in assessing subjective probability, and factors that might affect subjective probability must be controlled in assessing utility; or these factors must be varied orthogonally and some A-POSTERIORI-DECOMPOSITION technique such as FUNCTIONAL MEASUREMENT (Shanteau, 1975) or CONJOINT MEASUREMENT (Tversky, 1967) must be used to measure them simultaneously. The method assumes, not only that probabilities can be separated from preferences, but also that the choice was OPTIMAL (Keeney & Raiffa, 1976, p. 18). Thus, a caution in the use of this method is suggested by those studies that suggest that people do not always MAXIMIZE SEU (though revealed preference can be based on models other than the SEU model). See PROSPECT THEORY, ALLAIS' PARADOX, ELLSBERG PARADOX.

Hammond, McClelland, & Mumpower (1980, p. 136) observe that "The Group I approaches [DT, BDT, and PDT] with their DECISION THEORY origins tend to use choice methods for collecting data.... On the other hand, the Group II approaches [SJT, IIT, and AT] usually have the subject make ratings on numerical scales...."

related terms: SUBJECTIVE PROBABILITY, UTILITY, ELLSBERG PARADOX, ANCHORING and ADJUSTMENT, ALLAIS' PARADOX, PROSPECT THEORY.

RIDGE REGRESSION

definition: A method of REGRESSION ANALYSIS for use with intercorrelated predictors that achieves a "major reduction" (Marquardt, 1970, p. 591) in the variance of the REGRESSION

COEFFICIENTS by adding small positive quantities to the diagonal of the correlation matrix. This reduction in variance is achieved at the cost of introducing a "small amount of BIAS" (Marquardt, 1970, p. 591).

comment: When the predictor VARIABLES are intercorrelated, the regression coefficients estimated by ordinary least-squares regression analysis "are often too large in absolute value and the sign of the coefficients can be wrong" (Newman, 1977, p. i). Because those estimated by ridge regression tend, despite the bias, to be closer to the "true" coefficients, they tend to cross-validate better and to make better sense in terms of the underlying psychological processes. On the basis of accumulating evidence (e.g., Lawless & Wang, 1976; Hoerl, Kennard, & Baldwin, 1975; Price, 1977; Dempster, Schatzoff, & Wermuth, 1975; Newman, 1977), Newman (1977, p. 44) concludes:

> "...With proper choice of k, the bias constant, [ridge regression] will always be better than OLS [ordinary least-squares regression] when there are intercorrelations between the predictor variables and will do as well as OLS when the intercorrelations between the predictors are zero or near zero. On the basis of what has been discovered so far, it is now clear that OLS should not, in general, be used by behavioral scientists."

However, Rozenboom (1979, p. 242) states:

> "...Ridge regression can indeed improve upon the accuracy of traditional estimates of regression parameters if background circumstances are right. But if they are not right--and how to diagnose this remains obscure--ridge regression incurs a loss of estimational accuracy."

related terms: REGRESSION ANALYSIS, REDUNDANCY, LINEAR MODEL.

RISK

definition 1: A situation in which there are a number of alternative states of nature and one does not know which of them has occurred or will occur--as used in the terms RISKY and RISKLESS DECISION MAKING or

CHOICE, RISK PREMIUM, RISK AVERSION, and RISK PRONENESS (Raiffa, 1968; Keeney & Raiffa, 1976).

comment regarding definition 1: Hammond, McClelland, & Mumpower (1980, p. 181) observe that "DT, BDT, and PDT are ordinarily concerned with such 'risky' DECISION MAKING, or decision making under conditions of UNCERTAINTY, although DT and BDT are increasingly also concerned with 'riskless' decision making, or decision making under conditions of certainty. SJT, IIT, and AT, on the other hand, are ordinarily concerned with riskless decision making...."

synonym for definition 1: Definition 1 of UNCERTAINTY.

definition 2: A situation where there are a number of alternative possible states of nature and one does not know which of them has occurred or will occur (as in Definition 1), but one *does* know the PROBABILITY of occurrence of each (Knight, 1921; Luce & Raiffa, 1957, p. 13). An earlier usage explicitly contrasted with definition 2 of UNCERTAINTY.

comment regarding definition 2: The usual basis for knowledge of probabilities of alternative states of nature is past relative frequency of occurrence (see OBJECTIVE PROBABILITY). The PRESCRIPTIVE strategy for decision making under risk is MAXIMIZATION of EXPECTED UTILITY (Raiffa, 1968). Definition 2 is passing out of common use.

definition 3: "The possibility of loss, injury, disadvantage, or destruction" (Webster's Unabridged, 1976, p. 1962). A situation where there are a number of alternative states of nature (as in Definition 1) and at least one of them would involve serious loss, as in the phrase "at risk" or RISK ASSESSMENT (Kates, 1978;; Otway & Pahnen, 1976; Slovic & Fischhoff, in press). "I prefer to define 'risk' as a compound measure of the probability and magnitude of adverse effect" (Lowrance, 1980, p. 6). One may or may not know the probabilities of occurrence of the alternative states.

related terms: RISKY DECISION MAKING, RISK PREMIUM, RISK ASSESSMENT, OBJECTIVE PROBABILITY, EXPECTED UTILITY, UNCERTAINTY, ELLSBERG PARADOX, VARIANCE PREFERENCES, RISK DIMENSIONS, CONFLICT, CONFLICT THEORY, TECHNOLOGY ASSESSMENT.

RISK ASSESSMENT.

See ENVIRONMENTAL IMPACT ASSESSMENT.

RISK AVERSION.

See EXPECTED UTILITY, VON NEUMANN-MORGENSTERN UTILITY.

RISK DIMENSIONS.

See VARIANCE PREFERENCES.

RISK NEUTRALITY.

See VON NEUMANN-MORGENSTERN UTILITY.

RISK PREMIUM

definition: The premium (**INSURANCE PREMIUM**, in the broadest sense) one would be willing to pay in order to avoid risk. The EXPECTED VALUE of a LOTTERY minus its CERTAINTY EQUIVALENT.

example: If a person is indifferent between $100 for certain and a lottery that gives a .50 chance on $200 and a .50 chance on $0, the certainty equivalent for the lottery is $100. The risk premium is, then, the expected value of .50($200) + .50($0) = $100 minus the certainty equivalent of $100, or $0. Most persons would prefer $100 for certain to a .50 .50 chance on $200 or $0. Their certainty equivalent for this lottery would be less than $100. If the certainty equivalent for this lottery is, say, $75, then the risk premium is $100 - $75 = $25.

comment: A positive risk premium indicates RISK AVERSION; a negative risk premium, RISK PRONENESS.

synonym: INSURANCE PREMIUM.

related terms: UTILITY, WILLINGNESS to PAY.

RISK PRONENESS.

See VON NEUMANN-MORGENSTERN UTILITY.

RISK SEEKING.

See RISK PRONENESS.

RISKLESS.

See RISK.

RISKY.

See RISK.

ROLLING BACK.

See FOLDING BACK.

RULE LEARNING.

See CONCEPT LEARNING.

SATISFICING

definition: Selecting the first course of action that is satisfactory, in that it meets a certain ASPIRATION LEVEL, or set of aspiration levels (Simon, 1957, pp. 204-205; 1976.) An executive looking for a new job, for example, is likely to settle for the first one to come along that meets his minimal requirements--satisfactory pay, good chance for advancement, adequate working conditions, and location within commuting distance of his home. To be contrasted with MAXIMIZATION.

comment: Simon (1957, 1976) argues that satisficing fits the limited information-processing capabilities, or BOUNDED RATIONALITY, of human beings. Our limited ability to foresee future consequences and to obtain information about the variety of available alternatives inclines us to settle for a course of action that is simply better than things are now.

related terms: BOUNDED RATIONALITY, HEURISTICS, MAXIMIZATION, ASPIRATION LEVEL, CONJUNCTIVE and DISJUNCTIVE MODELS, NONCOMPENSATORY MODEL.

SCALES of MEASUREMENT

definition: "The type of scale achieved when we deputize the numerals to serve as representatives for a state of affairs in nature depends upon the character of the basic empirical operations performed on nature. These operations are limited ordinarily by the peculiarities of the thing being scaled and by our choice of concrete procedures, but, once selected, the procedures determine that there will eventuate one or another of four types of scale: *nominal*, *ordinal*, *interval*, or *ratio*. Each of these four classes of scales is best characterized by its range of invariance--by the kinds of transformations that leave the 'structure' of the scale undistorted. And the nature of the invariance sets limits to the kinds of statistical manipulations that can legitimately be applied to the scaled data" (Stevens, 1951, p. 23).

examples: The most commonly considered scales of measurement are nominal, ordinal, ordered-metric, interval, ratio, and absolute. (See Stevens, 1951, pp. 23 ff; Coombs, Dawes, & Tversky, 1970, pp. 14 ff.)

A NOMINAL scale represents simply identity. Any distinctness-preserving transformation is permitted. An example of a nominal scale would be numbers used to identify alternative courses of action: A1, A2, A3, etc. Alternatives identified as 1, 2, and 3 can be represented by any other numbers whatsoever, so long as no two alternatives are assigned the same number.

An ORDINAL scale represents ordinal relations among points. Only order-preserving, or MONOTONIC, transformations are permitted. An example of an ordinal scale would be ORDINAL UTILITY, or PREFERENCE. Preference of strawberry to chocolate, and chocolate to vanilla can be represented by assigning the numbers 1, 2, and 3 to vanilla, chocolate, and strawberry, respectively. These ordinal relations could just as well be represented, however, by 1, 20, and 300; -5, 0, and +.33; etc.

An ORDERED-METRIC scale represents ordinal relations among differences between points. The allowable transformations for ordered-metric scales are not easy to state (see Krantz, Luce, Suppes, & Tversky, 1971, p. 431; and McClelland & Coombs, 1975). An ordered metric scale could be constructed, for example, if one were to rank order different automobile brands according to say, luxuriousness and in addition rank order the differences between brands (e.g., "the difference between a Buick and a Cadillac in terms of luxuriousness is smaller than the difference between a Buick and a Rabbit"). Ordered-metric scales are produced by UNFOLDING (Coombs, 1964) and by finite additive CONJOINT MEASUREMENT (Krantz, Luce, Suppes, & Tversky, 1971, p. 431). Given enough information on the ordering of distances between points it is possible to produce "interval-like" scales (McClelland & Coombs, 1975).

An INTERVAL scale, sometimes called a LINEAR SCALE, represents ratios among differences between points. Only interval-preserving or positive LINEAR, transformations are permitted. An example of an interval scale would be CARDINAL UTILITY (including von NEUMANN-MORGENSTERN UTILITY). Thus, the utilities .10, .20, and .30, for example, indicate that the difference in utility between the first and second elements is equal to that between the second and third elements. This fact could just as well be represented by the numbers 1, 2, and 3 (multiplication by a constant), or 1.1, 1.2, and 1.3 (addition of a constant); or 15, 25, and 35 (both multiplication by a constant and addition of a constant.)

A RATIO scale represents ratios among points. The difference between an interval scale and a ratio scale is illustrated by the Centigrade and Kelvin scales of temperature. While both have arbitrary units, only the Kelvin scale has a true zero (one that represents no temperature at all.) Another way of saying this is that an interval scale has two degrees of freedom (its zero and its unit); two numbers can be changed arbitrarily, but then the rest are determined by the scale. A ratio scale has only one degree of freedom (its unit); one number can be changed arbitrarily, but then (since the zero is already fixed) the rest are determined by the scale. Only ratio-preserving transformations (multiplication by a constant) are permitted by a ratio scale. One example of a ratio scale is importance WEIGHT. To assign weights of .10, .20, and .30 to different dimensions is to assert that the second is twice as important as the first and that the third is three times as important as the first. The numbers 1, 2, and 3; or 7, 14, and 21, for example, would do as well. Another example of a ratio scale is PROBABILITY. While zero probability is fixed, the unit can be varied by allowing the probabilities to sum to numbers other than 1 (i.e., by multiplying by a constant.)

An ABSOLUTE scale represents absolute quantities. No transformation whatsoever is permitted. Counting, viewed as MEASUREMENT, provides an example of an absolute scale.

A METRIC scale is one that has a metric, or unit of measurement. Metric scales include interval, ratio, and absolute scales and may, depending upon the writer, include ordered-metric scales.

related terms: MEASUREMENT.

SCALING.

  See MEASUREMENT.

SCALING CONSTANT.

  See WEIGHT.

SCENARIO

definition 1: A possible future course of events.

comment: Each ENDPOINT on a DECISION TREE corresponds to a scenario.

definition 2: A detailed consideration of a possible future course of events.

related terms: ENDPOINT.

SCHEMATIC REDUNDANCY.

See REDUNDANCY.

SCORING RULE.

See PROPER SCORING RULE.

SCREENING.

See CONJUNCTIVE and DISJUNCTIVE MODELS.

SCRIPT

definition: Defined by Abelson (1976; Shank & Abelson, 1977), the originator of the term, as a coherent sequence of events expected by the individual, involving him either as a participant or as an observer.

comment: Scripts, according to Abelson (1976), may be episodic, categorical, or hypothetical. Abelson illustrates these kinds of scripts in terms of the example of a faculty admissions committee member deciding on the likely success in graduate school of an applicant.

In the episodic case, "a past single case would be recalled [see AVAILABILITY], similar to the present applicant. ('Mr. Kolodny reminds me very much of Paul Pippik, who hung around for eight years never writing his dissertation. Let's not get into that again')" (Abelson, 1976, p. 37).

"In the categorical variant, a generic type would be invoked by assimilating [see REPRESENTATIVENESS] the applicant to a category (She's one of those shy women types. They do well in courses, but don't have enough initiative in research,' or 'He's one of those guys who writes about all this existential stuff, and ends up wanting to go into clinical psych')" (Abelson, 1976, p. 37).

"At a more abstract level, the applicant can be seen as a bundle of pros and cons, whose success is a hypothetical variable darkly contingent on all the important enumerable features. An obscure computation is necessary to compare one applicant with another ('Her letters are better than his, although she's from a less well-known place. Her verbal GRE is much higher than his. On the other hand, he's had more math and his quantitative is higher. However, ...'). It is at this level that judges evidently function as if they were mediocre linear processors." (See LINEAR MODEL.) Decisions at this level are "conflictful and unconfident" (Abelson, 1976, p. 37.)

related terms: CAUSAL SCHEMA, AVAILABILITY, REPRESENTATIVENESS, LINEAR MODEL.

SELLING PRICE.

See WILLINGNESS to PAY.

SENSITIVITY ANALYSIS

definition: Determination of the extent to which the decision is affected by, or sensitive to, variations in various aspects of the process by which the final ordering of the alternatives was arrived at.

example: To perform a sensitivity analysis on a given PROBABILITY estimate, one would determine how much this probability estimate would have to be changed in order to change which alternative is ranked first. If a small change in the probability is sufficient to change the decision, the decision is said to be "sensitive" to this probability estimate. If a large change in the probability is necessary to change the decision, the decision is said to be "insensitive" to this probability estimate.

comment: Sensitivity analyses help to identify critical assumptions, those areas in which more precise information is desirable. See BREAK-EVEN ANALYSIS.

related terms: UNCERTAINTY, RISK, BREAK-EVEN ANALYSIS.

SEU.

See SUBJECTIVE EXPECTED UTILITY.

SHADOW PRICE (ACCOUNTING PRICE)

definition 1:   Shadow prices (accounting prices) are "Estimates of social benefits or social losses that are either unpriced or not satisfactorily priced" in existing markets (see MARKET PRICE); (Mishan, 1976, p. 82). Unpriced benefits or losses largely involve NONMARKETED GOODS. Unsatisfactory pricing can be due to numerous market imperfections, including the existence of major EXTERNALITIES.

definition 2:   In MATHEMATICAL PROGRAMMING, shadow (accounting) prices are those "implicit in exchanges that should be made to maximize a particular OBJECTIVE FUNCTION (or to minimize a cost function)" (McKean, 1968, p. 33). See MAXIMIZATION. "The shadow price tells us what it would be worth [in terms of level achieved of an objective function] to relax a particular constraint by one unit." (Stokey & Zeckhauser, 1978, p. 188; see also Sen, 1972, p. 487).

comment: Definition 1 is the most relevant to COST-BENEFIT ANALYSIS and to COST-EFFECTIVENESS ANALYSIS. A theme common to both definitions is the notion that market prices will often, if not always, be insufficient for complete valuation of benefits and costs. Another common theme (evident particularly in Definition 2) is the importance of clarifying the OPPORTUNITY COSTS of action and of constraints on action. Opportunity costs are usually less evident than direct financial costs, but are no less important for rational decision making (Rothenberg, 1975; Stokey & Zeckhauser, 1978).

related terms: COST-BENEFIT ANALYSIS, COST-EFFECTIVENESS ANALYSIS, MARKET PRICE, NONMARKETED GOODS, EXTERNALITIES, MATHEMATICAL PROGRAMMING, MAXIMIZATION, OPPORTUNITY COST, SURROGATE PRICE.

SIA.

See SOCIAL IMPACT ASSESSMENT.

SIMPLE MULTIATTRIBUTE RATING TECHNIQUE.

See SMART.

SINGLE-PEAKED PREFERENCE FUNCTION.

See PORTFOLIO THEORY.

SINGLE-SYSTEM CASE.

See COGNITIVE SYSTEM.

SJT.

See SOCIAL JUDGMENT THEORY.

SMART

definition: A *S*imple *M*ulti*A*ttribute *R*ating *T*echnique (Edwards, 1971) for MULTIATTRIBUTE UTILITY MEASUREMENT, designed "not toward mathematical sophistication" but for usefulness "in environments in which time is short and DECISION MAKERS are multiple and busy." (Gardiner & Edwards, 1975, pp. 13.) The technique consists of the following ten steps (Gardiner & Edwards, 1975, pp. 12-19):

"*Step 1*. Identify the person or organization whose utilities are to be MAXIMIZED.

"*Step 2*. Identify the issue or issues (that is, decisions) to which the utilities needed are relevant.

"*Step 3*. Identify the entities to be evaluated" (OUTCOMES of possible actions).

"*Step 4*. Identify the relevant DIMENSIONS of VALUE.

"*Step 5*. Rank the dimensions in order of importance.

"*Step 6.* Rate the dimensions on importance, preserving ratios.

"*Step 7.* Sum the importance WEIGHTS, divide each by the sum, and multiply by 100.

"*Step 8.* Measure the location of each entity being evaluated on each dimension.

"*Step 9.* Calculate utilities for entities."

$$U_i = \Sigma w_i u_i.$$

"*Step 10.* Decide." Ordinarily this means selecting the act that maximizes U(i). If one of the dimensions is subject to an upper bound (a budget constraint), however, steps 4 through 10 should be done ignoring the constrained dimension, and the ratios U(i)/C(i) should be chosen "in decreasing order of that ratio until the budget constraint is used up" (Gardiner & Edwards, 1975, pp. 12-19.) (See B/C RATIO.)

comment: SMART is a technique that approximates more complex utility assessment techniques on the assumptions of RISK NEUTRALITY, PREFERENTIAL INDEPENDENCE, LINEAR FUNCTION FORMS, and the desire by judges to maximize EXPECTED UTILITY.

related terms: POLICY, DECISION TREE, PIP, EXPECTED UTILITY, EXPECTED VALUE, DECISION THEORY, MAXIMIZATION, RATIONALITY.

SOCIAL DILEMMA

definition: A situation in which (a) "each individual receives a higher PAYOFF for a socially defecting CHOICE (e.g., having additional children, using all the energy available, polluting his or her neighbors) than for a socially cooperative choice, no matter what the other individuals in society do," yet (b) "all individuals are better off if all cooperate than if all defect" (Dawes, 1980, p. 169.) See PRISONER'S DILEMMA.

comment: Sometimes referred to as the "TRAGEDY of the COMMONS" or "COMMONS DILEMMA", using the problem faced by herdsmen sharing a common pasture as an analogy for social dilemmas, in general (Hardin, 1968.)

synonyms: TRAGEDY of the COMMONS, COMMONS DILEMMA.

related terms: PRISONER'S DILEMMA, EXTERNALITIES.

SOCIAL IMPACT ASSESSMENT.

See ENVIRONMENTAL IMPACT ASSESSMENT.

SOCIAL JUDGMENT THEORY

definition: A DESCRIPTIVE and NORMATIVE approach to JUDGMENT and DECISION MAKING developed by Kenneth Hammond (1955, 1965, 1971, 1976; Brehmer & Hammond, 1973; Hammond, Stewart, Brehmer, & Steinmann, 1975) on the basis of Egon Brunswik's (1952, 1956) PROBABILISTIC FUNCTIONALISM. Social Judgment Theory (SJT) has been applied to the analysis of MULTIPLE CUE PROBABILITY LEARNING (Brehmer, 1969a, 1976b; Peterson, Hammond, & Summers, 1965a, 1965b), INTERPERSONAL CONFLICT (Brehmer & Hammond, 1977), INTERPERSONAL LEARNING (Brehmer, 1969b), and social POLICY DECISIONS (Hammond, Rohrbaugh, Mumpower, & Adelman, 1977; Hammond & Adelman, 1976). It has also produced the "POLICY" DECISION AID.

comment: The major emphasis of SJT is on the CAUSAL AMBIGUITY of the environment and its relationship to judgment.

synonym: SJT.

related terms: JUDGMENT vs. DECISION THEORIES, PROBABILISTIC FUNCTIONALISM, LENS MODEL, REPRESENTATIVE DESIGN, MULTIPLE CUE PROBABILITY LEARNING, CONFLICT, "POLICY" AID.

SOCIAL WELFARE FUNCTION

definition: A procedure for the AGGREGATION of individual PREFERENCES to yield a preference for the society (Luce & Raiffa, 1957, p. 328).

examples: Some of the more common procedures are convention, religious code, authority, dictatorial decree, voting, and economic MARKET institutions (Luce & Raiffa, 1957, p. 328).

related terms: ARROW's PARADOX, AGENDA PROBLEM.

SPURIOUS CORRELATION.

See ILLUSORY CORRELATION.

St. PETERSBURG PARADOX

definition: A famous paradox that led to the concept of UTILITY. "A 'fair' coin, which is defined by the property that the PROBABILITY of heads is $1/2$, is tossed until a head appears. The gambler receives 2^n dollars if the first head occurs on trial n.... [Because the EXPECTED VALUE does not sum to any finite number], one should be willing to pay any sum, however large, for the privelege of participating in such a gamble" (Luce & Raiffa, 1957, p. 20). The paradox is that few, if any, people would be willing to pay an unlimited amount to participate in the St. Petersburg gamble. "...Originally set out by Nicholas Bernoulli and later used by Daniel Bernoulli (1738, reprinted 1954) in the formulation of his concept of moral expectation" (Lopes, in press).

comment: "The pertinent variable to be averaged, [Bernoulli] argued, is not the actual monetary worth of the outcomes, but rather the intrinsic worths of their monetary VALUES" (Luce & Raiffa, 1957, p. 20), that is, their UTILITIES. The paradox is avoided if decisions are based on EXPECTED UTILITY, rather than expected value. More recently, however, Lopes (in press) has argued that the St. Petersburg paradox does not have "much or anything to do with the distinction between utility and monetary value" (p. 3) but relates to the distinction between expected returns in the short run and expected returns in the long run: "In evaluating gambles such as these, we do not consider the large amounts that we are prodigiously unlikely to get, but rather consider the amounts that we are likely to get most of the time" (p. 5).

related terms: UTILITY, EXPECTED UTILITY, VALUE, EXPECTED VALUE.

STANDARD GAMBLE

definition: A technique for measuring von NEUMANN-MORGENSTERN UTILITY by asking for PREFERENTIAL equivalences between RISKY and RISKLESS alternatives. One form of the standard gamble begins by presenting a risky alternative, or **LOTTERY**, in which there is a .50 chance of winning the highest objective amount and a .50 chance of winning the lowest objective amount. BIDDING techniques are used to determine the CERTAINTY EQUIVALENT for this lottery, that is, the objective amount offered for certain that the respondent JUDGES to be equal in VALUE (definition 2b) to the lottery. Another form of the standard gamble is to begin with a riskless alternative, a fixed amount on the objective dimension, and to ask for PROBABILITIES that would make the judge indifferent between a lottery on the highest and lowest objective amounts and the riskless option.

comment: In obtaining ORDINAL judgments for *pairs* of values (one from each of two dimensions, here, probability and value) one obtains information on at least an ORDERED-METRIC scale about the *intervals* between values.

related terms: UTILITY THEORY, von NEUMANN-MORGENSTERN UTILITY, RISK PREMIUM, BIDDING GAME, TRADEOFF.

STANDARD REGRESSION WEIGHT.

   See WEIGHT, BETA WEIGHT.

STATISTICAL PREDICTION.

   See ACTUARIAL PREDICTION.

STATISTICAL TRIALS.

   See MONTE CARLO METHOD.

STOCHASTIC TRANSITIVITY.

See TRANSITIVITY.

STRATEGIC EQUIVALENCE

definition: If the final ordering of the alternatives in terms of EXPECTED UTILITY is not SENSITIVE to the CHOICE between alternative inputs to the DECISION-MAKING process (e.g., alternative PROBABILITY estimates, alternative VALUE JUDGMENTS, alternative decision rules), then these alternative inputs are strategically equivalent.

related terms: SENSITIVITY ANALYSIS.

STRUCTURAL MODELING

definition: The use of geometric models to assist in organizing and analyzing data. A structural model "represents a system as a set of elements with pairwise relations linking some or all of the elements. It is graphically represented by points (or nodes) and connecting lines (or arcs)" (Linstone, Hays, Rogers, & Lendaris, 1978, p. 7). Structural models, in contrast to CROSS-IMPACT MODELS, are intended only to obtain a qualitative appreciation of the "geography" of a complex system and not for quantitative output. The analysis may yield identification of critical elements and subsystems or illumination of behavior, such as stability, evolution over time, and sensitivity to changes (Linstone, et al., 1978, pp. 6-7).

related terms: PROBLEM STRUCTURING, CROSS-IMPACT ANALYSIS, GRAPHIC AIDS.

SUBCERTAINTY

definition: The assumed property (Kahneman & Tversky, 1979b, pp. 281f) that

$$p_i(p) + p_i(1 - p) < 1,$$

where p_i is the DECISION WEIGHT attached to a PROBABILITY. "Subcertainty entails that decision weights are REGRESSIVE with respect to *p*, i.e., that PREFERENCES are generally less sensitive to variations of probability than the expectation principle (see EXPECTED UTILITY) would dictate" (Kahneman & Tversky, 1979b, p. 282).

related terms: DECISION WEIGHT, CONSERVATISM.

SUBJECTIVE ATTRIBUTE

definition: An ATTRIBUTE for which no commonly understood SCALE exists and for which a scale must be constructed (Keeney & Raiffa, 1976, pp. 40, 62.)

example: Examples are prestige and goodwill.

comment: Keeney & Raiffa (1976, pp. 56ff) list three options for assessing the UTILITY of a subjective attribute: DIRECT PREFERENCE MEASUREMENT, a SUBJECTIVE INDEX, and a PROXY ATTRIBUTE.

synonyms: PURELY SUBJECTIVE DIMENSION.

related terms: DIRECT PREFERENCE MEASUREMENT, SUBJECTIVE INDEX, PROXY ATTRIBUTE.

SUBJECTIVE EXPECTED UTILITY MODEL

definition: A DESCRIPTIVE MODEL of DECISION behavior that asserts that individuals choose so as to MAXIMIZE subjective expected utility. The SUBJECTIVE EXPECTED UTILITY of an alternative with UNCERTAIN consequences is the sum of the UTILITIES of its OUTCOMES, each WEIGHTED by its SUBJECTIVE PROBABILITY of occurrence (Edwards, 1954). The subjective utility model was introduced by Savage (1954) and named and explored empirically by Edwards (1954; 1961, p. 474).

comment: The historical trend in expectation models is towards accepting subjective JUDGMENTS as inputs to the COMBINING RULE. The EXPECTED VALUE model accepts OBJECTIVE PROBABILITIES and objective VALUES. The EXPECTED UTILITY model (originally proposed by Bernoulli, 1738) accepts objective probabilities but subjective utilities. And the subjective expected utility model (proposed by Ramsey, 1926, reprinted 1964; Savage, 1953; von Neuman & Morgenstern, 1947) accepts both subjective probabilities and subjective utilities.

synonym: SEU MODEL

related terms: SUBJECTIVE PROBABILITY,   BAYESIAN,   EXPECTED   UTILITY,
EXPECTED VALUE, VARIANCE PREFERENCES, RISK DIMENSIONS.

SUBJECTIVE EXPTECTED UTILITY.

  See SUBJECTIVE EXPECTED UTILITY MODEL.

SUBJECTIVE INDEX

definition: An   index,   or   SCALE, on which the location of entities
must be determined through subjective judgment rather   than   objective
measurement.   It is constructed to represent an attribute (SUBJECTIVE
ATTRIBUTE) for   which   no   adequate   objective   measurement   scale   or
objectively   measurable   proxy   attribute   (INDICATOR)   exists,   often
because the attribute represented is   abstract   rather   than   concrete
(Keeney & Raiffa, 1976, pp. 40, 62).

example: Indices for measurement (scaling) of prestige, goodwill, and
scenic beauty.

comment: Keeney & Raiffa (1976, p.   62) identify   three   options   for
assessing   the   utility   of   an alternative on a subjective attribute:
use of a subjective index; a PROXY ATTRIBUTE;   and   DIRECT   PREFERENCE
MEASUREMENT.

synonym: Purely subjective dimension.

related   terms: SUBJECTIVE   ATTRIBUTE,   PROXY   ATTRIBUTE,   DIRECT
PREFERENCE   MEASUREMENT,   RELEVANCE   TREE,   DECISION   THEORY,
MULTIATTRIBUTE UTILITY THEORY.

SUBJECTIVE PROBABILITY

definition: The encoding of BELIEFS about the likelihood of events in
terms of numbers that, like all probabilities, (a) range from   0,   for
impossibility,   to 1, for certainty, (b) can be added to yield the p's

for sets of events that are mutually exclusive, and (c) add to 1 for sets of events that are mutually exclusive and exhaustive. Subjective probabilities are based on JUDGMENTS, in contrast to OBJECTIVE PROBABILITIES, which are most commonly based on counting.

Actually, the early subjectivist approach to probability (Bernoulli, 1713; De Morgan, 1847; La Place, 1825) later divided into two. One, the RATIONALIST approach (Jeffreys, 1961; Keynes, 1921), asserts that a probability expresses the rational degree of belief that should hold *logically* between a set of propositions (taken as given hypotheses) and another proposition (taken as the conclusion). The other, the SUBJECTIVIST approach (De Finetti, 1937, reprinted 1964; Ramsey, 1926, reprinted 1964; Savage, 1954), asserts that a probability simply expresses subjective degree of belief, interpreted operationally in terms of willingness to act.

comment: Edwards, a subjectivist, argues that subjective probabilities are no more vague than objective probabilities (1968b, p. 39) "[The rules for objective probability] are very vague and subjective while pretending to be otherwise: this fact is most conspicuous in the specification that relative frequencies are supposed to be observed under 'substantially similar conditions,' which means that the conditions should be similar enough but not too similar. (A coin always tossed in *exactly* the same way would presumably fall with the same face up every time.) Perhaps most important, the FREQUENTISTIC set of rules is just not applicable to many, perhaps most, of the questions about which men might be uncertain."

Feller (1966, pp. 4-5), an objectivist, acknowledges that at least the CLASSICAL version of the objective approach to probability does not apply to inductive reasoning, for example, coming up with a probability that the sun will rise tomorrow, for "we should have to agree on an (idealized) model which would presumably run along the lines 'out of infinitely many worlds one is selected at random....' Little imagination is required to construct such a model, but it appears both uninteresting and meaningless" (pp. 4-5.)

For an excellent review of the history of approaches to probability, see Raiffa (1968, pp. 273-278.)

synonyms: INTUITIVE PROBABILITY, PERSONAL PROBABILITY.

related terms: OBJECTIVE PROBABILITY, UNCERTAINTY, CHANCE FORK, BAYESIAN, SEU MODEL, CLINICAL PREDICTION, IMPRESSION FORMATION, ATTRIBUTION.

SUBJECTIVIST APPROACH to PROBABILITY.

See SUBJECTIVE PROBABILITY.

SUBOPTIMIZING

definition: Choosing an alternative that is not optimal.

related terms: OPTIMIZATION.

SUCCESSIVE ACCUMULATION

definition: A technique for studying the influence of a number of VARIABLES by beginning with an artificial situation (see SYSTEMATIC DESIGN) in which only one of these variables is present and observing the effects of adding various combinations of others (Postman & Tolman, 1959, p. 531; Brunswik, 1956.)

comment: The standard technique in psychology. To be contrasted with SUCCESSIVE OMISSION. For example, if one compares size constancy with and without binocular cues, the two methods yield different results (Brunswik, 1956, p. 25.) A large effect of binocular cues is obtained, if one observes this variable under impoverished conditions (successive accumulation); yet no effect at all is obtained under more nearly normal conditions (successive omission.)

related terms: SUCCESSIVE OMISSION, SYSTEMATIC DESIGN.

SUCCESSIVE OMISSION

definition: A technique for studying the influence of a number of VARIABLES by beginning with a lifelike situation (see REPRESENTATIVE DESIGN) in which all are present and observing the effects of omitting various combinations of them (Postman & Tolman, 1959, p. 531.)

comment: To be contrasted with SUCCESSIVE ACCUMULATION. For example, if one compares size constancy with and without binocular cues, the two methods yield results that point to different conclusions (Brunswik, 1956, p. 25.) A large effect of binocular cues is obtained, if one observes this variable under impoverished stimulus conditions (successive accumulation); yet no effect at all is obtained under more nearly normal conditions (successive omission.)

The great advantage of the technique of successive omission is that it preserves intact the multiplicity of minimal PROXIMAL CUES, *many of which are unknown*, and evaluates the contribution of the major well-established cues against this background (Postman & Tolman, 1959, p. 532.)

related terms: SUCCESSIVE ACCUMULATION, REPRESENTATIVE DESIGN.

SUPPRESSOR VARIABLE

definition: A VARIABLE that, while having little or no correlation with the criterion, improves prediction of the criterion by suppressing within-group variation through its positive correlation with a variable that *is* correlated with the criterion (Bock, 1975, p. 420.) "...A suppressor variable improves prediction in the population when it is given a negative WEIGHT....A variable receives a negative weight in a regression equation if the ratio between its correlation with the error in the rest of the equation, and its correlation with the criterion variable, exceeds a certain amount" (Darlington, 1968, pp. 163, 179).

example: An example is shown below, with X_1 as the predictor, X_2 as the suppressor variable, and Y as the criterion. X_2 is uncorrelated with Y but correlated with X_1 and functions as a predictor of error variance in X_1.

X_1	X_2	Y
0	0	0
1	1	0
1	0	1
2	1	1

related terms: REDUNDANCY.

SURE-THING PRINCIPLE

definition: The principle, first enunciated by Savage (1954, p. 21), that an alternative, A, that is at least as good as another, B, in all possible futures and better in at least one is to be preferred to that alternative.

example: Savage's example is of a businessman contemplating buying a certain piece of property and thinking about the outcome of the next presidential election relevant to the attractiveness of the purchase. "Seeing that he would buy in either event, he decides that he should buy, even though he does not know which event will obtain" (p. 21).

related terms: DOMINANCE, RATIONALITY.

SURFACE.

See LENS MODEL, CUE.

SURROGATE PRICE.

See SHADOW PRICE.

SYNERGISM.

See CONFIGURAL.

SYSTEMATIC DESIGN

definition: Experimental design, first formalized by J. S. Mill (1843), in which (a) a small number of VARIABLES is examined, (b) the distribution of VALUES on each of the separate variables is made to be uniform (i.e., each value is made to occur with the same frequency), and (c) the degree of covariation among pairs of variables is usually artificially set at either 0 (orthogonal variables) or 1.00 (completely confounded variables) (Brunswik, 1956, pp. 7ff.) The main aim is to disentangle the effects of various independent variables by examining the "concomitant variation" of each with the dependent variable (Mill, 1843). It is the standard method in psychology, best exemplified by the analysis-of-variance design. To be contrasted with the less commonly employed REPRESENTATIVE DESIGN, in which representativeness of natural conditions is emphasized more than control.

related terms: REPRESENTATIVE DESIGN, COVARIATION PRINCIPLE.

SYSTEMATIC ERROR.

See BIAS.

SYSTEMIC RATIONALITY.

See RATIONALITY.

TA.

See TECHNOLOGY ASSESSMENT.

TECHNOLOGY ASSESSMENT

definition: The obtaining of information useful to POLICY makers on the IMPACTS of a technology (Linstone, Hays, Rogers, & Lendaris, 1978.)

related terms: IMPACT ASSESSMENT.

TERMINAL FOCUS.

See LENS MODEL.

TIME-SERIES FORECASTING.

See FORECASTING.

TRADEOFF

definition 1: The amount one must give up on one dimension to achieve a given amount on another.

synonym for definition 1: MARGINAL RATE of TRANSFORMATION (MRT), ENVIRONMENTAL TRADEOFF.

definition 2: The amount one is willing to give up on one objective in order to achieve a given amount on another.

synonym for definition 2: MARGINAL RATE of SUBSTITUTION (MRS), SUBSTITUTION RATIO (Samuelson, 1976, p. 446), VALUE TRADEOFF.

comment: The first type of tradeoff (MRT) is a characteristic of the environment external to a decision maker and thus of the set of options facing him. It is represented symbolically by a production function, and depicted graphically by a PRODUCTION POSSIBILITY frontier, or simply POSSIBILITY FRONTIER (Baumol, 1977, Ch. 11; Samuelson, 1976, Ch. 27; Stokey & Zeckhauser, 1978, Ch. 3). The second type of tradeoff (MRS) is a characteristic of the decision maker's preferences among whatever options his environment provides. It is represented symbolically by a UTILITY (Definition 1), or preference, function, and depicted graphically by an INDIFFERENCE MAP (see INDIFFERENCE CURVE).

The two types of tradeoff are logically independent (see FACT-VALUE SEPARATION) but must be considered jointly for RATIONAL DECISION MAKING. (See Stokey & Zeckhauser, 1978, Ch. 3, regarding the "fundamental model of choice," a PRESCRIPTIVE MODEL.)

Methods for assessing tradeoffs of the first type (MRT) are beyond this book. Methods for assessing tradeoffs of the second type (MRS) are discussed extensively by MacCrimmon and his associates (MacCrimmon & Siu, 1974; MacCrimmon & Toda, 1969; MacCrimmon & Wehrung, 1977) as well as in the literatures of DT, BDT, SJT, and IIT. MacCrimmon and Wehrung (p. 127) distinguish the INDIFFERENCE and PREFERRED PROPORTIONS approaches to assessing value tradeoffs. In the indifference approach, a tradeoff is the change in one attribute, X, that is necessary to offset a given change in another attribute, Y, so that the new alternative A_1 (= X_1, Y_1) produced by the changes is indifferent to a reference alternative A_O (= X_O, Y_O)--that is, so that the two alternatives yield equal UTILITY (Definition 1), or VALUE (Definition 2a) and thus lie on the same indifference curve. In the preferred proportions approach, a tradeoff is the proportion of change in attributes X and Y that the decision maker would most prefer if he could move away from the reference alternative A_O to whatever other alternative A_1 yields the greatest possible increase in UTILITY (Definition 1) or VALUE (Definition 2a). Relating the two approaches to a preference function U(X, Y) on the attributes, MacCrimmon & Wehrung (p. 129) state: "An indifference curve is a contour of this function; that is, a locus of points of equal height or preference. A preferred proportions curve is a path up the preference surface under particular, allowable moves away from a given point."

Both the indifference approach and the preferred proportions approach can be implemented in either the equivalence (direct) mode on the choice (successive choice) mode (MacCrimmon & Siu, 1974, pp. 683-684; MacCrimmon & Wehrung, 1977, pp. 130-131). In the equivalence mode, the decision maker must specify the level of X and/or Y in the new alternative A_1. In the choice mode, the analyst generates hypothetical levels of X and Y for new alternatives A_1, A_2, ... A_n and then for each of these alternatives asks the decision maker simply whether it is (in the indifference approach) superior, equal, or inferior in UTILITY (Definition 1) to reference alternative A_O, or (in the preferred proportions approach) yields the greatest possible improvement in utility over A_O. MacCrimmon and Wehrung (p. 130-131) state that the direct (equivalence) mode is more efficient in principle because it requires less iteration, but the (successive) choice mode is better in practice because it is easier for decision makers and yields more reliable results, since "the direct [equivalence] mode requires the decision maker to perform the multiple operations of 'generate and test' rather than the single operation of 'test' required by the successive choice mode."

related terms: UTILITY, VALUE, MULTIATTRIBUTE UTILITY THEORY, MULTI-ATTRIBUTE DECISION MAKING, INDIFFERENCE CURVE, PRESCRIPTIVE MODEL, DT, BDT, SJT, IIT.

TRAGEDY of the COMMONS.

See SOCIAL DILEMMA.

TRANSITIVE.

See TRANSITIVITY.

TRANSITIVITY

definition: The relation, r, is said to exhibit transitivity if and only if,' for all A, B, and C,

ArB & BrC --> ArC.

"If [one] prefers A to B and B to C, then he prefers A to C. Similarly, if he is indifferent between A and B and between B and C, then he is indifferent between A and C" (Edwards, 1954, p. 381).

This kind of transitivity, often called ALGEBRAIC TRANSITIVITY, is to be distinguished from STOCHASTIC TRANSITIVITY. A distinction is also made between strong and weak stochastic transitivity. "WEAK STOCHASTIC TRANSITIVITY simply asserts that if the PROBABILITIES of preferring A to B and B to C are both equal to or greater than .5, the probability of preferring A to C is also equal to or greater than .5. STRONG STOCHASTIC TRANSITIVITY asserts that if the probabilities of preferring A to B and B to C are both equal to or greater than .5, the probability of preferring A to C is equal to or greater than the larger of the other two probabilities" (Edwards, 1961, p. 483).

comment: Transitivity is generally considered to be a very compelling principle of RATIONALITY, since persons who violate it can be used as "MONEY PUMPS." Assume a person prefers A to B and B to C, yet prefers C to A. If he has A and C and you have B, you can arrange to exchange B for C plus a price, say $1. Then he will have A and B, and you will have C, and you can arrange to exchange C for A plus, say, another $1. Then he will have C and B, and you will have A, and you can arrange to exchange A for B plus $1, which will put you back at the start and ready to go again!

However compelling transitivity may be from a NORMATIVE point of view, the only kind of transitivity that it is realistic to incorporate into a DESCRIPTIVE MODEL of human behavior is one of the forms of stochastic transitivity, for, as Edwards (1961, p. 483) has said, "...As a basis for psychological theorizing, algebraic transitivity is dead...."

related terms: RATIONALITY, AXIOM.

TREE

definition: A graph with a single point as source and in which no two points are connected by more than one path (that is, in which cycles or loops do not occur).

examples: Examples of trees are DECISION TREES, PROBABILITY TREES, RELEVANCE TREES, PREFERENCE TREES, FAULT TREES, and GOAL TREES.

comment: A tree structure is a HIERARCHICAL structure. In a hierarchical structure, a division at any level may be further subdivided, but this subdivision applies only to divisions directly above it in the hierarchy. Thus, living things may be divided into plants and animals, and animals may be further subdivided into vertebrates and invertebrates, but the vertebrate-invertebrate division applies only to animals, not to plants. Similarly, in a tree structure, any branch may be further branched, but this branching applies only to directly preceding branches. For example, a DECISION TREE may branch into the decision to have children and the decision not to have children, and the branch for the decision to have children may be further branched into various possibilities for numbers and sexes of children; however, this further branching would not apply to the branch for the decision not to have children.

Trees, or hierarchies, seem to be virtually indispensable in the study and practice of decision making. Keeney & Raiffa (1976, p. 41), for example, state that "Almost everyone who has seriously thought about the objectives in a complex problem has come up with some sort of hierarchy of objectives."

related terms: DECISION TREE, PROBABILITY TREE, RELEVANCE TREE, PREFERENCE TREE, FAULT TREE, GOAL TREE.

TRIANGULATION

definition: The use of multiple methods for obtaining JUDGMENTS, for example, FRACTILE ESTIMATION and PROBABILITY ESTIMATION (see ANCHORING and ADJUSTMENT) or WILLINGNESS to PAY and WILLINGNESS to ACCEPT PAYMENT (see WILLINGNESS to PAY), in order to converge on more nearly correct judgments.

related terms: BIAS, DECISION AID.

TRIPLE-SYSTEM CASE.

See COGNITIVE SYSTEM.

UNCERTAINTY

definition 1:   A situation where there are a number of alternative possible states of nature and one does not know *which* of them has occurred or will occur.

synonym for definition 1: Definition 1 of RISK.

definition 2:   A situation where there are a number of alternative possible states of nature, and one does not know which of them has occurred or will occur (as in Definition 1), *or* even the PROBABILITY of occurrence of each (Knight, 1921).   Explicitly contrasted with Definition 2 of RISK.

example of definition 2: A firm is deciding whether or not to market a totally new type of product. That decision depends on the potential demand for the product: if high the product should be marketed; if low, it should not.

The various potential demand levels are alternative states of nature, and since the firm does not know which demand level would actually be found if the product were marketed, it is uncertain in the sense of definition 1.   Moreover, since the firm has no past experience with this product or other basis on which to estimate the probabilities of the various potential demand levels, the firm is uncertain in the sense of Definition 2, as well.

definition 3: A mathematical measure that reflects the number of alternative states of nature and the extent to which they are equiprobable (Garner, 1962).

general comment: Uncertainty is a pervasive problem in JUDGMENT and DECISION MAKING, since KNOWLEDGE is virtually always imperfect. One is almost never certain about which state of nature existed before, exists now, or (especially) will exist in the future. Even certainty about the relative probabilities of alternative states of nature is usually lacking as well. See SUBJECTIVE PROBABILITY and ELLSBERG PARADOX.

The most widely recommended strategies for decision making under uncertainty are MAXIMIZING SUBJECTIVE EXPECTED UTILITY and MINIMAX REGRET.

related terms: SUBJECTIVE PROBABILITY, SUBJECTIVE EXPECTED UTILITY, MINIMAX REGRET, RISK, ELLSBERG PARADOX.

UNCONFLICTED ADHERENCE.

See CONFLICT THEORY.

UNCONFLICTED CHANGE.

See CONFLICT TEHHEORY.

UNCORRELATED.

See INDEPENDENCE.

UNFOLDING THEORY

definition: A SCALING theory designed to construct a space with a set of points for the JUDGES and a set of points for the objects judged, on the assumption that an individual's PREFERENCES "fold" the underlying preference scale about his/her own position (the "ideal point") on that scale (Coombs, 1950; Coombs, Dawes, & Tversky, 1970, pp. 36f.).

example: Assume that an individual who normally drives 55 mph on the highway is asked to indicate his/her preference for highway speeds of 30, 40, 50, 60, and 70 mph. One possible outcome is that he/she would rank them from most preferred to least preferred as follows: 60, 50, 40, 70, 30. The underlying scale is thus folded about the preferred speed of 55, and the ordering represents relative distances from this point along the folded scale.

related terms: SCALING, MEASUREMENT, PORTFOLIO THEORY.

USEFULNESS.

See BETA WEIGHT.

UTILITY

definition 1: According to the utilitarian philosophers, such as Jeremy Bentham and James Mill, positive utility is the property of giving pleasure, and negative utility is the property of giving pain (see Edwards, 1954, p. 382). D. Bernoulli (1738, reprinted 1954) defined it as "moral worth," not distinguishing positive from negative. Modern writers also have tended not to distinguish positive from negative in their definitions of utility, as "satisfaction" (Samuelson, 1976, p. 433), "personal value" (Brown, Kahr, & Peterson, 1974, p. 47), ."subjective value" (Edwards, 1961, p. 474), or "welfare" (Stokey & Zeckhauser, 1978, p. 264). However, PROSPECT THEORY (Kahneman & Tversky, 1979b) distinguishes between GAINS and LOSSES.

This concept of utility applies to both riskless and risky alternatives; that is, to both "consequences" and "acts" (Savage, 1954).

comment regarding Definition 1: The distinction between VALUE (Definition 2b or 3) and UTILITY (Definition 1) was central to the neo--classical school of economics, prevalent during the late nineteenth and early twentieth centuries (e.g., Marshall, 1927). It is- exemplified by the "law" of DIMINISHING MARGINAL UTILITY: "As the

amount consumed of a good increases, the MARGINAL UTILITY of the good
(or the extra utility added by its last unit) tends to decrease"
(Samuelson, 1976, p. 433). Neo-classical economists applied the
diminishing marginal utility concept both to specific commodities and
to money, which serves as a proxy for all marketed commodities
(Savage, 1954). Though diminishing marginal utility was first
proposed by D. Bernoulli (1738, reprinted 1954) to account for the
St. PETERSBURG PARADOX, a problem in risky decision making, but "For
a long period economists accepted Bernoulli's idea of moral wealth
[worth] as the measurement of a person's well-being apart from any
consideration of probability" (Savage, 1954, p. 96).

More recent "ordinalist" economists and others have argued,
however, that the diminishing marginal utility concept is meaningless
for the riskless case. Their premise is that utility (Definition 1)
is measurable only on an ordinal, not a cardinal (interval) SCALE of
MEASUREMENT (see CARDINAL UTILITY, ORDINAL UTILITY), because people
can only *rank* states of the world in order of desirability, not say
how much they prefer one state to another (Baumol, 1977, pp. 193-4
and 431-2; Pareto, 1906, cited by Edwards, 1954, p. 384; Stigler,
1950). And it clearly "is meaningless to speak of the slope, or
marginal utility, of an ordinal utility function" (Edwards, 1954, p.
384).

Lange (1933, cited by Edwards, 1954, p. 385) and Edwards (1954,
p. 385), however, argue that riskless cardinal utility *is* rigorously
measurable and the concept of riskless marginal utility therefore
meaningful. They make two main points: First, *if* people can reliably
judge utility on an ORDERED-METRIC scale by ranking pairs of utility
differences (intervals)--that is, say whether the utility difference
between states A and B is greater than, equal to, or less than the
utility difference between states C and D, utility is cardinally
measurable. Such comparisons are the basis of the psychophysical
Method of Equal Sense Differences, which yields an interval measure of
subjective sensation. Second, even Pareto, the initiator of the
ordinalist movement, acknowledged (1906) that people generally *can*
make reliable comparisons of utility differences. Many other judgment
and decision analysts such as Keeney and Raiffa (1976, pp. 91-94) and
Anderson (1976) support this view. See also von Neumann & Morgenstern
(1947, pp. 19-20), as quoted under INDIFFERENCE CURVE.

synonym: VALUE (Definition 2a).

definition 2: The VALUE (Definition 2b) of risky alternatives (see RISK), which incorporates ATTITUDE TOWARD RISK. (See von NEUMANN-MORGENSTERN UTILITY.) "The economist's [riskless] concept of utility and the von Neumann-Morgenstern [risky] concept are completely different. Knowing one implies very little about the other. One function can easily be convex and the other concave for the same attribute" (Keeney & Raiffa, 1976, p. 150).

comment regarding Definition 2: Utility in this sense is equated with VALUE Definition 2b (measured on a descriptive variable) rather than Definition 2a (measured on an intrinsically evaluative abstract variable) because in assessment of von NEUMANN-MORGENSTERN UTILITY, the utility of a risky alternative (i.e., of a STANDARD GAMBLE providing some most desirable outcome with probability p and some least desirable outcome with probability $[1 - p]$, where the outcomes are defined in terms of VALUE Definition 2b) is indicated by preferential equivalence, or indifference, to a CERTAINTY EQUIVALENT (i.e., a level on the same descriptive scale provided with $p = 1.0$) rather than by direct rating on an abstract desirability scale.

The particular absolute desirability level shared by the risky alternative and certainty equivalent remains implicit (Baumol, 1977, pp. 431-432). True, the certainty equivalent is then mapped onto an apparently abstract scale of utility measured in "utils" (or "utiles"), but the levels of this scale are just proxies for levels of the descriptive variable, normalized to range from the least desirable (0.00) to the most desirable (1.00) outcome of the gamble. Any scale level represents an EXPECTED VALUE, represented as the corresponding probability of obtaining the most desired outcome (p X $1.0 = p$). Any expected value itself, however, is measured on the same descriptive scale as the values of the outcomes from which it is derived.

Utility in the sense of Definition 2 includes utility in the sense of Definition 1, though implicitly.

synonym: von NEUMAN-MORGENSTERN UTILITY.

related terms: VALUE, PROSPECT THEORY, GAINS AND LOSSES, DIMINISHING MARGINAL UTILITY, MARGINAL UTILITY, ST. PETERSBURG PARADOX, ATTITUDE TOWARD RISK, RISKY, VON NEUMANN-MORGENSTERN UTILITY, SCALE OF MEASUREMENT.

UTILITY CURVE.

See UTILITY, FUNCTION FORM.

UTILITY INDEPENDENCE

definition: "...*Y* is *utility independent* of *Z* when conditional preferences for LOTTERIES on *Y* given *Z* do not depend on the particular LEVELS of *Z*.... When *Y* is utility independent of *Z*, there is a single utility FUNCTION over *Y*" (Keeney & Raiffa, 1976, pp. 226, 227). (See INDEPENDENCE.)

example: The kind of questions used to assess utility independence (Keeney & Raiffa, 1976, p. 226) would be ones like:

> Assuming a 0% population increase in either case, what level of income would make you indifferent between (a) a guarantee of $ _____ and (b) a 50-50 chance on either $20,000 or $40,000?

> Assuming a 10% population increase in either case, what level of income would make you indifferent between (a) a guarantee of $ _____ and (b) a 50-50 chance on·either $20,000 or $40,000?

If the same level (CERTAINTY EQUIVALENT) on the income VARIABLE is given as the answer to both questions, then income is utility independent of population, at least over these ranges.   Though $20,000, $*X*, and $40,000 will almost surely have different values depending on whether they are paired with a 0% or a 10% increase in population, the difference between $20,000 and $*X* should bear the same relation to that between $*X* and $40,000 in each case.   The INTERVAL relations among value judgments produced by different levels of income should be independent of level of population.

comment: Independence   is   important   in   the   assessment   of MULTIATTRIBUTE PREFERENCE, VALUE, or UTILITY. So long as (mutual) utility independence obtains, it is possible to DECOMPOSE multiattribute problems, that is, (a) to assess VALUE or UTILITY FUNCTIONS ATTRIBUTE by attribute, (b) to assess WEIGHTS for the attributes, and then (c) to combine weighted values by either an

ADDITIVE MODEL (if the weights sum to 1) or a MULTIPLICATIVE MODEL (if the weights do not sum to 1)(Keeney & Raiffa, 1976, pp. 293ff).

While PREFERENTIAL INDEPENDENCE is sufficient in RISKLESS cases for eliminating DOMINATED alternatives, and for dealing with TRADEOFFS among attributes that are MUTUALLY PREFERENTIALLY INDEPENDENT, UTILITY INDEPENDENCE (more precisely, MUTUAL UTILITY INDEPENDENCE) is necessary for dealing with tradeoffs in RISKY cases (Keeney & Raiffa, 1976, Ch. 5). "The concept of utility independence can be viewed as a specialization of the concept of preferential independence" (Keeney & Raiffa, 1976, p.225). (See PREFERENTIAL INDEPENDENCE.) No stronger form of independence that mutual utility independence is ever required for decision making, however, because in comparing alternatives, only differences among them, and not ABSOLUTE values of each, need to be taken into account.

synonym: CONSTANT SUBSTITUTION (Keeney & Raiffa, 1976, p. 85f).

related terms: INDEPENDENCE, PREFERENTIAL INDEPENDENCE, MULTILINEAR MODEL, TRADEOFF, RISK, SCALES of MEASUREMENT, UTILITY, DIMENSION, ATTRIBUTE, MULTIATTRIBUTE UTILITY THEORY, DECOMPOSITION, FUNCTION FORM, ADDITIVE MODEL, MULTIPLICATIVE MODEL, DOMINANCE, RISK.

VALUE

definition 1: A level on a DIMENSION.

synonym: LEVEL.

definition 2: The noun form denotes a level on an evaluative dimension. The adjective form (as in "value dimension", "VALUE JUDGMENT") denotes concern with evaluation, in contrast with description. Numerous authors distinguish description from evaluation: for example, Hammond and Adelman (1976) distinguish "scientific judgments" from "social value judgments." Matheson & Howard (1977) distinguish "outcomes" from "values"; Stokey & Zeckhauser (1978) distinguish "predictions" from "values"; and Weber (1949) distinguishes "empirical facts" from "practical evaluations", all reflecting the same logical distinction (see FACT-VALUE SEPARATION).

There are two principal types of evaluative dimension, or

NUMERAIRE:

    a. Those defined in terms of an intrinsically evaluative abstract variable representing the absolute degree of satisfaction produced by the good, action, situation, etc. evaluated, or the capacity of that good, etc., to produce such satisfaction.

     synonyms:: Desirability, quality, worth, UTILITY (Definition 1).

    b. Those defined in terms of a descriptive variable which is not intrinsically evaluative but is used as a surrogate for one that is so. This descriptive variable is defined in terms of some type of entity, event, or characteristic thereof, external to the judge. Judgments indicate subjective equivalence in desirability, value (Definition 2a), or utility (Definition 1), between levels of the dimension being evaluated and levels of the evaluative dimension. (Baumol, 1977, Chs. 9 & 17; Edwards, 1954; Keeney & Raiffa, 1976, Ch. 3; Sinden & Worrell, 1979, Ch. 4).

     examples: monetary value, MONETARY WORTH.

comment regarding Definition 2: Dimension type (a) is often used as the response scale in studies of value judgment (SINGLE-SYSTEM CASE) conducted by SJT and IIT researchers (Hammond et al., 1980, p. 180).

    Dimension type (b) is used as the response scale in BIDDING GAMES for assessment of WILLINGNESS to PAY and WILLINGNESS to ACCEPT PAYMENT, among other uses.

    The descriptive variable used as a value (Definition 2b) indicator may be *any* valued good (entity, event, or characteristic thereof). This is often money but need not be. Money has no special theoretical status; its usefulness derives from the fact that it is convertible into many other goods and thus can serve as a proxy, or surrogate, for them (i.e., as a "composite good"). (Baumol, 1977, Ch. 9; Edwards, 1954; Rothenberg, 1975, p. 67; Sinden & Worrell, 1979, p.

44; Solow, 1975, pp. 31-33; and Stokey & Zeckhauser, 1978, pp. 170-71.)

The two types of evaluative dimension may be used in sequence, 2b then 2a, wherein:

1. Descriptive variable X is used as a numeraire for one or more other descriptive variables, A...N, yielding the value function:

   $$X = f(A, B...N); \text{ then}$$

2. The value of X is determined in terms of an intrinsically evaluative dimension of desirability, value, utility, etc., yielding the function:

   $$V \text{ (or } U) = g(X).$$

Such an approach would be necessary for riskless assessment of the marginal utility of money or of any other numeraire good, for example.

definition 3: A level on a non-evaluative dimension.

example: EXPECTED VALUE, in this sense, is contrasted with EXPECTED UTILITY.

synonym: OUTCOME, IMPACT, FACT.

related terms: DIMENSION, FACT-VALUE SEPARATION, UTILITY, COMMENSURATION, NUMERAIRE, SINGLE-SYSTEM CASE, SJT, IIT, BIDDING GAMES, WILLINGNESS TO PAY, WILLINGNESS TO ACCEPT PAYMENT, MARGINAL RATE OF SUBSTITUTION, VALUE TRADEOFF, OUTCOME, IMPACT, FACT.

VALUE CONFLICT.

　　See CONFLICT.

VALUE CURVE (OR FUNCTION).

See VALUE, FUNCTION FORM.

VALUE DIMENSION.

See VALUE.

VALUE JUDGMENT.

See VALUE, FACT-VALUE SEPARATION.

VARIABLE.

See DIMENSION.

VARIANCE PREFERENCES

definition: PREFERENCES for UTILITY distributions with either high or low variances (but most commonly for low variances). Following the lead of the economist Irving Fisher (1906), "Allais (1952, 1953a, 1953b) and Georgescu-Roegen (1953) have argued that it is not enough to apply a transform on objective VALUE and on OBJECTIVE PROBABILITY (see SEU MODEL) in order to predict RISKY DECISIONS from EXPECTED UTILITY (see also Tintner, 1942); it is also necessary to take into account at least the variance, and possibly the higher moments, of the utility distribution" (Edwards, 1954, p. 401; Lopes, in press). (See also Atkinson, 1957; Atkinson, Bastian, Earl, & Litwin, 1960.) "Insofar as the notion of 'utility of gambling' can be given an operational meaning, it must correspond with variance preferences since, clearly, any CHOICE whose OUTCOME is UNCERTAIN will have a higher variance than the (zero) variance of not gambling at all" (Edwards, 1961, p. 486).

example: "You would probably prefer the certainty of a million dollars to a 50-50 chance of getting either four million or nothing. I do not think that this preference is due to the fact that the expected utility of the 50-50 bet is less than the utility of one million dollars to you, although this is possible. A more likely explanation is simply that the variances of the two propositions are different. Evidence in favor of this is the fact that if you know you would be offered this choice 20 times in succession, you would probably take the 50-50 bet each time" (Edwards, 1954, p. 401). Increasing the number of times the choice is offered, of course, changes the variance but not the mean.

comment: An alternative to variance preferences for describing the way people take risk into account in making decisions is the concept of RISK DIMENSIONS. People seem to base their decisions on the amount to be won in some cases and on the probability of losing in others (Lichtenstein Slovic, 1971; Payne, 1973). (See ANCHORING and ADJUSTMENT, PROCESS-TRACING MODEL.)

related terms: ALLAIS PARADOX, RISK DIMENSIONS, SUBJECTIVE EXPECTED UTILITY, PORTFOLIO THEORY.

VICARIOUS FUNCTIONING

definition: A term used originally by Brunswik (e.g., 1956, p. 93) to refer to the mutual substitutability in cognitive functioning of (a) CUES or (b) responses. When cues function vicariously, one or another may be used to achieve the same end. For example, relative size and relative motion function vicariously in the JUDGMENT of object size. Similarly, when responses function vicariously, one or another may be used to achieve the same end. For example, a judgment of object size could be communicated either verbally or by drawing.

comment: The mutual substitutability of cues is what system theorists (e.g., von Bertalanffy, 1956) have called "EQUIPOTENTIALITY." It is represented by associationists e.g., Hull, 1952) in terms of a stimulus hierarchy, or convergent hierarchy.

The mutual substitutability of responses is what system theorists (e.g., von Bertalanffy, 1956) have called "EQUIFINALITY." It is represented by associationists (e.g., Hull) in terms of a habit-family hierarchy, or divergent hierarchy. Vicarious functioning, particularly the substitutability of responses, has been widely taken to be the defining characteristic of purposive behavior (Brunswik, 1956, p. 141; Hunter, 1928; Tolman, 1932; Ashby, 1956, 1960).

Brunswik discussed both disjunctive and conjunctive use of

REDUNDANT cues. He used the phrase "or-assembly" of cues (Brunswik, 1956, p. 50) to refer to the fact that, when cues are redundant, one or another may be used to achieve the same end. This is the essence of vicarious functioning. Vicarious functioning takes advantage of VICARIOUS MEDIATION, or cue REDUNDANCY. Hammond (1955) has suggested that it is the vicarious functioning of cues in INTUITIVE judgment that makes it difficult for the judge to verbalize the basis of judgment, that, in other words, leads to lack of RETRACEABILITY.

Brunswik also pointed out that redundant cues can be conjoined to reduce the PROBABILITY of error (Brunswik, 1956, p. 140.) pointing (p. 143) to the fact that the overall FUNCTIONAL VALIDITY of, for example, size judgments is .99, although the ECOLOGICAL VALIDITY of the best single cue is only .70. More recently, Garner (1962, pp. 197f) has expressed a similar view, saying that the purpose of redundancy is to ensure against error (random distortion of the signal) due to either failure to receive information or reception of incorrect information. For NORMATIVE approaches to combining information from redundant or nonredundant cues that are probabilistic, see REGRESSION ANALYSIS, BAYES' THEOREM.

synonyms: EQUIPOTENTIALITY, EQUIFINALITY, REDUNDANCY.

related terms: VICARIOUS MEDIATION, PROBABILISTIC FUNCTIONALISM, QUASI-RATIONALITY, LENS MODEL, COMPENSATORY MODEL.

VICARIOUS MEDIATION.

See REDUNDANCY.

VIGILANCE.

See CONFLICT THEORY.

Von NEUMANN-MORGENSTERN UTILITY

definition: A scaling of objective VALUES in terms of PROBABILITIES that, when entered in a LOTTERY on the lowest versus the highest objective value, capture the DECISION MAKER's ATTITUDE TOWARD RISK (von Neumann & Morgenstern, 1947.) The lowest value is always assigned a probability of 0; the highest value is always assigned a probability of 1; and intermediate values are assigned probabilities that depend on the decision maker's attitude toward risk. For

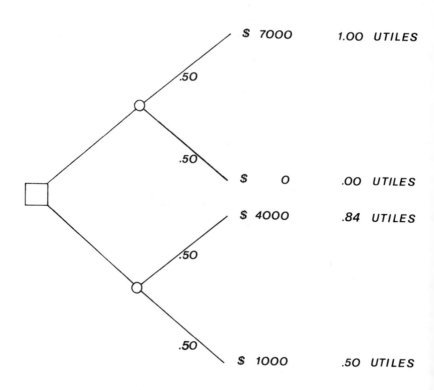

Initial Decision Tree

example, an objective value halfway between the lowest and highest will be assigned a probability of .50 if the decision maker is RISK NEUTRAL, a probability greater than .50 if he/she is RISK AVERSE, and a probability less than .50 if he/she is RISK PRONE (see RISK PREMIUM). The resulting probability scale is called a scale of UTILITY.

example: "To give a simple example: Assume that an individual prefers the consumption of a glass of tea to that of a cup of coffee, and the cup of coffee to a glass of milk. If we

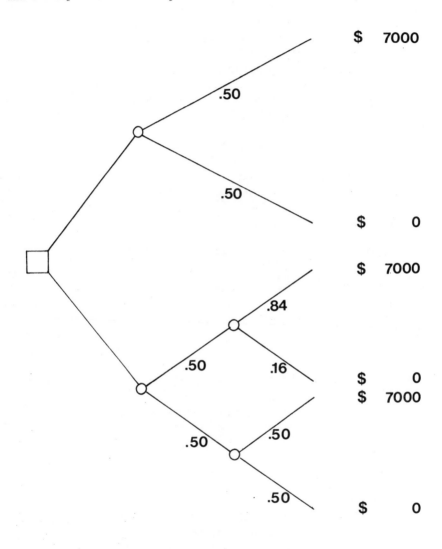

Substitution of Equivalent Lotteries

now want to know whether the last preference--i.e., difference in utilities--exceeds the former, it suffices to place him in a situation where he must decide this: Does he prefer a cup of coffee to a glass the content of which will be determined by a 50%-50% chance device as tea or milk" (von Neumann & Morgenstern, 1947, p. 18).

comment: MAXIMIZATION of EXPECTED UTILITY is widely considered to be a defining characteristic of RATIONALITY. To see why, consider the following example (from Barclay, Brown, Kelly, Peterson, Phillips, & Selvidge, 1977, pp. 39ff.)

Consider a choice between two gambles: (a) a .50-.50 chance on $0 vs. $7000, and (b) a .50-.50 chance on $1000 vs. $4000. And assume the following utility scaling: $0 = 0 utiles, $1000 = .50 utiles, $4000 = .84 utiles, and $7000 = 1.00 utiles. (Note that these utilities reflect risk aversion.) The choice can be represented by the first DECISION TREE above.

Because .84 utiles, to take it as an example, has been previously judged (in the utility assessment phase) to be equivalent in value to a .84 chance on $7000 and a .16 chance on $0, however, the ENDPOINT labelled .84 utiles can be replaced by an EVENT FORK representing this gamble. By the same kind of argument, any other endpoints can be replaced by a similar event fork. (The pros and cons of this substitution, which lies at the core of utility theory, are discussed in Raiffa (1968) and Kahneman & Tversky (1979b). This substitution has been accomplished in the second decision tree.

Now we no longer have to be concerned about TRADEOFFS between probabilities and amounts to be won, because the amounts to be won are held constant across all alternatives. What varies from alternative to alternative is only the probability of winning, which, in this case is .50 for Alternative A and .67 for Alternative B. (Note that, whereas Alternative A maximizes EXPECTED VALUE, Alternative B maximizes expected utility.) Any rational decision maker faced with a choice between two probabilities of winning the same amount will select the higher probability. This is all that maximizing expected utility (in the von Neumann-Morgenstern sense of "utility") means.

The first experimental study of expected utility was that of Mosteller & Nogee (1951). A problem with the Mosteller & Nogee study was that, while they gave their subjects the true probabilities, there was no assurance that their subjects used these probabilities. Davidson, Suppes, & Siegel (1957), instead, used an event that they had experimentally determined to have a subjective probability of .5. Savage (1954) had developed an axiomatic theory leading to the simultaneous measurement of subjective probability and utility. Tversky (1967) was the first to measure subjective probability and utility simultaneously, finding utility to be LINEAR for GAINS and POSITIVELY ACCELERATED for LOSSES. More recently, Shanteau (1975) applied FUNCTIONAL MEASUREMENT to the simultaneous measurement of subjective probability and utility and found that, while the MULTIPLYING relation in the SEU MODEL holds, the ADDING relation may more correctly be an AVERAGING one.

related terms: RISK, UNCERTAINTY, UTILITY, RISK PREMIUM, ALLAIS' PARADOX, PROSPECT THEORY.

VOTING PARADOX.

    See ARROW'S PARADOX.

WEIGHT

definition: A numerical value that is presumed to represent the importance of (a) a DIMENSION or (b) a LEVEL on a dimension. Whether the weights in question are constant or variable across the levels of a dimension, multiplying the appropriate weight by each level of an input dimension renders the dimension COMMENSURABLE with other input dimensions in terms a common scale. In the case of FACT JUDGMENTS, the common scale is the criterion (in REGRESSION ANALYSES) or the CONDITIONAL PROBABILITY of some value on the criterion (in BAYESIAN analyses). In the case of VALUE JUDGMENTS, it is a scale of value or UTILITY. When a constant, or dimension, weight is employed, the transformation of the input dimension is LINEAR, and the weight is the slope of the function that transforms the input dimension to the common scale. When variable weights are employed, the transformation of the input dimension is NONLINEAR. Multiplication of weights by scale values assumes that weights are measured on at least a RATIO scale and that scale values are measured on at least an INTERVAL scale (See SCALES of MEASUREMENT.)

comment: "Weight" has been operationally defined in a variety of ways. A fundamental operational distinction is between direct and indirect assessment. In DIRECT ASSESSMENT, the judge is asked to judge weights (and usually also scale values) by producing numerical values for each. This is the technique employed by BDT in its SMART procedure (see Edwards, Guttentag, & Snapper, 1975).

In INDIRECT ASSESSMENT, the judge is asked only to provide an overall judgment for each of the entities being evaluated or to make choices among them. Various techniques (experimental in the case of A PRIORI DECOMPOSITION, statistical or AXIOMATIC in the case of A POSTERIORI DECOMPOSITION) are then employed to separate these overall judgments into scale value and weight components.

Techniques for the indirect assessment of weights are considered in two categories: (a) those that apply the weights directly to objective scale values, and (b) those that first transform objective scale values into subjective scale values and apply the weights to the subjective scale values. Two possibilities fall into the first category:

> 1. *untransformed objective scale values.*
> REGRESSION WEIGHTS (*b* WEIGHTS) reflect the importance of unit changes on the objective scales in terms of the units of the criterion scales, with the effects of other variables partialled out (Cohen & Cohen, 1975, pp. 75-78). Regression weights are used in PDT and SJT. Because they are defined in terms of units on the objective scale, regression weights are sensitive to unit changes but not to range changes on these scales. Because the effects of other variables have been partialled out, these weights are sensitive to inter-correlations among the objective scales. Because the objective scales are not transformed, the units on these scales have no psychological significance, and all psychological significance resides in the weights. (Regression weights that have been normalized to sum to 1 are called RELATIVE WEIGHTS (Hoffman, 1960); however, see (4) below for a different use of this term.)

2. *variance-normalized objective scale values.*
   Another possibility is to normalize all scales
   to the same variance, and then to use STANDARD
   REGRESSION WEIGHTS (BETA WEIGHTS) to reflect
   the importance of a change of one standard
   deviation on each objective scale in terms of
   standard deviations on the criterion scale,
   with the effects of other variables partialled
   out (Cohen & Cohen, 1975, pp. 75-78). Beta
   weights are used in PDT and SJT. Because they
   are defined in terms of standard deviations,
   beta weights are not sensitive to unit or range
   changes on the objective scales, but are
   sensitive to changes in the distribution of
   cases along these scales. Because the effects
   of other variables have been partialled out,
   these weights are sensitive to
   intercorrelations among the objective scales.
   Because the objective scales are not
   transformed, the units on these scales have no
   psychological significance, and all psychological significance resides in the weights.

Two possibilities fall into the category of those techniques that
apply weights to subjective scale values:

3. *range-normalized subjective scale values.* One
   possibility in this category is to normalize
   all subjective scales to the same range and
   then to use weights to reflect the importance
   of a full-range change on the subjective scale
   in terms of the underlying value scale. This
   is the approach taken by SJT, as one option in
   its "POLICY" program (Hammond, Stewart,
   Brehmer, & Steinmann, 1975, pp. 282-283), and
   by DT (Keeney & Raiffa, 1976, pp. 121-123,
   271-273). RANGE-ADJUSTED WEIGHTS (SJT) and
   SCALING CONSTANTS (DT) reflect the importance
   of a full-range change on the subjective scale
   in terms of a common underlying scale of value.
   Because they are defined in terms of ranges on
   the subjective scales, these weights are

sensitive to range changes, but not unit
changes, on the objective scales. (It is this
sensitivity to range changes that has led
Keeney & Raiffa (1976, p. 272) to insist that
"scaling constants *do not* indicate the relative
importance of attributes".) Because the
objective scales are transformed, by means of
FUNCTION FORMS (SJT) or UTILITY FUNCTIONS (DT),
to subjective scales before the weights are
applied, the units on the subjective scales, as
well as the weights, have psychological
significance. (CONJOINT ANALYSIS (Green &
Wind, 1973) employs a similar measure of
weight.)

4. *untransformed subjective scale values.* IIT has
the most complex weighting scheme. While
weights are not defined for the cases of ADDING
and MULTIPLYING MODELS, all psychological
significance residing in the scale values in
these models, both ABSOLUTE and RELATIVE
WEIGHTS are defined for the case of the
AVERAGING MODEL (Anderson, 1981, pp. 68-77).
Absolute weights (w_1, w_2, w_3, ...) are assumed
to be constant across different sets of
stimuli. Relative weights (w_i/W), on the other
hand, are assumed to vary across different sets
of stimuli (because of variation in $W = w_1 + w_2$
$+ w_3 + ...$). It is the manipulation of the
number of stimuli in the set that makes
possible the assessment of relative weights and
that provides a foundation, both conceptual and
empirical, for establishing the psychological
reality of the weight parameter. The absolute
weights (w_i) in Anderson's (1981) averaging
model can be either constant across levels
within a dimension EQUAL WEIGHTS) or variable
across levels within a dimension (DIFFERENTIAL
WEIGHTS). The arguments for differential
weights include greater salience and
informativeness of extreme levels on a
dimension (Manis, Gleason, & Dawes, 1966; Oden
and Anderson, 1971; Osgood & Tannenbaum, 1955).

Relative weights (equal or differential) reflect the importance of unit changes on the subjective scales in terms of a common underlying scale of value. Because they are defined in terms of units on subjective scales, the relative weights of IIT should be independent of the units, ranges, and variances of the objective values presented. Because they depend on the other stimuli in the set, relative weights can account for certain CONFIGURAL properties of judgment. Because the objective scales are transformed to subjective scales before the weights are applied, the units on the subjective scales, as well as the weights, have psychological significance.

The BAYESIAN equivalent of weight is DIAGNOSTICITY. Whereas weights in correlational and (except for IIT) analysis-of-variance studies generally reflect "importance across an entire dimension," the Bayesian measure of weight reflects the "impact of each individual datum" (Slovic & Lichtenstein, 1973, p. 39). Related psychological measures are SUBJECTIVE PROBABILITY and DECISION WEIGHT (which see).

related terms: COMMENSURATION, FUNCTION FORM, FACT-VALUE SEPARATION, DIAGNOSTICITY, SUBJECTIVE PROBABILITY, DECISION WEIGHT.

WELFARE.

See UTILITY.

WHOLISTIC

definition: Intact, not DECOMPOSED.

example: Phelps & Shanteau (1978) presented judges with photographs or verbal descriptions of pigs, varying on such dimensions as ham thickness, muscle trimness, body weight, and number of nipples, as a basis for wholistic evaluation of each pig. In evaluating police handgun ammunition, Hammond and Adelman (1976) presented representatives of the public with profiles of hypothetical bullets that differed in terms of weight, muzzle velocity, stopping effectiveness, severity of injury, and threat to bystanders, as a basis for wholistic evaluation of the corresponding bullets. Decomposed judgments, by way of contrast, would have involved obtaining judgments DIMENSION by dimension, rather than judgments of "whole bullets".

synonym: GLOBAL.

related terms: DECOMPOSITION.

WILLINGNESS to PAY, WILLINGNESS to ACCEPT PAYMENT

definition: Willingness to Pay (**WTP**) and Willingness to Accept Payment (**WTAP**) are both TRADEOFFS (Definition 2) between a given dimension, or set of dimensions (X) and another dimension (Y) which is used as a common indicator of VALUE (Definition 2a), or UTILITY (Definition 1). Dimension X may be risky or riskless (i.e., may or may not involve lotteries). Dimension Y, the NUMERAIRE, is often money.

One's WTP or WTAP for a given change in X, (ΔX), is the change in Y, (ΔY), whose UTILITY (Definition 1) exactly equals that of ΔX; that is WTP (or WTAP) for ΔX is that ΔY at which $U(\Delta Y) = U(\Delta X)$. In INDIFFERENCE terms, define x^O and x^* as one's initial and final levels of X and y^O and y^* as one's initial and final levels of Y Assume that the changes from initial to final levels are voluntary and that one is indifferent between initial state (y^O, x^O) and final state (y^*, x^*). Then one's WTP or WTAP for $[\Delta X = (x^* - x^O)]$ equals $[\Delta Y = (y^* - y^O)]$. The difference between WTP and WTAP depends on the sign of ΔY: If negative, ΔY means WTP since one would willingly sacrifice some of Y for ΔX; if positive, ΔY means WTAP since one would demand payment in Y to accept ΔX. (See, for example, Keeney & Raiffa, 1976, pp. 125-127; Mishan, 1976, p. 122). WTP is sometimes termed maximum BUYING PRICE and WTAP termed minimum SELLING PRICE.

Economists customarily *define* the VALUE of any ΔX as one or more individuals' WTP or WTAP for it, using VALUE in the sense of Definition 2b. The greater the UTILITY (Definition 1) of ΔX, the more of Y one will pay or demand in payment for it, all else equal. (See, for example, Baumol, 1977, p. 192; Freeman, 1976, p. 3; Mishan, 1976, p. 122;; Sinden & Worrell, 1979, p. 12; Stokey & Zeckhauser,

1978, p. 150.)

comment: Measurement, or COMMENSURATION, of the value of changes on one or more dimensions $X_i (i = 1 \dots n)$ in terms of a single numeraire dimension Y is often termed COSTING OUT or PRICING OUT when Y is defined as money.

In general, one's WTP (or WTAP) in Y for a given ΔX_i may depend on the levels of all other preference-relevant dimensions $X_j \dots X_n$, (see INDEPENDENCE) and the starting levels of X_i and Y, as well as on ΔX_i (see FUNCTION FORM). The levels of other dimensions $X_j \dots X_n$ can properly be ignored only if the (X_i, Y) tradeoff is "PREFERENTIALLY INDEPENDENT" of those other dimensions. Starting levels of X_i and Y can be ignored only if the MARGINAL UTILITY of each is constant throughout its range. (Keeney & Raiffa, 1976, p. 125-127). Keeney & Raiffa assert, however, that these assumptions unfortunately are usually not checked before pricing out changes on X_i into Y.

WTP and WTAP concepts are applicable to valuation of absence as well as occurrence of change on X_i. Insurance premiums indicate WTP to offset (probabilistically) adverse changes in one's income or wealth (here X_i and Y are the same variable, money); economists and public officials must often assess citizens' WTP to prevent adverse changes in the social or physical environment; and accident victims often seek through lawsuits monetary compensation (indicating WTAP) for the future income and other satisfactions their injuries will force them to forego.

WTP and WTAP can be estimated through analysis of aggregate behavior or through direct questioning of individuals. Economists rely on MARKET PRICES to indicate societal WTP (WTAP) for change (or absence of change) in levels of marketed goods, and sometimes of NONMARKETED GOODS as well (see SHADOW PRICE). JUDGMENT and DECISION analysts normally rely on various direct questioning methods (see TRADEOFF), including BIDDING GAMES, though sometimes relying on records of aggregate behavior such as committee decisions (e.g., Dawes, 1971). Economists also use direct questioning methods, particularly bidding games, for valuation of nonmarketed goods.

related terms: TRADEOFF, INDIFFERENCE CURVE, VALUE, UTILITY, NUMERAIRE, COMMENSURATION, MARKET PRICE, NONMARKETED GOOD, SHADOW PRICE, BIDDING GAME, COST-BENEFIT ANALYSIS, COST-EFFECTIVVENESS

ANALYSIS, ECONOMIC MAN, GAINS and LOSSES.

WORTH.

See VALUE.

ZERO-SUM GAME

definition: A game where the gain of one player equals the loss of the other, and, hence, these two quantities sum to zero (von Neumann & Morgenstern, 1947; Luce & Raiffa, 1958; Rapoport, 1960). The zero-sum property applies to each turn of the game, as well as to the game as a whole.

related terms: GAME THEORY, CONFLICT.

ZONE of AMBIGUITY

definition: The conceptual space between the observable PROXIMAL STIMULI and the unobservable DISTAL VARIABLES (Hammond, Stewart, Brehmer, & Steinmann, 1975, p. 275), so named because its CAUSAL TEXTURE is characterized by great AMBIGUITY. (See CAUSAL TEXTURE for dimensions that have been used to describe the zone of ambiguity.)

related terms: CAUSAL TEXTURE, AMBIGUITY, UNCERTAINTY, PROBABILISTIC FUNCTIONALISM, LENS MODEL.

A COCITATION MAP of AUTHORS

in

JUDGMENT and DECISION RESEARCH

Howard D. White and Belver C. Griffith

School of Library and Information Science
Drexel University
Philadelphia, PA 19104

A variety of methods have been devised recently to display the structure of research and scholarship. One of these, author cocitation analysis, examines the way in which the works of authors are cited together, uses this as a measure of the similarity or the "relatedness" of their contributions, and then creates maps of the authors.

The Frontispiece is a map commissioned by the authors of this book to show interrelationships of 41 representative authors in studies of human judgment and decision making during 1972-1980. The map was produced by computer using nonmetric multidimensional scaling (Kruskal's M-D-SCAL) and Johnson hierarchical clustering programs [1, 2]. It may be thought of as a kind of "snapshot" of major groupings in the field at the end of that period. Authors close together, particularly within boundaries, may be thought of as similar; authors far apart, as relatively dissimilar.

Our similarity measure, described below, is based on author cocitation data--that is, counts of the times each pair of authors has been cited together in new papers over the nine years. These counts are publicly available in Social Scisearch, the online version of *Social Sciences Citation Index*, as provided by Lockheed DIALOG. Our data-gathering took place in late 1980 and early 1981; the counts will have increased by now, since new cocitations occur constantly, but nine years' worth are sufficient to yield trustworthy patterns, we think. It should be stressed that the patterns in the Frontispiece are based on hundreds of citers' use of the 41 authors, and not on the judgment of any one person or coterie. Hence, the map is about as objective as possible, assuming the 41 authors are reasonably well chosen to define the field.

To find the cocitation count for a given pair, e.g., Paul Slovic and Amos Tversky, one's input to Lockheed DIALOG might look like this:

SELECT CR=Slovic P? AND CR=Tversky A?

which means, "Select all papers having among their cited references (CR) anything by Slovic and anything by Tversky." The truncator ? obviates having to specify particular works by either author. (In conventional searches on cited authors, works are specified.) Here we are able to avoid specification, in the belief that someone who cites these two authors together will choose works of theirs that are appropriately connected in subject matter, to which the citer's paper is also connected. This belief, interestingly enough, very often holds true. In any case, Social Scisearch will respond to input like the above with a count of all papers meeting the requirement. Identifications of these papers can then be printed out, if wanted, since bibliographic retrieval is the main function of Social Scisearch. In such a retrieval, the names Slovic and Tversky act much like a subject heading, "Aspects of Psychological Decision Theory." Many other pairs of names can also be read as implicit subject headings. See White [3] and White and Griffith [4].

When large numbers of cocitation counts are to be obtained (e.g., in a mapping project, as here) technical knowledge is needed to form the sets economically. The first author, HDW, may be contacted for advice on shortcuts and limitations in this kind of online searching.

WHAT THE NUMBERS MEAN

Each author's point on the map, as given by M-D-SCAL, has been replaced by his or her *mean cocitation count* (as of December 1980) with all other authors shown. These averages, taken from highly skewed distributions, are a crude indicator of eminence or "recognized usefulness" within the field. Means greater than 30 have been circled to set off authors of highest use. (This is rather like distinguishing the magnitude of stars on star maps.) The highest mean is Slovic's 54, followed closely by Tversky's 52.

To assess the means properly, one must know that an "author" on this map is a corpus of writings, not an individual person. By

convention of the Institute for Scientific Information, which produces
Social Scisearch, any writing that has a person as its sole author *or*
first author will go into that person's corpus, but will not be
entered if the person is an author other than first.   Thus Slovic's
count is increased by citations to important papers he did in
collaboration with, e.g., Lichtenstein and Fischhoff; counts of the
latter two are not incremented when they are second authors.
Similarly, only von Neumann's count is incremented by citations to
Theory of Games and Economic Behavior, on which Morgenstern was second
author; if the latter shared citations to this very influential work,
his own count would not be so different from von Neumann's.
Generally, however, we think the mean counts are a valuable "third
dimension" to the two-dimensional positioning in subject space
accomplished by M-D-SCAL. Authors with high means relative to the
field correspond well with one's historical sense of important
contributors.

CHOICES AND LABELS

    The orienting work for the map is Hammond, McClelland, and
Mumpower's *Human Judgment and Decision Making*--hereafter *HJDM* [5].
Repeating a method we have used elsewhere [6], we drew as our initial
sample every author with two or more lines of page references in the
HJDM index. This gave 25 names who were important enough to receive
multiple mentions in a book-length review of the field and its major
subdivisions. About 25 more names were then added jointly by the ONR
research group at the University of Colorado and one of us (BCG), a
psychologist by training who has maintained some familiarity with the
decision science literature over the years. Subsequently, authors
with fewer than 40 citations in all, or lacking cocitation counts of
one or more with at least a third of the other authors on the list,
were dropped from the analysis. The 41 remaining authors, given in
Table 1, produced 41(40)/2 = 820 unique pairs. Of these, 730 pairs or
89 percent had actually been cocited in the journal literature one or
more times by the end of 1980. This is the highest percentage of
connectedness we have seen in several such studies. Plainly there has
been a great deal of cociting across specialty boundaries during
1972-80, which suggests that the field as defined here is highly
coherent despite its distinct subdivisions.

    The labeling of the subdivisions on the map is drawn largely from
HJDM, in which each chapter compares and contrasts aspects of Decision
Theory, Behavioral Decision Theory, Psychological Decision Theory,

Social Judgment Theory, Information Integration Theory, and Attribution Theory. The group we label "Game Theory, Utility Theory" comprises authors added in the second round of choosing; they are

Anderson NH*	Keeney RL*
Arrow KJ	Kelley HH*
Beach LR	Lichtenstein S*
Becker GM	Lindley DV
Brehmer B*	Luce RD
Brown RV	Meehl PE
Brunswik E*	Morgenstern O
Coombs CH*	Peterson CR
Edwards W*	Raiffa H*
Einhorn HJ	Rapoport A
Fishburn PC	Savage LJ
Fischhoff B*	Schlaifer RO
Goldberg LR	Shanteau JC*
Green PE	Shepard RN
Hammond KR*	Shuford EH
Heider F*	Simon H
Hoffman PJ	Slovic P*
Howard RA	Stewart TR*
Janis I	Tversky A*
Jones EE*	von Neumann J
Kahneman D*	

*Selected from the index to *Human Judgment and Decision Making*

Table 1

AUTHORS APPEARING in the STUDY

mostly famous generalists who have brought high mathematical formalization to the borderline area between psychology and economics. The group we label "Preference Theory," also second-round choices, includes three major figures in multidimensional scaling research, Green, Shepard, and Coombs, who may be cited more as methodologists than as theorists on preferences.

We tried several clustering routines, including factor analysis, to examine the various "theory groups" of authors in the Frontispiece. Five of the groups--Decision Theory, Social Judgment Theory,

Attribution Theory from *HJDM*, plus the later additions Game and Utility Theory and Preference Theory--always emerged as distinct clusters. Cocitation evidence, in other words, bears out the view that these groups have distinctive subject matters and methodologies. The map shows them as an "outer five" around three other groups whose labels, as stated above, are from *HJDM*. Both the Johnson clustering routine (see Figure 1) and our factor analysis suggest that the "inner three" are not so clearly separate as the "outer five." Rather, they are a densely interlinked core of studies within the larger field; in the factor analysis they load on one factor. We have partitioned them on the basis of the Johnson clusters around major figures identified in *HJDM*--Edwards, Tversky, and Anderson. But the Johnson routine does not always group authors quite like the book. Slovic and Lichtenstein, for example, are put with Edwards, and by implication Behavioral Decision Theory (on which they and Fischhoff did a chapter in the 1977 *Annual Review of Psychology*); *HJDM* puts them with Tversky and Psychological Decision Theory. We think these discrepancies not too important. Cocited author analysis probably will not always reflect distinctions that are valid to writers on theoretical content. It may also be the case that citers have used authors in somewhat different combinations than those based strictly on content would suggest. What seems clear from our data is that authors in the Psychological Decision Theory and Behavioral Decision Theory groups are perceived by citers as highly related. This may partly be due to collaborative relationships that cross group boundaries--e.g., Edwards and Tversky co-edited a book; Slovic, Fischhoff, and Lichtenstein have co-authored papers. Anderson and Shanteau, in Information Integration Theory, are also apparently seen as highly related to the other two "inner" groups.

THE MEASURE OF SIMILARITY

M-D-SCAL places the authors in subject space on the basis of their perceived similarity. We measure similarity by a Pearson r correlation coefficient for each pair, computed from their vectors of cocitation counts over all 40 others in the study. A Pearson r for each pair is preferable to their simple raw cocitation count because it makes use of much more information--in this case 40 data points instead of one--and because it eliminates unwanted effects of scale, so that, e.g., two authors with a cocitation count of 100 are not necessarily mapped as five times more similar than two authors with a count of 20. Authors who have the greatest number of high positive correlations with other authors take the center of any M-D-SCAL map.

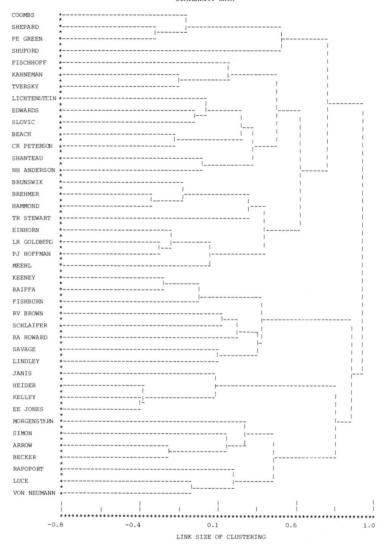

JOHNSON CLUSTERING DIAGRAM

SIMILARITY DATA

LINK SIZE OF CLUSTERING

Figure 1

JOHNSON CLUSTERING ROUTINE

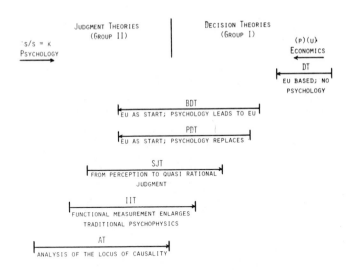

Figure 2a. Origins, overlapping interests, and directions of research among the six approaches and two groups.

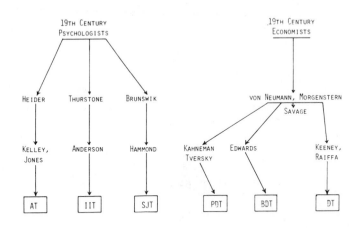

Figure 2b. First- and second-generation theorists.

Figure 2

MAPS from *HUMAN JUDGMENT and DECISION MAKING*

In this sense they, and the approach or specialization they represent, are central to the field. Here the author set closest to the map's origin by M-D-SCAL is obviously Tversky, with Coombs close by. The central work in the field, in the sense that it is correlated with work in all surrounding directions, has been done in Psychological and Behavioral Decision Theory, Information Integration Theory, and Preference Theory. Authors holding a more or less central place within group boundaries (e.g., Raiffa and Keeney) are central to specialities, if not to the field as a whole. Generally they are highly correlated with their surrounding near neighbors.

Stress 2, a measure of fit between the rank-ordered input pairs and the computer-derived distances in two dimensions on the map, is here 0.30. Given a square matrix as input, we regard this fit as tolerably good.

A COMPARISON OF MAPS

This trial of cocited author mapping to delineate a field's subdivisions differs from our previous trials in one important respect: for the first time we had existing maps of sorts by "insiders" against which to compare our results. The insiders in this case were Hammond, McClelland, and Mumpower, whose one-dimensional maps serve to organize the first chapters of HJDM. Two of them are reproduced in Figure 2. Figure 2a depicts, from left, three "Judgment Theories," which have their roots in psychology--Attribution Theory, Information Integration Theory, and Social Judgment Theory; and three "Decision Theories," which have their roots in economics (and the idea of expected utility, EU)--Psychological Decision Theory, Behavioral Decision Theory, and Decision Theory proper. These are ranged on a continuum in which Attribution Theory at left is "most psychological" and Decision Theory at right is "most economic"; the others represent various mixes of the two parent disciplines. The bulk of HJDM explicates differences among these six subdivisions. The important point here, however, is that the six were arrived at judgmentally by experts, who placed them thus after pondering their relations in one-dimensional subject space.

It will be seen that if the horizontal axis of our cocited author map is taken as this continuum, with psychology leftward and economics rightward, and if the theory groups are moved to it from their present positions, they line up very much as in HJDM. Further, and remarkably, if one moves major contemporary figures identified in

Figure 2b to the horizontal axis of our map, the line-up is virtually identical to that in 2b. Without introducing another figure, the result can be suggested by a line or two of type:

Kelley		Kahneman			Keeney
Jones	Anderson	Hammond	Tversky	Edwards	Raiffa

The cocitation map even captures something of the "apartness" of the two extreme groups, Attribution Theory and Decision Theory--the sense that they differ sharply in certain respects from the other specialties--that is conveyed by several passages in *HJDM*.

Why should our result, obtained wholly independently of Hammond, McClelland, and Mumpower's original analysis, square so well with their conceptual organization? While we can only speculate, it seems plausible that human judges of the structure of the literature in a field take many of their cues from what we might call "co-occurrence data"--e.g., co-occurrences of nouns and noun phrases in particular contexts. The joint appearance of authors' names in the textual references, footnotes, and endnotes of a paper may be an especially notable and memorable kind of co-occurrence. In other words, persons who have read extensively within a field--extensively enough to judge the structure of its literature--probably have "processed" a great deal of cocitation data impressionistically. As a consequence, their view of the field might well resemble what we get when we process cocitation data systematically, by introducing all possible pairs within a given set of authors. Persons well read in a field also know when its subdivisions have been explicitly linked. They know, for example, that Anderson has explicitly linked Attribution Theory with his own work on cognitive algebra in an integrative paper, and that therefore he should somehow be "close to" Attribution Theory. Our cocitation data say that this perception is indeed widespread among citers: Anderson's point is "pulled toward" Attribution Theory in a way that, say, Raiffa's is not. Thousands of such judgments underlie the positioning of points in the Frontispiece.

The vertical axis in our map is not so readily interpretable as the horizontal axis. It does not seem to represent a continuum from hard to soft science, or from relatively theoretical work to relatively applied—two dimensions that have appeared in earlier studies of fields. Instead, it seems to represent another subject dimension: perhaps (and we must be very tentative here) the importance of *utility* as a principal concept in organizing theory. This would account for the wide separation on the vertical axis between Social Judgment Theory and Attribution Theory, both of which originate in psychology. *HJDM*, p. 71, states, "The concept of utility (as this term is used in Group I approaches [i.e., those originating in economics] has no special role in [Social Judgment Theory]." In contrast, on p. 76 we find, "*Utility*...is given considerable importance by [Attribution Theory], but it is discussed in terms of valence or value." The clusters above and to the right of Social Judgment Theory on the map, including those in Group I—Psychological Decision Theory, Behavioral Decision Theory, and Decision Theory—of course make much use of utility as a technical concept, and for some it is absolutely central. But should Attribution Theory, which is portrayed as the most psychological and least quantitative specialty in *HJDM*, be ranged with Group I specialties on the vertical axis? Again *HJDM*, pp. 62-63, offers a tempting lead: "A recent [1976] article by Jones and McGillis indicates that [Attribution Theory] may have taken an entirely new turn that will link it more closely to Group I approaches." Noting that these two authors compare what they are doing to the work of Edwards, *HJDM* continues: "Jones and McGillis go much further and suggest that they are producing a normative or prescriptive theory similar to decision theory or game theory."

If cocitation patterns have picked up the difference between Attribution Theory and Social Judgment Theory that these quotes imply, that could account for their relative positions on the vertical axis. We know that cocitation mapping is capable of rendering such differences, including shifts in the perceived relationships of authors that occur through intellectual realignments. However, the resolution of this matter would take a much deeper analysis of the past and present history of the decision sciences than we, as outsiders, can undertake. Our map will have served its purpose if it stimulates additional analysis by insiders, along the lines of *Human Judgment and Decision Making*.

REFERENCES

1. Kruskal, J. B., & Wish, M. *Multidimensional scaling*.

Beverly Hills, CA: Sage, 1978.

2. Johnson, S. C. Hierarchical clustering schemes. *Psychometrika*, 1967, *32*, 241-254.

3. White, H. D. Cocited author retrieval online: An experiment with the social indicators literature. *Journal of the American Society for Information Science*, 1981, *32*, 16-21.

4. White, H. D., & Griffith, B. C. Author cocitation: A literature measure of intellectual structure. *Journal of the American Society for Information Science*. In press.

5. Hammond, K. R., McClelland, G. H., & Mumpower, J. *Human judgment and decision making: Theories, methods, and procedures*. New York: Praeger, 1980.

6. In addition to 4 above, which may be consulted for methodological details in general, and which maps the field of information science, we have in progress a mapping of studies in science, technology, and society. Both projects started with samples of heavily referenced authors in works purporting to survey the field.

BIBLIOGRAPHY

Abelson, R. P. Script processing in attitude formation and decision making. In J. S. Carroll & J. W. Payne (Eds.), Cognition and social behavior. New York: Erlbaum, 1976.

Adelman, L. A. The influence of formal, substantive, and contextual task properties on the relative effectiveness of diffferent forms of feedback in multiple-cue probability learning tasks (Center for Research on Judgment and Policy, Report No. 199). Unpublished manuscript, University of Colorado, Institute of Behavioral Science, 1977.

Allais, M. Fondements d'une theorie positive des choix comportant un risque et critique des postulats et axiomes de l'ecole americaine. Colloque Internationale du Centre National de la Recherche scientifique, 1952, No. 36.

Allais, M. Le comportement de l'homme rationnel devant le risque: Critique des postulats et axiomes de l'ecole americaine. Econometrica, 1953, 21, 503-546. (a)

Allais, M. L'Extension des theories de l'equilibre economique general et du rendement social au cas du risque. Econometrica, 1953, 21, 269-290. (b)

Allport, G. W. Personality: A psychological interpretation. New York: Holt, 1937.

Alluisi, E. A. On the use of information measures in studies of form perception. Perceptual and Motor Skills, 1960, 11, 195-203.

Alpert, M., & Raiffa, H. A progress report on the training of probability assessors. Unpublished manuscript, Harvard University, 1969.

Anderberg, M. R. Cluster analysis for applications. New York: Academic Press, 1973.

Anderson, B. F. The complete thinker: A handbook of techniques for creative and critical problem solving. Englewood Cliffs, NJ: Prentice-Hall, 1980.

Anderson, N. H. Application of an additive model to impression formation. Science, 1962, 138, 817-818.

Anderson, N. H. Averaging versus adding as a stimulus-combination rule in impression formation. Journal of Experimental Psychology, 1965, 70, 394-400.

Anderson, N. H. Algebraic models in perception. In E. L. Carterette

&   M. P. Friedman   (Eds.),   Handbook   of   perception   (Vol. 2),
Psychophysical judgment and measurement.   New York: Academic   Press,
1974 (a).

Anderson, N. H. Cognitive algebra. In L. Berkowitz (Ed.), Advances
in Experimental Social Psychology (Vol. 7). New York: Academic
Press, 1974. (b)

Anderson, N. H. Information integration theory: A brief survey. In
D. H. Krantz,   R. C. Atkinson,   R. D. Luce,   &   P. Suppes   (Eds.)
Contemporary   developments   in   mathematical   psychology   (Vol. 2),
Measurement, psychophysics, and neural information processing.   San
Francisco: Freeman, 1974. (c)

Anderson, N. H.   How functional measurement can yield validated
interval scales of mental quantities. Journal of Applied Psychology,
1976, 61, 677-692.

Anderson, N. H.   Foundations of information integrating theory. New
York: Academic Press, 1981.

Anderson, N. H., & Cuneo, D. O. The height + width rule in children's
judgments of quantity. Journal of Experimental Psychology: General,
1978, 107, 335-378.

Anderson, N. H., & Farkas, A. J. Integration theory applied to models
of inequity.   Personality & Social Psychology Bulletin, 1975, 1,
588-591.

Anderson, N. H., & Jacobson, A. Effect of stimulus inconsistency and
discounting instructions in personality impression formation. Journal
of Personality and Social Psychology, 1965, 2, 531-539.

Armelius, B., & Lenntoft, K. Effect of cue intercorrelation in a
multiple cue probability learning task with different cue validities
(Umea Psychological Report No. 20).   Department of Psychology,
University of Umea, 1970.

Arrow, K. J.   Social choice and individual values. New York: Wiley,
1951.

Arrow, K. J. Social choice and individual values (2nd ed.).   New
York: Wiley, 1963.

Asch, S. Forming impressions of personality. Journal of Abnormal &
Social Psychology, 1946, 41, 258-290.

Asch, S. E. Opinions and social pressure. Scientific American, 1955,
193(5), 31-35.

Ashby, W. R. Introduction to cybernetics. New York: Wiley, 1956.

Ashby, W. R. Design for a brain (2d ed.). New York: Wiley, 1960.

Atkinson, J. W. Motivational determinants of risk-taking behavior. Psychological Review, 1957, 64, 359-372.

Atkinson, J. W., Bastian, J. R., Earl, R. W., & Litwin, G. H. The achievement motive, goal setting, and probability preferences. Journal of Abnormal & Social Psychology, 1960, 60, 27-36.

Attneave, F. Transfer of experience with a class-schema to identification learning of patterns and shapes. Journal of Experimental Psychology, 1957, 54, 81-88.

Azuma, H., & Cronbach, L. J. Cue response correlations in the attainment of a scalar concept. The American Journal of Psychology, 1966, 79, 38-49.

Baird, J. C., & Moma, E. Fundamentals of scaling and psychophysics. New York: Wiley, 1978.

Barclay, S., Brown, R. V., Kelly, C. W., III, Peterson, C. R., Phillips, L. D., & Selvidge, J. Handbook for decision analysis. McLean, VA: Decisions & Designs, Inc., 1977.

Bass, F. M., Pessemier, E. A., & Lehmann, D. R. An experimental study of relationships between attitudes, brand preference, and choice. Behavioral Science, 1972, 17, 532-541.

Baumol, W. J. Economic theory and operations analysis (4th ed.). Englewood Cliffs, NJ: Prentice-Hall, Inc., 1977.

Bayes, T. An essay towards solving a problem in the doctrine of chances. Biometrika, 1958, 45, 296-315. (Originally published, 1764.)

Beach, L. R., Wise, J. A., & Barclay, S. Sample proportion and subjective probability revisions. Organizational Behavior and Human Performance 1970, 5, 183-190.

Becker, G. M. Decision making: Objective measures of subjective probability and utility. Psychological Review, 1962, 69, 136-148.

Becker, G. M., De Groot, M. H., & Marschak, J. Measuring utility by a single-response sequential method. Behavioral Science, 1964, 9, 226-232.

Becker, G. M., & McClintock, C. G. Value: Behavioral decision theory. Annual Review of Psychology, 1967, 18, 239-286.

Becker, G. S. The economic approach to human behavior. Chicago: University of Chicago Press, 1976.

Becker, S. W., & Brownson, F. O. What price ambiguity of ambiguity in decision-making. Journal of Political Economy, 1964, 72, 62-73.

Bell, D. E., Keeney, R. L., & Raiffa, H. (Eds.). Conflicting objectives in decisions. New York: Wiley, 1977.

Bellman, R. E. Dynamic programming. Princeton, NJ: Princeton University Press, 1957.

Bem, D. J. Self-perception theory. In L. Berkowitz (Ed.), Advances in experimental social psychology (Vol. 6). New York: Academic, 1972.

Ben-Dak, J. D. Gaming and simulation in the service of social impact assessment. In K. Finsterbusch & C. P. Wolf (Eds.), Methodology of social impact assessment. Stroudsburg, PA: Dowden, Hutchinson, & Ross, 1977.

Berlin, I. Karl Marx: His life and environment (4th ed.). Fairlawn, NJ: Oxford University Press, 1978.

Bernoulli, J. Ars conjectandi. Basel, 1713.

Bernoulli, D. [Exposition of a new theory on the measurement of risk] (L. Sommer, trans.). Econometrica, 1954, 22, 23-36. (Reprinted from Petropolitanae, 1738, 5, 175-192.

Black, D. On the rationale of group decision making. Journal of Political Economics, 1948, 56, 23-34. (a)

Black, D. The decisions of a committee using a special majority. Econometrica, 1948, 16, 245-261. (b)

Blin, J.-M. Fuzzy sets in multiple criteria decision making. In M. K. Starr & M. Zeleny (Eds.), Multiple Criteria Decision Making. (TIMS Studies in Management Sciences. Vol. 6). Amsterdam: North-Holland, 1977.

Bock, R. D. Multivariate statistical methods in behavioral research. New York: McGraw-Hill, 1975.

Borel, E. [The theory of play and integral equations with skew symmetric kernels] (L. J. Savage, trans.). Econometrica, 1953, 21, 97-100. (Reprinted from C. R. Aca. Sci., Paris, 1921, 173, 1304-1308.

Borel, E. [On games that involve chance and the skill of the players] (L. S. Savage, trans.). Econometrica, 1953, 21, 101-105. (Originally published, 1924.)

Borel, E. [On systems of linear forms of skew symmetric determinants and the general theory of play] (L. J. Savage, trans.). Econometrica, 1953, 21, 116-117. (Reprinted from C. R. Acad. Sci., Paris, 1927, 184, 52-53.)

Borgida, E., & Nisbett, R. E. The differential impact of abstract vs. concrete information on decisions. Journal of Applied Social Psychology, 1977, 7(3), 258-271.

Bourne, L. E., Jr. Human conceptual behavior. Boston: Allyn & Bacon, 1966.

Bourne, L. E. Jr., & Restle, F. Mathematical theory of concept identification. Psychological Review, 1959, 66, 278-296.

Bowman, E. H. Consistency and optimality in managerial decision making. Management Science, 1963, 9, 310-321.

Bradford, D. Benefit-cost analysis and demand curves for public goods. Kyklos, 1970, 23, 775-791.

Brams, S. J. Game theory and politics. New York: Free Press, 1975.

Brandle, J. E. Satisficing, feedback, and decision rules in government. In S. Nagel (Ed.), Improving policy analysis. Beverly Hills: SAGE Publications, 1980.

Brehmer, B. Cognitive dependence on additive and configural cue-criterion relations. The American Journal of Psychology, 1969, 82, 490-503. (a)

Brehmer, B. The roles of policy differences and inconsistency in policy conflict (Umea Psychological Report No. 18). Department of Psychology, University of Umea, 1969. (b) (Also published as Program on Cognitive Processes, Report No. 118, Institute of Behavioral Science, University of Colorado, 1969.)

Brehmer, B. Effects of communication and feedback on cognitive conflict. Scandinavian Journal of Psychology, 1971, 12, 205-216. (a)

Brehmer, B. Subjects' ability to use functional rules. Psychonomic Science, 1971, 24, 259-260. (b)

Brehmer, B. Policy conflict as a function of policy differences and policy complexity. Scandinavian Journal of Psychology, 1972, 13, 208-221.

Brehmer, B. Hypotheses about relations between scaled variables in the learning of probabilistic inference tasks. Organizational Behavior and Human Performance, 1974, 11, 1-27.

Brehmer, B. Learning complex rules in probabilistic inference tasks (Umea Psychological Reports 88). University of Umea, Department of Psychology, 1975.

Brehmer, B. Social judgment theory and the analysis of interpersonal conflict. Psychological Bulletin, 1976, 83, 985-1003. (a)

Brehmer, B. Subjects' ability to find the parameters of functional rules in probabilistic inference tasks (Umea Psychological Reports 97). Umea, Sweden: University of Umea, Department of Psychology, 1976. (b)

Brehmer, B., & Hammond, K. R. Cognitive sources of interpersonal conflict: Analysis of interactions between linear and nonlinear cognitive systems. Organizational Behavior and Human Performance, 1973, 10, 290-313.

Brehmer, B., & Hammond, K. R. Cognitive factors in interpersonal conflict. In D. Druckman (Ed.), Negotations: Social-psychological perspectives. Beverly Hills, CA: Sage, 1977.

Brehmer, B. & Kuylenstierna, J. Task information and performance in probabilistic inference tasks. Organizational Behavior and Human Performance, 1978, 22, 445-464.

Brehmer, B., & Lindberg, L. A. The relation between cue dependency and cue validity in single-cue probability learning with scaled cue and criterion variables. Organizational Behavior and Human Performance, 1970, 5, 542-554.

Broadbent, D. E. The magic number seven after fifteen years. In A. Kennedy & A. Wilkes (Eds.), Studies in Long Term Memory. New York: Wiley, 1975.

Brookshire, D., Ives, B., & Schulze, W. The valuation of aesthetic ʌeferences. Journal of Environmental Economics and Management, 1976, 3, 325-346.

Brookshire, D., Randall, A., & Stoll, J. Valuing increments and decrements in natural resource service flows. American Journal of Agricultural Economics, 1980, August, 478-488.

Brown, R. U., Kahr, A. S., & Peterson, C. Decision analysis for the manager. New York: Holt, Rinehart, and Winston, 1974.

Brunswik, E. The organism and the causal texture of the environment. Psychological Review, 1935, 42, 43-77.

Brunswik, E. The conceptual framework of psychology. In International Encyclopedia of Unified Science (Vol. 1(10)). Chicago: University of Chicago Press, 1952.

Brunswik, E. Representative design and probabilistic theory in a functional psychology. Psychological Review, 1955, 62, 193-217.

Brunswik, E. Perception and the representative design of psychological experiments (2nd ed.). Berkeley: University of California Press, 1956.

Brunswik, E. Reasoning as a universal behavior model and a functional differentiation between "perception" and "thinking". In K. R. Hammond (Ed.), The Psychology of Egon Brunswik. New York: Holt, Rinehart, & Winston, 1966. (Originally published, 1954.)

Bush, R. R., Galanter, E., & Luce, R. D. Characterization and classification of choice experiments. In R. D. Luce, R. R. Bush & E. Galanter (Eds.), Readings in mathematical psychology (Vol. 1). New York: Wiley, 1963.

Campbell, N. R. Symposium: Measurement and its importance for philosophy. Aristotelian Society for the Systematic Study of Philosophy, London: Proceedings, Supplementarl Volume, 1938, 17, 121-142.

Campbell, N. R., and others. Final report. The Advancement of Science, 1940, No. 2, 331-349.

Canter, L. W. Environmental impact assessment. New York: McGraw-Hill, 1977.

Cardano, G. The book on games of chance. In O. Ore (Ed.), Cardano, the gambling scholar. Princeton, N. J.: Princeton University Press, 1953.

Carroll, J. D. Categorical conjoint measurement. Paper presented at the meeting of Mathematical Psychology, Ann Arbor, August 1969.

Carroll, J. D. Individual differences and multidimensional scaling. In R. N. Shepard, A. K. Romney & S. Nerlove (Eds.), Multidimensional Scaling: Theory and application in the behavioral sciences, (Vol. 1). New York: Seminar Press, 1972.

Carroll, J. D., & Arabie, P. Multidimensional scaling. In M. R. Rosenzweig & L. W. Porter (Eds.), Annual Review of Psychology. Palo Alto, CA: Annual Reviews, Inc., 1980.

Carroll, J. D., & Wish, M. Multidimensional scaling of individual differences in perception and judgment. Unpublished manuscript, 1977.

Cattell, R. B. The three basic factor analytic research designs - their interrelations and derivatives. In D. N. Jackson & S. Messick (Eds.), Problems in human assessment. New York: McGraw-Hill, 1967.

Chapman, L. J., & Chapman, J. P. Genesis of popular erroneous psychodiagnostic observations. Journal of Abnormal Psychology, 1967, 72, 193-204.

Chernoff, H. Rational selection of decision functions. Econometrica, 1954, 22, 422-443.

Chernoff, H. Decision theory. In W. H. Kruskal & J. M. Tanur (Eds.),

International Encyclopedia of Statistics (Vol. 1). New York: Free Press, 1968.

Christensen, S. Decision making and socialization. In J. G. March & J. P. Olsen (Eds.), Ambiguity and choice in organizations. Bergen: Universitetsforlaget, 1976.

Clawson, M., & Knetsch, J. L. Economics of outdoor recreation. Baltimore: Johns Hopkins University Press (for Resources for the Future), 1966.

Coates, J. F. The role of formal models in technology assessment. Technological Forecasting & Social Change, 1976, 9, 139-190. (a)

Coates, J. F. Technology assessment - A tool kit. Chem Tech-Chemical Technology, 1976, June, 372-383. (b)

Cohen, J., & Cohen, P. Applied multiple regression/correlation analysis for the behavioral sciences. Hillsdale, NJ: Erlbaum, 1975.

Cohen, M. D., & March, J. G. A garbage can model of organizational choice. Administrative Science Quarterly, 1972, 17, 1-25.

Cohen, M. D., & March, J. G. Leadership and ambiguity: The American college president. New York: McGraw-Hill, 1974.

Cohen, M. R., & Nagel, E. An introduction to logic and the scientific method. New York: Harcourt, Brace, & World, 1934.

Cohon, J. L. Multiobjective programming and planning. New York: Academic Press, 1978.

Cook, R. L. An interactive and iterative approach to computer-aided policy capturing (Center for Research on Judgment and Policy Report No. 164). Unpublished manuscript, University of Colorado, 1974.

Cooley, W. W., & Lohnes, P. R. Multivariate data analysis. New York: Wiley, 1971.

Coombs, C. H. Psychological scaling without a unit of measurement. Psychological Review, 1950, 57, 145-158.

Coombs, C. H. A theory of data. New York: Wiley, 1964.

Coombs, C. H. Portfolio theory: A theory of risky decision making. La decision. Paris: Centre National de la Recherche Scientifique, 1969.

Coombs, C. H. Portfolio theory and the measurement of risk. In M. F. Kaplan & S. S. Schwartz (Eds.), Human judgment and decision processes. New York: Academic Press, 1975.

Coombs, C. H., & Avrunin, G. S. Single-peaked functions and the theory of preference. Psychological Review, 1977, 84, 216-230.

Coombs, C. H., Dawes, R. M., & Tversky, A. Mathematical Psychology. Englewood Cliffs, NJ: Prentice-Hall, 1970.

Coombs, C. H., & Huang, L. C. Polynomial psychophysics of risk. Journal of Mathematical Psychology, 1970, 7, 317-338.

Coombs, C. H., & Meyer, D. E. Risk-preference in coin-toss games. Journal of Mathematical Psychology, 1969, 6, 514-527.

Coombs, C. H., & Pruitt, D. G. Components of risk in decision making: Probability and variance preferences. Journal of Experimental Psychology, 1960, 60, 265-277.

Cyert, R. M., & March, J. G. A behavioral theory of the firm. Englewood Cliffs, N.J.: Prentice-Hall, 1963.

Dale, H. C. A. Weighing evidence: An attempt to assess the efficiency of the human operator. Ergonomics, 1968, 11, 215-230.

Dalkey, N. C. An elementary cross-impact model. In H. A. Linstone & M. Turoff (Eds.), The Delphi method: Techniques and applications. Reading, Mass.: Addison-Wesley, 1975.

Dalkey, N., & Helmer, O. An experimental application of the Delphi method to the use of experts. Management Science, 1963, 3, 458.

Dannenbring, D. G., & Starr, M. K. Management science: An introduction. New York: McGraw-Hill, 1981.

Darlington, R. B. Multiple regression in psychological research and practice. Psychological Bulletin, 1968, 69, 161-182.

Dawes, R. M. Social selection based on multi-dimensional criteria. Journal of Abnormal and Social Psychology, 1964, 68, 104-109.

Dawes, R. M. Graduate admissions: A case study. American Psychologist, 1971, 26, 180-188.

Dawes, R. M. The mind, the model, and the task. In F. Restle, R. M. Shiffrin, N. J. Castellan, H. R. Lindman & D. P. Pisoni (Eds.), Cognitive theory (vol. 1). Hillsdale, N. J.: Erlbaum, 1975.

Dawes, R. M. The robust beauty of improper linear models in decision making. American Psychologist, 1979, 34, 571-582.

Dawes, R. M. Social dilemmas. In M. R. Rosenzweig & L. W. Porter (Eds.), Annual Review of Psychology. Palo Alto, CA: Annual Reviews, Inc., 1980.

Dawes, R. M., & Corrigan, B. Linear models in decision making. Psychologcial Bulletin, 1974, 81, 95-106.

Day, R. H., & Groves, T. (Eds.). Adaptive economic models. New York: Academic Press, 1975.

De Finetti, B. Foresight: Its logical laws, its subjective sources. In H. E. Kyberg & H. Smokler (Eds.), Studies in subjective probability. New York: Wiley, 1964. (Originally published, 1937.)

De Morgan, A. Formal logic. London: Taylor and Walton, 1847.

Deane, D. H., Hammond, K. R., & Summers, D. A. Acquisition and application of knowledge in complex inference tasks. Journal of Experimental Psychology, 1972, 92, 20-26.

Delbecq, A. L., Van de Ven, A. H., & Gustafson, D. H. Group techniques for program planning. Glenview, Ill.: Scott Foresman, 1975.

Dempster, A. P., Schatzoff, M., & Wemuth, N. A simulation study of alternatives to ordinary least squares (Department of Statistics, Report No. S-35). Unpublished manuscript, Harvard University, 1975.

Dudycha, A. L. A Monte Carlo evaluation of JAN and PROF: Two techniques for capturing and clustering rater policies. Unpublished doctoral dissertation, the Ohio State University, 1967.

Dudycha, A. L. & Naylor, J. C. Characteristics of the human inference process in complex choice behavior situations. Organizational Behavior and Human Performance, 1966, 1, 110-128.

Dudycha, L. W., & Naylor, J. C. The effect of variations in the cue R matrix upon the obtained policy equation of judges. Educational and Psychological Measurement, 1966, 26, 583-603.

Earle, T. C. Task learning, interpersonal learning, and cognitive complexity. Oregon Research Institute Research Bulletin, 1970, 10(2).

Eckstein, O. Water-resource development. Cambridge, Mass.: Harvard University Press, 1958.

Edelman, M. The symbolic uses of politics. Champaign, Ill.: University of Illinois Press, 1960.

Edgeworth, F. Y. Mathematical Physics. London: Kegan Paul, 1881.

Edwards, W. The theory of decision making. Psychological Bulletin, 1954, 51, 380-417.

Edwards, W. The prediction of decisions among bets. Journal of Experimental Psychology, 1955, 51, 201-214.

Edwards, W. Behavioral decision theory. Annual Review of Psychology, 1961, 12, 473-498.

Edwards, W. Dynamic decision theory and probabialistic information processing. Human Factors, 1962, 4, 59-73.

Edwards, W. Conservatism in human information processing. In B. Kleinmuntz (Ed.), Formal representation of human judgment. New York: Wiley, 1968. (a)

Edwards, W. Decision making: Psychological aspects. In D. L. Sills (Ed.), International encyclopedia of the social sciences, (Vol. 4). New York: Macmillan & Free Press, 1968. (b)

Edwards, W. Social utilities. The Engineering Economist, Summer Symposium Series, 1971, 6.

Edwards, W. Social utilities. In A. Cesser, Jr. (Ed.), Decision and risk analysis: powerful new tools for management. Hoboken, NJ: The Engineering Economist, 1972.

Edwards, W., Guttentag, M., & Snapper, K. A decision-theoretic approach to evaluation research. In E. L. Struening & M. Guttentag (Eds.), Handbook of evaluation research (Vol. 1). Beverly Hills: SAGE Publications, 1975.

Edwards, W., Lindman, H., & Phillips, L. D. Emerging technologies for making decisions. In F. Barron, W. C. Dement, W. Edwards, H. Lindman, C. D. Phillips & J. Miolds (Eds.), New Directions in Psychology II. New York: Holt, Rinehart, and Winston, 1965.

Edwards, W., Lindman, H., & Savage, L. J. Bayesian statistical inference for psychological research. Psychological Review, 1963, 70, 193-242.

Edwards W., & Phillips, L. D. Man as transducer for probabilities in Baysian command and control systems. In M. W. Shelly, II & G. L. Bryan (Eds.), Human judgments and optimality. New York: Wiley, 1964.

Edwards, W., Phillips, L. D., Hays, W. L., & Goodman, B. C. Probabilistic information processing systems: Design and evaluation. IEEE Transactions on Systems Science and Cybernetics, 1968, SSC-4, 248-265.

Eilon, S. Goals and constraints in decision-making. Operational Research Quarterly, 1972, 23(1), 3-15.

Einhorn, H. J. The use of nonlinear, noncompensatory models in decision making. Psychological Bulletin, 1970, 73, 221-230.

Einhorn, H. J. Use of nonlinear, noncompensatory models as a function of task and amount of information. Organizational Behavior and Human Performance, 1971, 6, 1-27.

Einhorn, H. J., & Hogarth, R. M. Unit weighting schemes for decision making. Organizational Behavior and Human Performance, 1975, 13, 171-192.

Einhorn, H. J., & Hogarth, R. M. Confidence in judgment: Persistence of the illusion of validity. Psychological Review, 1978, 85, 395-416.

Einhorn, H. J., & Hogarth, R. M. Behavioral decision theory: Processes of judgment and choice. Annual Review of Psychology, 1981, 32, 53-88.

Einhorn, H. J., Kleinmuntz, D. N., & Kleinmuntz, B. Linear regression and process tracing models of judgment. Psychological Review, 1979, 86(5), 465-485.

Einhorn, H. J., & McCoach, W. A simple multiattribute utility procedure for evaluation. Behavioral Science, 1977, 22, 270-282.

Ellsberg, D. Risk, ambiguity, and the Savage axioms. Quarterly Journal of Economics, 1961, 75, 643-669.

Emery, D. R., & Barron, F. H. Axiomatic and numerical conjoint measurement: An evaluation of diagnostic efficacy. Psychometrika, 1979, 44, 195-210.

Evans, S. H. Redundancy as a variable in pattern perception. Psychological Bulletin, 1967, 67(2), 104-113.

Farquharson, R. Theory of voting. New Haven: Yale University Press, 1969.

Feller, W. Introduction to probability theory and its applications (2nd ed. 2 vols.). New York: John Wiley & Sons, Inc., 1966 and 1971.

Finsterbusch, K., & Wolf, C. P. (Eds.) Methodology of social impact assessment. Stroudsburg, PA: Dowden, Hutchinson, & Ross, 1977.

Fischer, G. W. Multidimensional utility models for risky and riskless choice. Organizational Behavior and Human Performance, 1976, 17, 127-146.

Fischhoff, B. Hindsight foresight: The effect of outcome knowledge on judgment under uncertainty. Journal of Experimental Psychology: Human Perception and Performance, 1975, 1(3), 288-299.

Fischhoff, B., Slovic, P., & Lichtenstein, S. Knowing with certainty: The appropriateness of extreme confidence. Journal of Experimental Psychology: Human Perception and Performance, 1977, 3, 522-564.

Fischhoff, B., Slovic, P., & Lichtenstein, S. Fault trees: Sensitivity of estimated failure probabilities to problem representation. Journal of Experimental Psychology: Human Perception & Performance, 1978, 4, 330-344.

Fischhoff, B., Slovic, P., & Lichtenstein, S. Subjective sensitivity analysis. Organizational Behavior and Human Performance, 1979, 23, 339-359.

Fishburn, P. C. Utility Theory for Decision Making. New York: Wiley, 1970.

Fisher, I. The nature of capital and income. New York: Macmillan, 1906.

Fitzsimmons, S .J., Stuart, C .J., & Wolff, P. C. Social assessment manual. Boulder, CO: Westview Press, 1977.

Flood, M. M. Let's redesign democracy. Behavioral Science, 1978, 23, 429-440.

Franklin, B. Letter to Joseph Priestly. In The Benjamin Franklin sampler. New York: Fawcett, 1956.

Freeling, A. N. S. Fuzzy sets and decision analysis. IEEE Transactions on Systems, Man, & Cybernetics, 1980, SMC-10, 341-354.

Freeman, A. M. The benefits of environmental improvement. Baltimore: Johns Hopkins University Press, 1979.

Friedman, M., & Savage, L. J. The utility analysis of choices involving risk. Journal of Political Economy, 1948, 56, 279-304.

Gabrielli, W. F., Jr., & Winterfeldt, D. V. Are importance weights sensitive to the range of alternatives in multiattribute utility measurement? (SSRI Research Dept. Report 001922-6-T). Unpublished manuscript, University of Southern California, 1978.

Gardiner, P. C., & Edwards, W. Public values: Multiattribute utility measurement for social decision making. In M. F. Kaplan & S. Schwartz (Eds.), Human judgment and decision processes. New York: Academic Press, 1975.

Garner, W. R. Uncertainty and structure as psychological concepts. New York: Wiley, 1962.

Garner, W. R. The processing of information and structure. Potomac, Maryland: Erlbaum, 1974.

Garner, W. R., & Morton, J. Perceptual independence: Definitions, models, and experimental paradigms. Psychological Bulletin, 1969, 72, 233-259.

Georgescu-Roegen, N.   Utility,   expectations,   measurability, prediction. Paper presented at the meeting at the Econometric Society, Kingston, September 1953.

Gettys, C. F., Kelley, C., & Peterson, C. R. The best guess hypothesis in multistage inference. Organizational Behavior and Human Performance, 1973, 10, 364-373.

Gillis, J. S. Effects of chlorpromazine and thiothixene on acute schizophrenic patients. In K. R. Hammond & C. R. B.Joyce (Eds.), Psychoactive drugs and social judgment: Theory and research. New York: Wiley, 1975.

Gillis, J. S. Understanding the effects of psychiatric drugs on social judgment. In K. R. Hammond & N. E. Wascoe (Eds.), Realizations of Brunswik's representative design. SF: Jossey-Bass, 1980.

Goldberg, L. Diagnosticians vs. diagnostic signs: The diagnosis of psychosis vs. neurosis from the MMPI. Psychological Monographs, 1965, 79 (Whole No. 602).

Goldberg, L. R. Simple models or simple processes? American Psychologist, 1968, 23, 483-496.

Goldberg, L. R. Man versus model of man: A rationale, plus some evidence, for a method of improving on clinical inferences. Psychological Bulletin, 1970, 73, 422-432.

Goldman, T. A. (Ed.). Cost-effectiveness analysis. New York: Praeger, 1967.

Goldstein J. H. The effectiveness of manpower training programs: A review of research on the impact on the poor. In W. A. Niskanen and others (Eds.), Benefit-cost and policy analysis 1972. Chicago: Aldine, 1973.

Goodman, L. A., & Markowitz, H. Social welfare functions based on individual rankings. American Journal of Sociology, 1952, 58, 257-262.

Green, D. M., Luce, R. D., & Duncan, J. E. Variability and sequential effects in magnitude production and estimation of auditory intensity. Perception and Psychophysics, 1977, 22, 450-456.

Green, P. E. Mathematical tools for applied multivariate analysis. New York: Academic Press, 1976.

Green, P. E., & Srinivasan, V. Conjoint analysis in consumer research: Issues and outlook. Journal of Consumer Research, 1978, 5, 103-123.

Green, P. E., & Wind, Y. Multiattribute Decisions in Marketing: A measurement approach. Hinsdale, IL: The Dryden Press, 1973.

Greenberger, M., Crenson, M. A., & Crissey, B. L. Models in the policy process. New York: Russell Sage Foundation, 1976.

Grether, D. M., & Plott, C. R. Economic theory of choice and the preference reversal phenomenon. American Economic Review, 1979, 69(4), 623-638.

Guilford, J. P. Psychometric methods (29th ed.). New York: McGraw-Hill, 1954.

Hammond, K. R. Probabilistic functioning and the clinical method. Psychological Review, 1955, 62(4), 255-262.

Hammond, K. R. New directions in research on conflict resolution. Journal of Social Issues, 1965, 21, 44-66.

Hammond, K. R. Probabilistic functionalism: Egon Brunswik's integration of the history, theory, and method of psychology. In K. R. Hammond (Ed.) The psychology of Egon Brunswik. New York: Holt, Rinehart, and Winston, 1966.

Hammond, K. R. Computer graphics as an aid to learning. Science, 1971, 172, 903-908.

Hammond, K. R. Externalizing the parameters of quasi-rational thought. In M. Zeleny (Ed.), Multiple Criteria Decision Making. New York: Springer-Verlag, 1976.

Hammond, K. R. The integration of research in judgment and decision theory (Center for Research on Judgment and Policy, Report No. 226). Unpublished manuscript, Institute of Behavioral Science, University of Colorado, 1980.

Hammond, K. R., & Adelman, L. Science, values, and human judgment, Science, 1976, 194, 389-196.

Hammond, K. R., & Boyle, P. J. R. Quasi-rationality, quarrels, and new conceptions of feedback. Bulletin of the British Psychological Society, 1971, 24, 103-113.

Hammond, K. R., & Brehmer, B. Cognition, quarrels, and cybernetics (Center for Research on Judgment and Policy, Report No. 117). Unpublished manuscript, University of Colorado, Institute of Behavioral Science, 1970.

Hammond, K. R., & Brehmer, B. Quasi-rationality and distrust: Implications for international conflict. In L. Rappoport & D. Summers (Eds.), Human judgment and social interaction. New York: Holt, Rinehart, & Winston, 1973.

Hammond, K. R., Hursch, C. J. , & Todd, F. J. Analyzing the components of clinical inference. Psychological Review, 1964, 71, 438-456.

Hammond, K. R., McClelland, G. H., & Mumpower, J. Human judgment and decision making: Theories, methods, and procedures. New York: Praeger, 1980.

Hammond, K. R., Rohrbaugh, J., Mumpower, J., & Adelman, L. Social judgment theory: Applications in policy formation. In M. F. Kaplan & S. Schwartz (Eds.), Human judgment and decision processes in applied settings. New York: Academic Press, 1977.

Hammond, K. R., Stewart, T. R., Brehmer, B., & Steinmann, D. O. Social judgment theory. In M. F. Kaplan & S. Schwartz (Eds.), Human judgment and decision processes. New York: Academic Press, 1975.

Hammond, K. R., & Summers, D. A. Cognitive dependence on linear and non-linear cues. Psychological Review, 1965, 72, 215-224.

Hammond, K. R., & Summers, D. A. Cognitive control. Psychological Review, 1972, 79, 58-67.

Hammond, K. R., Summers, D. A., & Deane, D. H. Negative effects of outcome feedback in multiple-cue probability learning. Organizational Behavior and Human Performance, 1973, 9, 30-34.

Hanke, S. H., & Walker, R. A. Benefit-cost analysis reconsidered: An evaluation of the Mid-State Project. Water Resources Research, 1974, 10(5), 898-908.

Hardin, G. R. The tragedy of the commons. Science, 1968, 162, 1243-1248.

Harsanyi, J. C. Cardinal welfare, individualistic ethics, and interpersonal comparisons of utility. Journal of Political Economy, 1955, 63, 309-321.

Harsanyi, J. C. Nonlinear social welfare functions. Theory and Decision, 1975, 6, 311-332.

Harsanyi, J. C., & Selten, R. A generalized Nash solution for two-person bargaining games with incomplete information. Management Science, 1972, 18, 80-106.

Harvey, J. H., Ickes, W. J., & Kidd, R. F. (Eds.). New directions in attribution research (Vol. 1). Hillsdale, NJ: Erlbaum, 1976.

Harvey, J. H., Ickes, W. J., & Kidd, R. F. (Eds.). New directions in attribution research (Vol. 2). Hillsdale, NJ: Erlbaum, 1978.

Haveman, R. H. The ex-post evaluation of navagation improvements.

In W. A. Niskanen and others (Eds.), Benefit-cost and policy analysis 1972. Chicago: Aldine, 1972.

Haveman, R. H., & Margolis, J. (Eds.). Public expenditures and policy analysis. Chicago: Markham Publishing Co., 1970.

Hayes, J. R. Human data processing limits in decision making. In E. Bennett (Ed.), Information system science and engineering: Proceedings of the First Congress on the Information Systems Sciences. New York: McGraw-Hill, 1964.

Heider, F. Social perception and phenomenal causality. Psychological Review, 1944, 51, 358-374.

Heider, F. The psychology of interpersonal relations. New York: Wiley, 1958.

Helmer, O. Foreward. In H. A. Linstone & M. Turoff (Eds.), The Delphi method: Techniques and applications. Reading, Mass.: Addison-Wesley, 1975.

Herbert, J. A., Shikiar, R., & Perry, R. W. Valuing the environment via bidding games: A psychological perspective (Human Affairs Research Centers). Unpublished manuscript, Battelle Pacific Northwest Division, Seattle, Washington, 1978.

Himmelfarb, S. The impact of neutral information about a person. Unpublished manuscript, University of California at La Jolla, 1970.

Hinde, R. A. Animal behaviour: A synthesis of ethology and comparative psychology. New York: McGraw-Hill, 1966.

Hirsch, W. Z. Cost functions of an urban government service: Refuse collection. Review of Economics and Statistics, 1965, 47, 87-92.

Hirschman, A. O. Development projects observed. Washington, D. C.: The Brookings Institution, 1967.

Hoerl, A. E., & Kennard, R. W. Ridge regression: Biased estimation for nonorthogonal problems. Technometrics, 1970, 12, 55-67.

Hoerl, A. E., Kennard, R. W., & Baldwin, K. Ridge regression: Some simulations. Communcations in Statistics, 1975, 4, 105-123.

Hoffman, P. J. The paramorphic representation of clinical judgment. Psychological Bulletin, 1960, 57, 116-131.

Hoffman, P. J. Cue-consistency and configurality in human judgment. In B. Kleinmuntz (Ed.), Formal representation of human judgment. New York: Wiley, 1968.

Hoffman, P. J., & Blanchard, W. A. A study of the effects of varying amounts of predictor information on judgment. Oregon Research Institute Research Bulletin, 1961.

Hoffman, P. J., Slovic, P., & Rorer, L. G. An analysis-of-variance model for the assessment of configural cue utilization in clinical judgment. Psychological Bulletin, 1968, 69, 338-349.

Hogarth, R. M. Process tracing in clinical judgment. Behavioral Science, 1974, 19, 298-313.

Hogarth, R. Judgement and choice. Chichester, England: Wiley, 1980.

Howard, R. A. The foundations of decision analysis. IEEE Transactions on Systems Science and Cybernetics, 1968, SSC-42, 211-219.

Howell, W. C. Some principles for the design of decision systems: A review of six years of research on a command-control system simulation. Aerospace Medical Research Laboratories, Aerospace Medical Division, Air Force Systems Command (AMRL-TR-67-136). Wright-Patterson Air Force Base, Ohio, 1967.

Hudson, W. D. (Ed.) The is/ought question. New York: St. Martin's Press, 1969.

Hull, C. L. A behavior system. New Haven: Yale University Press, 1952.

Hume, D. A treatise of human nature. Reprinting edited by L. A. Selby-Bigge. Oxford: Clarendon, 1888.

Hunter, W. S. Human behavior. Chicago: University of Chicago Press, 1928.

Hursch, C. J., Hammond, K. R., & Hursch, J. L. Some methodological considerations in multiple-cue probability studies. Psychological Review, 1964, 71, 42-60.

Hurwicz, L. Optimality criteria for decision making under ignorance. Cowles Commission Discussion Paper, (Statistics, No. 370), 1951.

Jackson, D. N., & Messick, S. (Eds.). Problems in human assessment. New York: McGraw-Hill, 1967.

Jain, R. K., & Hutchings, B. L. (Eds.). Environmental impact analysis: Emerging issues in planning. Urbana: University of Illinois Press, 1978.

Jain, R. K., Urban, L. V., & Stacey, G. S. Environmental impact analysis: A new dimension in decision making. New York: Van Nostrand Reinhold, 1977.

Jamison, D., Fletcher, D., Suppes, P., & Atkinson, R. Cost and performance of computer-assisted instruction for education of disadvantaged children. Paper presented at the meetings of the National Bureau for Economic Research, Chicago, June 1971.

Janis, I. L. Victims of groupthink. Boston: Houghton Mifflin, 1972.

Janis, I. L. (Ed.). Counseling on personal decisions: Theory and field research on helping relationships. New Haven: Yale University Press, in press.

Janis, I. L., & Mann, L. A conflict-theory approach to attitude change and decision making. In A. Greenwald, T. Brock, & T. Ostrom (Eds.), Psychological foundations of attitudes. New York: Academic, 1968.

Janis, I. L., & Mann, L. Decision making: A psychological analysis of conflict, choice, and commitment. New York: The Free Press, 1977.

Jeffreys, H. Theory of probability (3rd ed.). Oxford: Clarindon Press, 1961. (Originally published, 1939.)

Jenkins, H. M., & Ward, W. C. The judgment of contingency between response and outcome. Psychological Monographs, 1965, 79. (Whole No. 594).

Jones, E. E. The rocky road from acts to dispositions. American Psychologist, 1979, 34, 107-117.

Jones, E. E., & Davis, K. E. From acts to dispositions: The attribution process in person perception. In L. Berkowitz (Ed.), Advances in experimental social psychology (Vol. 2). New York: Academic Press, 1965.

Jones, E. E., & Harris, V. A. The attribution of attitudes. Journal of Experimental Social Psychology, 1967, 3, 1-24.

Jones, E. E., Kanouse, D. E., Kelley, H. H., Nisbett, R. E., Valins, S., & Weiner, B. Attribution: Perceiving the causes of behavior. Morristown, NJ: General Learning Press, 1971.

Jones, E. E., & McGillis, D. Corrrespondent inferences and the attribution cube: A comparative reappraisal. In J. H Harvey, W. J. Ickes & R. F.Kidd (Eds.), New directions in attribution research (Vol. 1). Hillsdale, NJ: Erlbaum, 1976.

Kahneman, D., & Tversky, A. Subjective probability: A judgment of representativeness. (Technical Report). Oregon Research Institute, 1971, 2(2).

Kahneman, D., & Tversky, A. Subjective probability: A judgment of representativeness. Cognitive Psychology, 1972, 3, 430-454.

Kahneman, D., & Tversky, A. On the psychology of prediction. Psychological Review, 1973, 80, 237-251.

Kahneman, D., & Tversky, A. Intuitive prediction: Biases and corrective procedures. Management Science, 1979, 12, 313-327. (a)

Kahneman, D., & Tversky, A. Prospect theory: An analysis of decision under risk. Econometrika, 1979, 47, 263-291. (b)

Kain, J. F. An analysis of metropolitan transportation systems. In T. A. Goldman (Ed.), Cost-effectiveness analysis. New York: Praeger, 1967.

Kane, J. A primer for a new cross-impact language. Technological Forecasting & Social Change, 1972, 4, 129-142.

Kaplan, R. J., & Newman, J. R. Studies in probabilistic information processing. IEEE Transactions on Human Factors in Electronics, 1966, 7, 49-63.

Kates, R. (Ed.). Managing technological hazards: Research needs and opportunities. Boulder, CO: Institute of Behavioral Science, University of Colorado, 1977.

Kates, R. W. Risk Assessment of Environmental Hazard. New York: Wiley, 1978.

Katona, G. Psychological Analysis of Economic Behavior. New York: McGraw-Hill, 1951.

Keeney, R. L., & Raiffa, H. Decisions with multiple objectives: Preferences and value trade-offs. New York: Wiley, 1976.

Kelley, H. H. Attribution in social interaction. In D. N. Jackson & S. Messick (Eds.), Problems in human assessment. New York: McGraw-Hill, 1967. (a)

Kelley, H. H. Attribution theory in social psychology. In D. Levine (Ed.), Nebraska Symposium on Motivation, 1967. Lincoln, Neb.: University of Nebraska Press, 1967. (b)

Kelley, H. H. Causal schemata and the attribution process. In E. E. Jones, D. E. Kanouse, H. H. Kelley, H. H. Nisbett, S. Valins & B. Weiner (Eds.), Attribution: Perceiving the causes of behavior. Morristown, NJ: General Learning Press, 1972.

Kelley, H. H. Causal Schemata and the Attribution Process. New York: General Learning Press, 1972.

Kelley, H. H., & Michela, J. L. Attribution theory and research. Annual Review of Psychology, 1980, 31, 457-501.

Kelley, H. H., & Stahelski, D. J. The inference of intention from moves in the Prisoner's Dilemma game. Journal of Experimental Social Psychology, 1970, 6, 401-419.

Kendall, M. G. A course in multivariate analysis. London: Charles Griffin, 1957.

Kerlinger, F. N. Foundations of behavioral research. New York: Holt, Rinehart, & Winston, 1967.

Kerrick, J. S. The effect of relevant and non-relevent sources on attitude change. Journal of Social Psychology, 1958, 47, 15-20.

Keynes, J. M. A treatise on probability. New York: Macmillan, 1921.

Kiesler, C. A., Collins, B. E., & Miller, N. Attitude change: A critical analysis of theoretical approaches. New York: Wiley, 1969.

Kim, C. Quantitative analysis for managerial decisions. Reading, MA: Addison-Wesley, 1976.

Kim, K. H., & Roush, F. W. Mathematics for Social Scientists. New York: Elsevier, 1980.

Klahr, D. Decision making in a complex environment: The use of similarity judgments to predict preferences. Management Science, 1969, 15, 595-618.

Klitzner, M. D., & Anderson, N. H. Motivation x expectancy x value: A functional measurement approach. Motivation and Emotion, 1977, 1, 347-365.

Knight, F. H. Risk, uncertainty, and profit (London School of Economics and Political Science Series of Reprints of Scarce Tracts, No. 16). Unpublished manuscript, London School of Economics and Political Science, 1921. (a)

Knight, F. H. Risk, uncertainty, and profit. Boston: Houghton Mifflin, 1921. (b)

Krantz, D. H., Luce R. D., Suppes, P., & Tversky, A. Foundations of measurement (Vol. 1). New York: Academic Press, 1971.

Krantz, D. H. & Tversky, A. A critique of the applicability of cardinal utility theory (Michigan Mathematical Psychology Program Technical Report 65-4). Unpublished manuscript, University of Michigan, 1965.

Krantz, D. H. & Tversky, A. Conjoint measurement analysis of composition rules in psychology. Psychological Review, 1971, 78(2), 151-169.

Kreiner, K. Ideology and management in a garbage can situation. In J. G. March & J. P. Olsen (Eds.), Ambiguity and choice in organizations. Bergen: Universitetsforlagt, 1976.

Kriz, J. Der likelihood-quotient zur erfassung des subjektiven signifikanzniveaus (Forschungsbericht No. 9). Vienna: Institute for Advanced Studies, 1967.

Kruskal, J. B. Multidimensional scaling by optimizing goodness of fit to a nonmetric hypothesis. Psychometrika, 1964, 29, 1-27.

Kruskal, J. B. Analysis of factorial experiments by estimating monotone transformations of the data. Journal of the Royal Statistical Society - Series B, 1965, 27, 251-263.

La Place, P. S. de. Essai philosophique sur les probabilities. Paris: Mme Ve Courcier, 1814.

La Place, P. S. [A philosophical essay on probabilities] (F. W. Truscott & F. L. Emory, trans.). New York: Dover Press, 1952. (Originally published, 1825.)

Langbein, L. I., & Lichtman, A. J. Ecological inference. Beverly Hills, CA.: SAGE Publications, 1978.

Lange, O. The determinateness of the utility function. The Review of Economic Studies, 1933, 1, 218-225.

Langer, E. J. Rethinking the role of thought in social interaction. In J. H. Harvey, W. Ickes, & R. Kidd (Eds.), New directions in attribution research (Vol. 2). Hillsdale, NJ: Lawrence Erlbaum Associates, 1978.

Lawless, J. J., & Wang, P. A simulation study of some ridge and other regression estimators. Communications in Statistics, 1976, 4, 307-323.

Layard, P. R. G. (Ed.). Cost-benefit analysis. London: Penguin, 1972.

Lee, J. C., & Tucker, R. B. An investigation of clinical judgment: A study in method. Journal of Abnormal and Social Psychology, 1962, 64, 272-280.

Lehner, P. E. A comparison of portfolio theory and weighted utility models of risky decision making. Organizational Behavior & Human Performance, 1980, 26, 238-249.

Levin, H. M. Cost-effectiveness analysis in evaluation research. In M. Guttentag & E. Streuning (Eds.), Handbook of evaluation research (Vol. 2). Beverly Hills, CA.: SAGE Publications, 1975.

Lichtenstein, S., & Feeney, G. J. The importance of the data-generating model in probability estimation. Organizational Behavior and Human Performance 1968, 3, 62-67.

Lichtenstein, S., & Fischhoff, B. Training for calibration. Organizational Behavior and Human Performance, 1980, 26(2), 149-171.

Lichtenstein, S., Fischhoff, B., & Phillips, L. D. Calibration of probabilities: The state of the art. In H. Jungermann & G. de Zeeuw (Eds.), Decision making and change in human affairs. Dordrecht-Holland: Reidel, 1977.

Lichtenstein, S., & Slovic, P. Reversal of preference between bids and choices in gambling decisions. Journal of Experimental Psychology, 1971, 89, 46-55.

Lindblom, C. E. The science of muddling through. Public Administration Review, 1959, 19, 79-88.

Lindblom, C. E. The intelligence of democracy. New York: Macmillan, 1965.

Lindell, M. K. Factors affecting measures of linear achievement: Some methodological considerations (Center for Research on Judgment and Policy, Report No. 167). Boulder, CO: University of Colorado, Institute of Behavioral Science, 1974.

Lindman, H. R. The simultaneous measurement of utilities and subjective probabilities. Unpublished doctoral dissertation, University of Michigan, 1965.

Linstone, H. A., Hays, J., Rogers, S. D., Lendaris, G. E., Wakeland, W., & Williams, M. The use of structural modelling for technology assessment (Vol. 1). Portland, OR: Portland State University Press, 1978.

Linstone, H. A., & Turoff, M. (Eds.). The Delphi method: Techniques and applications. Reading, Mass.: Addison-Wesley, 1975.

Lonergan, B. J. F. Insight: A study of human understanding. New York: Philosophical Library, 1970.

Long, N. E. The local community as an ecology of games. American Journal of Sociology, 1958, 44, 251-261.

Lopes, L. L. Decision making in the short run. Journal of Experimental Psychology: Learning, Memory, & Cognition, in press.

Lord, W. B., Adelman, L., Wehr, P., Brown, C., Crews, R., Marvin, B., & Waterstone, M. Conflict management in federal water resources planning (Program on Technology, Environment and Man Monograph No. 28). Unpublished manuscript, University of Colorado, Institute of

Behavioral Science, 1979.

Luce, R. D. Conjoint measurement: A brief survey. In D. E. Bell, R. L. Keeney & H. Raiffa (Eds.), Conflicting Objectives in Decisions. New York: Wiley, 1977.

Luce, R. D., Bush, R. R., & Galanter, E. (Eds.). Readings in mathematical psychology (Vol. 2). New York: Wiley, 1965.

Luce, R. D., & Raiffa, H. Games and decisions: Introduction and critical survey. New York: Wiley, 1957.

Luce, R. D., & Tukey, J. W. Simultaneous conjoint measurement: A new type of fundamental measurement. Journal of Mathematical Psychology, 1964, 1, 1-27.

Maass, A., and others. Design of water-resources systems. Cambridge, Mass: Harvard University Press, 1962.

MacCrimmon, K. R. Descriptive and normative implications of the decision-theory postulates. In K. Borch & J. Mossin (Eds.), Risk and uncertainty. New York: St. Martin's Press, 1968.

MacCrimmon, K. R. An overview of multiple objective decision making. In J. L. Cochrane & M. Zeleny (Eds.), Multiple criteria decision making. Columbia, S. C.: University of South Carolina Press, 1973.

MacCrimmon, K. R., & Sui, J. K. Making trade-offs. Decision Sciences, 1974, 5(4), 680-704.

MacCrimmon, K. R., & Wehrung, D. A. Trade-off analysis: The indifference and preferred proportions approaches. In D. E. Bell, R. L. Keeney & H. Raiffa (Eds.), Conflicting objectives in decisions. New York: Wiley, 1977.

Makridakis, S. G., & Wheelwright, S. C. Forecasting methods for management. New York: Wiley, 1977.

Manis, M., Gleason, T. C., & Dawes, R. M. The evaluation of complex social stimuli. Journal of Personality & Social Psychology, 1966, 4, 404-419.

March, J. G. Model bias in social action. Review of Educational Research, 1973, 42, 413-429.

March, J. G. Bounded rationality, ambiguity, and the engineering of choice. The Bell Journal of Economics, 1978, 9, 587-608.

March, J. G., & Simon, H. A. Organizations. New York: Wiley, 1958.

Marks, M. R. Two kinds of regression weights that are better than betas in crossed samples. Paper presented at the meeting of the American Psychological Association, New York, September 1966.

Marquardt, D. W. Generalized inverses, ridge regression, biased linear estimation, and nonlinear estimation. Technometrics, 1970, 12, 591-611.

Marshall, A. Principles of economics (8th ed.). New York: Macmillan, 1927.

Matheson, J. E., & Howard, R. A. An introduction to decision analysis. In Readings in Decision Analysis (2d ed.). Menlo Park, CA: Stanford Research Institute (Decision Analysis Group), 1977.

Maxwell, J. C. On governors. Proceedings of the Royal Society (London), 1868, 16, 270-283.

McClelland, G. H. Equal versus differential weighting for multiattribute decisions: There are no free lunches (Center for Research on Judgment and Policy, Report No. 207). Unpublished manuscript, University of Colorado, Institute of Behavioral Science, 1978.

McClelland, G. H., & Coombs, C. H. ORDMET: A general algorithm for constructing all numerical solutions to ordered metric structures. Psychometrika, 1975, 40, 269-290.

McClelland, G. H., & Hackenberg, B. H. Subjective probabilities for sex of next child: U.S. college students and Philippine villagers. Journal of Population, 1978, 1(2), 132-147.

McClelland, G. H., & Rohrbaugh, J. Who accepts the Pareto axiom? The role of utility and equity in arbitration and decisions. Behavioral Science, 1978, 23, 446-456.

McKean, R. N. The use of shadow games. In S. B. Chase (Ed.), Problems in public expenditure analysis. Washington, D. C.: The Brookings Institution, 1968.

McNemar, Q. Psychological statistics. New York: Wiley, 1962.

Meehl, P. E. Clinical vs. statistical prediction: A theoretical analysis and a review of the evidence. Minneapolis: University of Minnesota Press, 1954.

Metropolis, N., & Ulam, S. The Monte Carlo method. Journal of the American Statistical Association, 1949, 44, 335-341.

Milgram, S. Behavvioral study of obedience. Journal of Abnormal and Social Psychology, 1963, 67, 371-378.

Mill, J. S. System of Logic. London, 1843.

Mill, J. S. Dissertations and discussions. Vol. 1. London, 1859-75.

Miller, D. C. Methods for estimating societal futures. In K. Finsterbusch & C. P. Wolf (Eds.), Methodology of social impact assessment. Stroudsburg, PA: Dowden, Hutchinson, & Ross, 1977.

Miller, D. W., & Starr, M. K. Executive decisions and operations research (2nd ed.). Englewood Cliffs, N. J.: Prentice-Hall, 1967.

Miller, G. A. The magical number seven, plus or minus two: Some limits on our capacity for processing information. Psychological Review, 1956, 63, 81-97.

Mishan, E. J. Cost-benefit analysis. New York: Praeger, 1976.

Mitroff, I. A., & Turoff, M. Philosophical and methodological foundations of Delphi. In H. A. Linstone & M. Turoff (Eds.), The Delphi method. Reading, Mass.: Addison-Wesley, 1975.

Mohring, H. Urban highway investments. In R. Dorfman (Ed.), Measuring benefits of public investments. Washington, D. C.: Brookings Institution, 1965.

Mushkin, S. J. Health as an investment. Journal of Political Economy, 1962, 70, 129-142.

Nash, J. F. The bargaining problem. Econometrica, 1950, 18, 155-162.

National Environmental Policy Act of 1969. U. S. Code, Title 42, Sec. 4321-4361.

Naylor, J. C., & Clark, R. D. Intuitive inference strategies in interval learning tasks as a function of validity magnitude and sign. Organizational Behavior and Human Performance, 1968, 3, 378-399.

Naylor, J. C., & Schenck, E. A. The influence of cue redundancy upon the human inference process for tasks of varying degrees of predictability. Organizational Behavior and Human Performance, 1968, 3, 47-61.

Naylor, J. C., & Wherry, R. J. The use of simulated stimuli and the "JAN" technique to capture and cluster the policies of raters. Educational & Psychological Measurement, 1965, 25, 969-986.

Nelson, R. R., & Winter, S. G. Towards an evolutionary theory of economic capabilities. The American Economic Review, 1973, 63, 440-449.

Newell, A., Shaw, J. C., & Simon, H. A. Elements of a theory of human problem solving. Psychological Review, 1958, 65, 151-166.

Newell, A., & Simon, H. A. Human problem solvving. Englewood Cliffs, New Jersey: Prentice-Hall, 1972.

Newman, J. R. Differential weighting for prediction and decision making studies: A study of ridge regression (Social Science Research Institute, Report No. 77-1). Unpublished manuscript, University of Southern California, 1977.

Newton, J. R. Judgment and feedback in a quasi-clinical situation. Journal of Personality and Social Psychology, 1965, 1, 336-342.

Nisbett, R. E., Borgida, E., Crandall, R., & Reed, H. Popular induction: Information is not always informative. In J. Carroll & J. Payne (Eds.), Cognitive and social behavior. Potomac, MD: Lawrence Erlbaum, 1976.

Nisbett, R., & Ross, L. Human inference: Strategies and shortcomings of social judgment. Englewood Cliffs, NJ: Prentice-Hall, 1980.

Nunnally, J. C. Psychometric Theory. New York: McGraw-Hill, 1967.

Oden, G. C., & Anderson, N. H. Differential weighting in integration theory. Journal of Experimental Psychology, 1971, 89, 152-161.

Oldfield, R. C. Memory mechanisms and the theory of schemata. British Journal of Psychology, 1954, 45, 14-23.

Osgood, C. E., & Tannenbaum, P. H. The principle of congruity in the prediction of attitude change. Psychological Review, 1955, 62, 42-55.

Oskamp, S. Overconfidence in case study judgments. Journal of Consulting Psychology, 1965, 29, 261-265.

Otway, H. J., & Pahner, P. D. Risk assessment. Futures, 1976, 282, 122-134.

Parducci, A. Range-frequency compromise in judgment. Psychological Monographs, 1963, 77 (Whole No. 565).

Parducci, A. Category judgment: A range-frequency model. Psychological Review, 1965, 72, 407-418.

Parducci, A. The relativism of absolute judgments. Scientific American, 1968, 219(6), 84-93.

Pareto, V. Manuale di economia politica, con una introduzione ulla scienza sociale. Milan, Italy; Societa Editrice Libraria, 1906.

Pareto, V. Manual of Political Economy. New York: A. M. Kelley, 1971. (Originally published, 1927.)

Pattanaik, P. K. Voting and collective choice. New York: Cambridge

University Press, 1971.

Payne, J. W. Alternative approaches to decision making under risk: Moments versus risk dimensions. Psychological Bulletin, 1973, 80, 439-453.

Payne, J. W., & Braunstein, M. L. Preferences among gambles with equal underlying distributions. Journal of Experimental Psychology, 1971, 87, 13-18.

Payne, J. W., Braunstein, M. L., & Carroll, J. S. Exploring pre-decisional behavior: An alternative approach to decision research. Organizational Behavior and Human Performance, 1978, 22, 17-44.

Pearl, J. A framework for processing value judgments. IEEE Transactions on Systems, Man, & Cybernetics, 1977, SMC-7, 349-354.

Peterson, C. R. (Ed.). Special issue: Cascaded inference. Organizational Behavior and Human Performance, 1973, 10, 315-432.

Peterson, C. R., Hammond, K. R., & Summers, D. A. Multiple probability learning with shifting cue weights. American Journal of Psychology, 1965, 78, 660-663. (a)

Peterson, C. R., Hammond, K. R., & Summers, D. A. Optimal responding in multiple-cue probability learning. Journal of Experimental Psychology, 1965, 70, 270-276. (b)

Phelps, R. H., & Shanteau, J. Livestock judges: How much information can an expert use? Organizational Behavior & Human Performance, 1978, 21, 209-219.

Phillips, L. D. Some components of probabilistic inference (Human Performance Center, Technical Report No. 1). Unpublished manuscript, University of Michigan, 1966.

Phillips, L. D., & Edwards, W. Conservatism in a simple probability inference task. Journal of Experimental Psychology, 1966, 72, 346-357.

Pitz, G. Subjective probability distributions for imperfectly known quantities. In G. W. Gregg (Ed.), Knowledge and cognition. New York: Wiley, 1974.

Plott, C. R. Axiomatic social choice theory: An overview and interpretation. American Journal of Political Science, 1976, 20, 511-596.

Podell, H. A., & Podell, J. E. Quantitative connotation of a concept. Journal of Abnormal and Social Psychology, 1963, 67, 509-513.

Poisson, S. D. Recherches sur la probabilite des judgements en matiere criminelle et en matiere civile, precedees des regles generales du calcul des probabilites, 1837.

Polya, G. Induction and analogy in mathematics. Princeton, NJ: Princeton University Press, 1954.

Postman, L., & Tolman, E. Brunswik's probabilistic functionalism. In S. Koch (Ed.), Psychology: A study of a science (Vol. 1). New York: McGraw-Hill, 1959.

Prest, A. R., & Turvey, R. Cost-benefit analysis: A survey. Economic Journal, 1965, 75, 685-705.

Price, M. Ridge regression: Application to nonexperimental data. Psychological Bulletin, 1977, 84, 759-766.

Quade, E. S. Analysis for public decisions. New York: Elsevier Publishing Co., 1975.

Radner, R. A behavioral model of cost reduction. The Bell Journal of Economics, Spring 1975, 6(1), 196-215. (a)

Radner, R. Satisficing. Journal of Mathematical Economics, 1975, 2, 253-262. (b)

Raiffa, H. Decision analysis: Introductory lectures on choices under uncertainty. Reading, Mass.: Addison-Wesley, 1968.

Raiffa, H., & Schlaifer, R. Applied statistical decision theory. Cambridge, Mass.: MIT Press, 1972.

Ramsey, F. P. Truth and probability. In R. B. Braithwaite (Ed.), The foundations of mathematics and other logical essays. New York: Harcourt Brace, 1931.

Ramsey, F. P. Truth and probability. In H. E. Kyberg & H. Smokler (Eds.), Studies in subjective probability. New York: Wiley, 1964. (Originally published, 1926.)

Randall, A., Ives, B., & Eastman, C. Bidding games for valuation of aesthetic environmental improvement. Journal of Environmental Economics and Management, 1974, 1, 132-149.

Rapoport, A. Fights, games, and debates. Ann Arbor: University of Michigan Press, 1960.

Rapoport, A., & Chammah, A. M. Prisoner's dilemma: A study in conflict and cooperation. Ann Arbor: University of Michigan Press, 1965.

Rapoport, A., & Wallsten, T. S. Individual decision behavior. Annual

Review of Psychology, 1972, 23, 131-176.

Rappoport, L., & Summers, D. A. (Eds.). Human judgment and social interaction. New York: Holt, Rinehart, and Winston, 1973.

Rawls, J. A Theory of Justice. Cambridge, Mass.: Harvard University Press, 1971.

Restle, F. A theory of discrimination learning. Psychological Review, 1955, 62, 11-19.

Restle, F. Psychology of Judgment and Choice: A theoretical essay. New York: Wiley, 1961.

Robinson, W. S. Ecological correlations and the behavior of individuals. American Sociological Review, 1950, 15, 351-357.

Romney, A. K., Shepard, R. N. & Nerlove, S. B. (Eds.). Multidimensional scaling: Theory and applications in the behavioral sciences (Vol. 2), Applications. New York: Seminar Press, 1972.

Ross, L. The intuitive psychologist and his shortcomings: Distortions in the attribution process. In C. Berkowitz (Ed.), Advances in Experimental social psychology (Vol. 10). New York: Academic Press, 1977.

Ross, L. Some afterthoughts on the intuitive psychologist. In L. Berkowitz (Ed.), Cognitive theories in social psychology. New York: Academic Press, 1978.

Rothenberg, J. Cost-benefit analysis: A methodological exposition. In M. Guttentag & E. Streuning (Eds.), Handbook of evaluation research (Vol. 2). Beverly Hills, CA.: SAGE Publications, 1975.

Rozeboom, W. W. Ridge regression: Bonanza or beguilement? Psychological Bulletin, 1979, 86, 242-249.

Russell, B. The principles of Mathematics (2nd ed.). New York: Norton, 1937.

Russell, B. A history of Western philosophy. New York: Simon & Schuster, 1945.

Russo, J. E., & Rosen, L. D. An eye movement analysis of multi-alternative choice. Memory and Cognition, 1975, 3, 267-276.

Samuelson, P. A. A note on the pure theory of consumer's behavior. Economica, 1938, 5, 61-71.

Samuelson, P. A. Foundations of economic analysis. Cambridge, Mass.: Harvard University Press, 1947.

Samuelson, P. A. Consumption theory in terms of revealed preference. Economica, 1948, 15, 243-253.

Samuelson, P. A. Economics (10th ed.). New York: McGraw-Hill, 1976.

Sarbin, T. R., Taft, R., & Bailey, D. E. Clinical inference and cognitive theory. New York: Holt, Rinehart, & Winston, 1960.

Savage, L. J. The theory of statistical decision. Journal of the American Statistical Association, 1951, 46, 55-67.

Savage, L. J. An axiomatic theory of reasonable behavior in the face of uncertainty (Statistical Research Center, No. SRC-21222S14). Unpublished manuscript, University of Chicago, 1953.

Savage, L. J. The foundations of statistics. New York: Wiley, 1954.

Sawyer, J. Measurement and prediction, clinical and statistical mimeo report. Psychological Bulletin, 1966, 66(3), 178-200.

Schelling, T. On the ecology of micro-motives. Public Interest, 1971, 25, 59-98.

Schlaifer, R. Probability and statistics for business decisions. New York: McGraw-Hill, 1959.

Schlaifer, R. O. Analysis of decisions under uncertainty. New York: McGraw-Hill, 1969.

Schmitt, N., Coyle, B. W., & King, L. Feedback and task predictability as determinants of performance in multiple-cue probability learning tasks. Organizational Behavioral and Human Performance, 1976, 16, 388-402.

Schulze, W. D., & Kneese, A. V. Risk in benefit-cost analysis (Environmental Economics Laboratory Discussion Paper No. 153). Unpublished manuscript, University of Wyoming, Department of Economics, 1980.

Schwing, R. C., & Albers, W. A., Jr. Societal risk assessment. New York: Plenum Press, 1980.

Sen, A. Interpersonal aggregation and partial comparability. Econometrica, 1970, 38, 393-409.

Sen, A. K. Control areas and accounting prices: An approach to economic evaluation. Economic Journal, 1972, 82, 486-501.

Sen, A. K. On economic inequality. Oxford: Clarendon Press, 1973.

Shank, R. C., & Abelson, R. P. Scripts, plans, goals, and

understanding. Hillsdale, N. J.: Erlbaum, 1977.

Shannon, C. E., & Weaver, W. The mathematical theory of communication. Urbana: University of Illinois Press, 1949.

Shanteau, J. C. An additive decision-making model for sequential estimation and inference judgments. Journal of Experimental Psychology, 1970, 85, 181-191.

Shanteau, J. C. An information-integration analysis of risky decision making. In M. F. Kaplan & S. Schwartz (Eds.), Human judgment and decision processes. New York: Academic Press, 1975.

Shanteau, J. C., & Anderson, N. H. Test of a conflict model for preference judgment. Journal of Mathematical Psychology, 1969, 6, 312-325.

Shaver, K. G. An introduction to attribution processes. Cambridge, MA: Winthrop, 1975.

Sheets, C., & Miller, M. J. The effect of cue-criterion function form on multiple cue probability learning. American Journal of Psychology, in press.

Shepard, R. N. The analysis of proximities: Multidimensional scaling with an unknown distance function. I. Psychometrika, 1962, 27, 125-140. (a)

Shepard, R. N. The analysis of proximities: Multidimensional scaling with an unknown distance function. II. Psychometrika, 1962, 27, 219-246. (b)

Shepard, R. N. On subjectively optimal selections among multiattribute alternatives. In M. Shelly & G. Bryan (Eds.), Human judgments and optimality. New York: Wiley, 1964.

Shepard, R. N. Introduction to Volume I. In R. N. Shepard, A. K. Romney & S. B. Nerlove (Eds.), Multidimensional scaling: Theory and applications in the behavioral sciences (Vol. 1), Theory. New York: Seminar Press, 1972. (a)

Shepard, R. N. A taxonomy of some principal types of data and of multidimensional methods for their analysis. In R. N. Shepard, A. K. Romney & S. B. Nerlove (Eds.), Multidimensional scaling: Theory and applications in the behavioral sciences (Vol. 1), Theory. New York: Seminar Press, 1972. (b)

Shepard, R. N., Romney, A. K. & Nerlove, S. B. (Eds.). Multidimensional scaling: Theory and applications in the behavioral sciences (Vol. 1), Theory. New York: Seminar Press, 1972.

Siemens, N., and others. Operations research: Planning, operating, and information systems. New York: The Free Press, 1973.

Simon, H. A. A behavioral model of rational choice. Quarterly Journal of Economics, 1955, 69, 99-118.

Simon, H. A. Rational choice and the structure of the environment. Psychological Review, 1956, 63, 129-138.

Simon, H. A. Models of Man: Social and rational. New York: Wiley, 1957.

Simon, H. A. Administrative behavior: A study of decision-making processes in administrative organization (3d ed.). New York: The Free Press, 1976.

Simon, H. A. Models of discovery: And other topics in the methods of science. Boston: D. Reidel, 1977. (a)

Simon, H. A. The new science of management decision (Rev. ed.). Englewood Cliffs, N. J.: Prentice-Hall, 1977. (b)

Simon, H. A. Rationality as process and as product of thought. American Economic Review, 1978, 68, 1-16.

Simon, H. A. Information processing models of cognition. Annual Review of Psychology, 1979, 30, 363-396. (a)

Simon, H. A. (Ed.) Models of thought. New Haven & London: Yale University Press, 1979. (b)

Sinden, J., & Worrell, A. Unpriced values. New York: Wiley-Interscience, 1979.

Slovic, P. Cue consistency and cue utilization in judgment. American Journal of Psychology, 1966, 79, 427-434.

Slovic, P., & Fischhoff, B. How safe is safe enough? Determinants of perceived and acceptable risk. In L. Gould & C. A. Walker (Eds.), Too Hot to Handle: Social and policy issues in the management of radioactive wastes. New Haven: Yale University Press, in press.

Slovic, P., Fischoff, B., & Lichtenstein, S. Cognitive processes and societal risk taking. In J. S. Carroll & J. W. Payne (Eds.), Cognition and social behavior. Hillsdale, NJ: Erlbaum Associates, 1976.

Slovic, P., Fischhoff, B. & Lichtenstein, S. Behavioral decision theory. Annual Review of Psychology, 1977, 28, 1-39.

Slovic, P., & Lichtenstein, S. Importance of variance preferences in gambling decisions. Journal of Experimental Psychology, 1968, 78(4), 646-654.

Slovic, P., & Lichtenstein, S. Comparison of Bayesian and regression approaches to the study of human information processing in judgment. Organizational Behavior and Human Performance, 1971, 6, 649-744.

Slovic, P. & Lichtenstein, S. Comparison of Bayesian and regression approaches to the study of human judgment. In L. Rappoport & D. A. Summers (Eds.), Human judgment and social interaction. New York: Holt, Rinehart and Winston, 1973.

Smedslund, J. Multiple-probability learning. Oslo: Akademisk Forlag, 1955.

Sobol, I. M.   The Monte Carlo   method   (R. Messer,   J. Stone   & P. Fortini, trans.). Chicago: University of Chicago Press, 1974.

Sokal, R., & Sneath, P. H.   Principles of numerical taxonomy. San Francisco: Freeman, 1963.

Solow, R. M. The intelligent citizen's guide to inflation.   The Public Interest, 1975, 38, 30-66.

Sproull, L. S., Weiner, S. S., & Wolf, D. B. Organizing an anarchy. Chicago: University of Chicago Press, 1978.

Stevens, S. S.   Mathematics, measurement, and psychophysics.   In S. S. Stevens (Ed.), Handbook of experimental psychology. New York: Wiley, 1951.

Stewart, T. R.   Generality of multidimensional representations. Multivariate Behavioral Research, 1974, 9, 507-519.

Stewart, T. R.   Components of correlation and extensions of the lens model equation. Psychometrika, 1976, 41, 101-120.

Stigler, G. J.   The development of utility theory.   Journal   of Political Economy, 1950, 58, Part I, 307-327, Part II, 373-396.

Stokey, E., & Zeckhauser, R. A primer for policy analysis. New York: Norton, 1978.

Summers, D. A. Rule versus cue learning in multiple probability tasks.   Proceedings of the 75th Annual Convention of the American Psychological Association, 1967, 2, 43-44.

Summers, D. A. Adaptation to change in multiple probability tasks. American Journal of Psychology, 1969, 82, 235-240.

Summers, D. A., & Hammond, K. R.   Inference behavior in multiple-cue tasks involving both linear and nonlinear relations.   Journal of Experimental Psychology, 1966, 71, 751-757.

Summers, S. A.   The learning of responses to multiple weighted cues.

Journal of Experimental Psychology, 1962, 64, 29-34.

Summers, S., Summers, R., Karkau, V. Judgments based on different functional relationships between interacting cues and a criterion. American Journal of Psychology, 1969, 82, 203-211.

Taguiri, R. Person perception. In E. Lindzey & E. Aronson (Eds.), Handbook of social psychology (Vol. 3). Reading, MA: Addison-Wesley, 1968.

Taha, H. A. Operations research: An introduction. New York: MacMillan, 1971.

Taha, H. A. Operations research: An introduction (2nd ed.). New York: Macmillan, 1976.

Takane, Y. On the relations among four methods of multidimensional scaling. Behaviormetrika, 1977, (4), 29-43.

Thorndike, E. L. Fundamental theorems in judging men. Journal of Applied Psychology, 1918, 2, 67-76.

Thurstone, L. L. The factor problem. In D. N. Jackson & S. Messick (Eds.), Problems in human assessment. New York: McGraw-Hill, 1967.

Tintner, G. A contribution to the non-static theory of choice. Quarterly Journal of Economics, 1942, 56, 274-306.

Todd, F. J., & Hammond, K. R. Differential feedback in two multiple-cue probability learning tasks. Behavioral Science, 1965, 10, 429-435.

Tolman, E. C. Purposive behavior in animals and men. New York: Appleton, 1932.

Tolman, E. C., & Brunswik, E. The organism and the causal texture of the environment. Psychological Review, 1935, 42, 43-77.

Torgerson, W. S. Multidimensional scaling: I. Theory and method. Psychometrika, 1952, 17, 401-419.

Torgerson, W. S. Theory and methods of scaling. New York: Wiley, 1958.

Torgerson, W. S. Multidimensional scaling of similarity. Psychometrika, 1965, 30, 379-393.

Tribe, L. H., Schelling, C. S., & Voss, J. (Eds.) When values conflict. Cmabridge: Ballinger, 1976.

Tribus, M. Rational descriptions, decisions and designs. New York: Pergamon, 1969.

Tryon, R. C. A theory of psychological components: An alternative to 'mathematical factors'. Psychological Review, 1935, 42, 425-454.

Tucker, L. R. A suggested alternative formulation in the developments by Hursch, Hammond, and Hursch, and by Hammond, Hursch, and Todd. Psychological Review, 1964, 71, 528-530.

Turoff, M. An alternative approach to cross-impact analysis. Technology Forecasting & Social Change, 1972, 3, 309-399.

Tversky, A. Additivity analysis of choice behavior: A test of utility theory (Michigan Mathematical Psychology Program Technical Report 65-4). Ann Arbor, Michigan, 1965.

Tversky, A. Additivity, utility, and subjective probability. Journal of Mathematical Psychology, 1967, 4, 175-201.

Tversky, A. The intransitivity of preferences. Psychological Review, 1969, 76, 31-48.

Tversky, A. Elimination by aspects: A theory of choice. Psychological Review, 1972, 79(4), 281-299.

Tversky, A. On the elicitation of preferences: Descriptive and prescriptive considerations. In D. E. Bell, R. L. Keeney & H. Raiffa (Eds.), Conflicting objectives in decisions. New York: Wiley, 1977.

Tversky, A., & Kahneman, D. Belief in the law of small numbers. Psychological Bulletin, 1971, 76, 105-110.

Tversky, A., & Kahneman, D. Availability: A heuristic for judging frequency and probability. Cognitive Psychology, 1973, 5, 207-232.

Tversky, A., & Kahneman, D. Judgment under uncertainty: Heuristics and biases. Science, 1974, 185, 1124-1131.

Tversky, A., & Kahneman, D. Causal schemata in judgments under uncertainty. In M. Fishbein (Ed.), Progress in social psychology. Hillsdale, NJ: Lawrence Erlbaum, 1977.

Tversky, A., & Kahneman, D. The framing of decisions and the rationality of choice. Engineering Psychology Program, Office of Naval Research Report (Contract N00014-79-C-0077), March 1980.

Tversky, A., & Krantz, D. H. Similarity of schematic faces. A test of interdimensional additivity. Perception & Psychophysics, 1969, 5, 124-128.

Tversky, A., & Sattath, S. Preference trees. Engineering Psychology Programs, Office of Naval Research Report (Contract N00014-79-C-0077) October 1979.

Uhl, C. Learning of interval concepts. I. Effects of differences in stimulus weights. Journal of Experimental Psychology, 1963, 66, 264-273.

Uhl, C. N. Effects of multiple stimulus validity and criterion dispersion on learning of interval concepts. Journal of Experimental Psychology, 1966, 72, 519-527.

Van de Geer, J. P. Introduction to multivariate analysis for the social sciences. San Francisco: Freeman, 1971.

Vlachos, E. The use of scenarios for social impact assessment. In K. Finsterbusch & C. P. Wolf (Eds.), Methodology of social impact assessment. Stroudsburg, PA: Dowden, Hutchinson, & Ross, 1977.

von Bertalanffy, L. General system theory. In General systems, Yearbook of the Society for the Advancement of General System Theory (Vol. 1), 1956.

von Neumann, J., & Morgenstern, O. Theory of games and economic behavior (2d ed.). Princeton, N. J.: Princeton University Press, 1947.

von Winterfeldt, D., & Edwards, W. Costs and payoffs in perceptual research. Manuscript submitted for publication, 1981.

Wainer, H. Estimating coefficients in linear models: It don't make no nevermind. Psychological Bulletin, 1976, 83, 213-217.

Wald, A. Contributions to the theory of statistical estimation and testing hypotheses. Annals of Mathematical Statistics, 1939, 10, 299-326.

Wald, A. Statistical decision functions. New York: Wiley, 1950.

Wallace, D. Cluster analysis. In International Encyclopedia of the Social Sciences. New York: Crowell Collier, 1968.

Wallace, H. A. What is in the corn judge's mind? Journal of the American Society of Agronomy, 1923, 15, 300-304.

Ward, J. H., Jr., & Davis, K. Teaching a digital computer to assist in making decisions. 6570th Personnel Research Laboratory, Aerospace Medical Division, Air Force Systems Command (PRL-TDR-63-16), June 1963.

Watson, S. R., Weiss, J. J., & Donnell, M. L. Fuzzy decision analysis. IEEE Transactions on Systems, Man, & Cybernetics, 1979, SMC-9, 1-9.

Weber, M. [The methodology of the social sciences.] (E. A. Shils & H. A. Finch, Eds. and trans.). New York: The Free Press, 1949.

Webster's Third New International Dictionary of the English Language Unabridged. Springfield, Mass.: Merriam, 1976.

Weick, K. E. The social psychology of organizing. Reading, Mass.: Addison-Wesley, 1969.

Weiner, S. S. Participation, deadlines, and choice. In J. G. March & J. P. Olsen (Eds.), Ambiguity and choice in organizations. Bergen: Universitetsforlaget, 1976.

Weisbrod, B. A. Economics of public health. Philadelphia: University of Pennsylvania Press, 1961.

Weiss, W. Scale judgments of triplets of opinion statements. Journal of Abnormal and Social Psychology, 1963, 66, 471-479.

Wheeler, D. D., & Janis, I. L. A practical guide for making decisions. New York: The Free Press, 1980.

Wickelgren, W. A. How to solve problems. San Francisco: W. H. Freeman & Co., 1974.

Wiener, N. The human use of human beings: Cybernetics and society. Boston: Houghton Mifflin, 1950.

Wiener, N. Cyberetics, or control and communication in the animal and the machine (2d ed.). Cambridge, Mass.: MIT Press, 1961.

Wiggins, N., & Hoffman, P. J. Three models of clinical judgment. Journal of Abnormal Psychology, 1968, 73, 70-77.

Willis, R. H. Stimulus pooling and social perception. Journal of Abnormal and Social Psychology, 1960, 60, 365-373.

Windelband, W. Geschichte und Naturwissenschaft. (3d ed.) 1904.

Winkler, R. L. An introduction to Baysian inference and decision. New York: Holt, Rinehart, and Winston, 1972.

Winter, S. G. Economic 'natural selection' and the theory of the firm. Yale Economic Essays, 1964, 4, 225-272.

Winter, S. G.. Satisficing, selection, and the innovating remnant. Quarterly Journal of Economics, 1971, 85, 237-261.

Winter, S. G. Optimization and evolution in the theory of the firm. In R. H. Day & T. Groves (eds.), Adaptive economic models. New York: Academic Press, 1975.

Wolf, C. P. Social impact assessment: The state of the art. In C. P. Wolf (Ed.), Social impact assessment. Milwaukee, WI: Environmental Design Research Association, 1974.

Wolf, C. P.   Getting social impact assessment into the policy arena. Environmental Impact Assessment Review, 1980, 1, 27-36.

Woodworth, R. S. Experimental psychology. New York: Holt, Rinehart & Winston, 1938.

WRC   Establishment of Principles and Standards for Planning. Federal Register, 1973, 38, (No.   174), Part 3, 82-83.

Wyer, R. S., Jr. The effects of information redundancy on evaluations of social stimuli. Psychonomic Science, 1968, 13, 245-246.

Wyer, R. S.   Information   redundancy,   inconsistency, and novelty and their role in impression formation. Journal of Experimental Social Psychology, 1970, 6, 111-127.

Yntema,   D. B., &   Torgerson, W. S.   Man-computer   cooperation   in decisions requiring common   sense.   IRE   Transactions   of   the Professional Group on Human Factors in Electronics, 1961, HFE 2(1), 20-26.

Zadeh, L. A. Fuzzy sets. Information & Control, 1965, 8, 338-353.

Zeckhauser, R., & Fisher, A.   Averting   behavior   and   external diseconomics.   Unpublished   manuscript,   Harvard   University, John F. Kennedy School of Government, 1976.

Zeleny, M. On the inadequacy of the regression paradigm used in the study of human judgment. Theory and Decision, 1976, 7, 57-65.